THE VANISHING VOTER

THE
VANISHING VOTER

Public Involvement in an Age of Uncertainty

THOMAS E. PATTERSON

ALFRED A. KNOPF   NEW YORK   2002

THIS IS A BORZOI BOOK
PUBLISHED BY ALFRED A. KNOPF

www.aaknopf.com

Library of Congress Cataloging-in-Publication Data
Patterson, Thomas E.
The vanishing voter : public involvement in an age of uncertainty /
Thomas E. Patterson.
p. cm.
Includes bibliographical references and index.
ISBN 0-375-41406-1 (alk. paper)
1. Voting—United States. I. Title.
JK1967 .P375 2002
324.6'5'0973—dc21   2002019021

Manufactured in the United States of America
First Edition

To my family

Contents

Acknowledgments

As a child growing up in a small Minnesota town, I remember elections as a time of activity and wonder. With eight children, my mom and dad voted in shifts, but vote they always did. Many of my grade-school classmates sported campaign pins. The "I Like Ike" buttons were more popular, but I wore my Adlai Stevenson pin proudly, even though something told me that ours was a losing cause. Campaign leaflets would appear at the house in the hands of neighbors or slipped between the doors. They were also found on store counters or on windshields when farmers came into town on Saturday night. Campaign posters were slapped on posts or taped to store windows. Summer evenings were spent watching the party conventions. There wasn't anything else available on TV, but the conventions would have been the program of choice in most homes anyway.

Elections don't look and feel like that anymore, and haven't for a long time. During the past four decades, the United States has had its longest sustained period of decline in election participation, including but not limited to the vote. Elections are now conducted on high, beamed from war rooms and newsrooms. We are invited to send a check and to vote on Election Day. Increasingly, we don't bother to do either one.

It is mythical, of course, to claim that elections were once bottom-up affairs that thrived solely on the effort and interest of ordinary citizens. But today's elections are unmistakably top-down affairs, conducted in ways that suit candidates, journalists, and officials. These professionals are not unmindful of or uncaring about the public, but they put their own needs first. The gap between the practitioner and the citizen—despite the intimacy of television and the immediacy of polling—has arguably never been greater. The world occupied by the hundreds at the top and the world populated by the millions at the bottom still overlap at points, but they do so less satisfactorily than before. The juice has been squeezed out of elections. The blinkered professionalism that marks other areas of American life has taken over politics and journalism, which are among the areas of modern life that actually work better when a spirit of amateurism prevails.

Absent that spirit, Americans are likely to continue to withhold their checks, their votes, and their attention. This prospect led to the Vanishing Voter Project on which this book is based. With the generous support of the Pew Charitable Trusts, we conducted weekly interviews with national samples of 1,000 Americans to discover how much attention they were paying to the 2000 presidential election campaign. We sought to discover what draws people to a campaign and what keeps them away. We did a lot of interviewing. Today's campaign lasts a full year, easily the longest among the world's major democracies. By the time the 2000 campaign ended, we had conducted nearly 90,000 interviews. We had not expected the outcome to go into overtime. But it did, and so did we, gathering an additional 10,000 interviews while Americans waited to hear whether George W. Bush's or Al Gore's legal team would win out.

Our Vanishing Voter Project benefited from the advice of a great many scholars, practitioners, foundation officers, and staff members. I begin my thanks with Sean Treglia of The Pew Charitable Trusts, who was the program officer for our research grant. Sean provided sound advice at critical stages of the project and represented Pew with distinction at our public forums. I am also indebted to Paul Light, who was at Pew when we proposed the project. Paul's backing was crucial. I am grateful for it, as well as for the support received from Michael Delli Carpini, Pew's Public Policy Program director, and Rebecca Rimel, Pew's president. Through its many grants, The Pew Charitable Trusts has made a singular contribution to improving American democracy.

It is a towering force in our civic life. It is also a hands-off foundation once a grant has been awarded. The opinions expressed in this book are my own and do not necessarily reflect the views of The Pew Charitable Trusts.

Throughout the Vanishing Voter Project—literally from beginning to end—I had support, counsel, and friendship from Marvin Kalb. Marvin and I hatched the idea of the project, secured funding for it, and directed it together. Marvin's experiences in journalism and the academy helped shape every aspect of the study. To my delight, but not to my amazement after having already worked with him for several years, Marvin was adept even at devising survey questions. Marvin also pulled together our two successful Washington conferences and our two stunning national party convention forums. Always generous in his advice and polite in his disagreements, Marvin is what one hopes for, and is lucky to find, in a collaborator and colleague.

The Vanishing Voter Project was also fortunate to have a dedicated research and administrative team. Tami Buhr was in charge of preparing the survey questions each week and getting the data in shape for analysis. She also participated in the preparation of the weekly news releases, our conference papers, and this book. Once the surveys were off and running, Tami was easily the project's most valuable player. I am thankful for her many efforts, some of which required her to work evenings and weekends. She is a marvelously talented research scholar and deserves a large chunk of the credit for the project's success. The Webmaster for our project was Ben Snowden, a skilled refugee from the private sector who is now in law school. Ben set up our Web site (www.vanishingvoter.com) and took charge of sending out our weekly news releases. The task of monitoring news coverage of the 2000 campaign fell to Alison Kommer. The data she so painstakingly prepared have found their way into this book. Also helping to shape the book were two first-rate editorial assistants, Parker Everett and Lynn Weil. Eric Anderson ably assisted in tracking news coverage of the project and in routing inquiries about the project to their proper place. Karen Hart capably handled the project budget. In Washington, Marvin Kalb had the assistance of Michael Barre. At the start of the project, my personal assistant was Melissa Ring. After the book was under way, Jamie

Arterton moved into the position. Melissa and Jamie did it all, from helping with project inquiries to assisting in manuscript preparation. These two very talented young women learned to work around my chronic disorganization, imposing an order on the project that was a marvel to all in the office.

The office in this case is the Joan Shorenstein Center on the Press, Politics and Public Policy at Harvard University's John F. Kennedy School of Government. Few places in academe are as stimulating or comfortable as the Shorenstein Center, a reflection of the two directors it has had, Marvin Kalb and Alex Jones. Alex came on board as the weekly surveys were in the final stretch and gave his full support to the project. Few things are more appealing to me than working with Alex in the years ahead. The mainstay in the Center throughout the project was Nancy Palmer. Superlatives are not enough in her case. She had her own job to do but always found time to help with the Vanishing Voter Project. I wore out the path to her office, two doors away, during our study. She was the first reader for every draft chapter, the first contact whenever a major problem arose, and a valued advisor at all times. Edith Holway was also there throughout the project, lending her special ability at bringing people together. Our conferences and meetings went off without a hitch as a result of Edie's skill.

Our surveys were conducted by International Communication Research. We paid for ICR's services but received a bonus when Melissa Herrmann was assigned to our project. Melissa went beyond what was required, cheerfully accommodating our frequent last-minute requests to add more questions to the weekly survey. ICR's A. J. Jennings and Chris Dinardo also helped enormously and have my thanks.

A project of this scope requires outside advice, and we had it in abundance. The scholars Robert Entman, Martin Wattenberg, Alex Keyssar, and Arthur LeGacy deserve special thanks. They served as readers of draft copies of chapters. Richard Morin needs to be singled out, too. Rich helped in preparing the initial survey and then worked with us on a special survey that became the basis for a *Washington Post* article. During various stages of the project, we received advice from numerous practitioners and scholars. With an apology to anyone inadvertently omitted, I would like to thank Iris Adler, Michael Alvarez,

Steve Ansolabehere, Paul Begala, Nolan Bowie, Bruce Buchanan, John Buckley, B. J. Bullert, Sheila Burke, Tim Cook, Kathleen deLaski, Len Downie, Sam Fleming, William Galvin, Curtis Gans, David Gergen, Anna Greenberg, Stephen Hess, Maxine Isaacs, Marion Just, Dan Kennedy, David King, Andrew Kohut, Taeku Lee, Robert Lichter, Jenny Mansbridge, Deborah Mathis, Jim Nicholson, Pippa Norris, David Nyhan, Michael Oreskes, Gary Orren, Richard Parker, Roy Romer, Tom Rosenstiel, Fred Schauer, Frank Sesno, Matthew Storin, Cheryl Sullivan, Paul Taylor, Evan Thomas, Bill Wheatley, and John Zaller.

Ashbel Green, my editor at Knopf, was for a second time the source of wise advice. He was also editor for my earlier Knopf book, *Out of Order* (a brilliant title that he suggested). I will always be indebted to Ash's kind and constructive response to a ragged first draft of this book. In addition to Ash, Knopf's Jonathan Fasman, Ellen Feldman, and Robert Olsson all helped and deserve my thanks.

An election project followed immediately by the hurried writing of a book based on it places a heavy toll on family members, one that I promise not to impose again, despite the encouragement and forbearance they showed. Lorie Conway, my wife, spent most of a summer and many nights and weekends alone, as I worked on the manuscript. Lorie's support was unflagging, as was that of her son Max. Lorie saw the light at the end of the tunnel long before I did, and she often mentioned it, perhaps to remind both of us that this strain would pass. I am thankful for her help and constant encouragement. She was the deep inspiration for this book. My children, Alex and Leigh, give me purpose that has sustained me through more than one book. They may not realize it, but time with them brings new energy and fascination. I like their company so much.

Thomas E. Patterson
Cambridge, Massachusetts
March 12, 2002

THE VANISHING VOTER

CHAPTER ONE

The Incredible Shrinking Electorate

I've lost interest in voting.
—twenty-six-year-old Pennsylvania voter[1]

I just don't vote.
—twenty-five-year-old North Carolina resident[2]

I don't have any time, and I'm not interested anyway.
—forty-year-old Washington resident[3]

I don't see any reason to vote.
—thirty-year-old Wisconsin resident[4]

SAM ROBERTS, a Miami resident, was kicking himself. A Gore supporter, he had not voted in the 2000 presidential election. "I should have voted," Roberts told a reporter. "Had planned to but didn't get around to it. Dumb."[5]

With the outcome of the 2000 election hanging by the thread of a few hundred votes in Florida, citizen regret was widespread. Nearly half of adult Americans had not voted, and a CNN poll indicated most of them wished they had.[6]

Even if more people go to the polls in the next election, and the terrorist attacks of September 11, 2001, could have that effect, the long-term prospects are anything but bright. The voting rate has fallen in nearly every presidential election for four decades. An economic recession and Ross Perot's spirited third-party bid sparked a healthy 5 percent increase in 1992, but turnout in 1996 plunged to 49 percent, the first time since the 1920s that it had slipped below 50 percent.

Many expected turnout to rise in 2000. The Clinton-Dole race four years earlier was one-sided from the start. The contest between Al Gore and George W. Bush, however, looked to be the tightest since 1960, when John F. Kennedy won by the slim margin of 100,000 votes. "Close elections tend to drive up voter interest," said CNN's political analyst Bill Schneider.[7] Turnout did rise, but only slightly: a mere 51 percent of U.S. adults voted in 2000.

That was a far cry from the 63 percent turnout for the Kennedy-Nixon race of 1960, which became the benchmark for evaluating participation in subsequent elections. In every presidential election for the next twenty years, turnout fell. It rose by 1 percentage point in 1984, but then dropped 3 points in 1988. Analysts viewed the trend with alarm, but the warning bells really sounded in 1996, when more Americans stayed home than went to the polls on Election Day. In 1960, 68.8 million adults voted and 40.8 million did not. In 1996, 96.3 million came out and 100.2 million passed.[8]

The turnout trend in the midterm congressional elections has been no less alarming. The voting rate was nearly 50 percent on average in the 1960s, barely stayed above 40 percent in the 1970s, and has averaged 37 percent since then. After a recent midterm vote the cartoonist Rigby showed an election clerk eagerly asking a stray cat that had wandered into a polling place, "Are you registered?"

The period from 1960 to 2000 marks the longest ebb in turnout in the nation's history. If in 2000, as in 1960, 63 percent of the electorate had participated, nearly 25 million more people would have voted. If that many queued up at a polling booth in New York City, the line would stretch all the way to Los Angeles and back, twice over.

Fewer voters are not the only sign that Americans are less interested in political campaigns. Since 1960, participation has declined in virtually every area of election activity, from the volunteers who work on campaigns to the viewers who watch televised debates. The United States had 100 million fewer people in 1960 than it did in 2000 but, even so, more viewers tuned to the October presidential debates in 1960 than did so in 2000.

Few today pay even token tribute to presidential elections. In 1974,

Congress established a fund to underwrite candidates' campaigns, financed by a checkoff box on personal income tax returns that allowed citizens to assign $1 (later raised to $3) of their tax liability to the fund. Initially, one in three taxpayers checked the box. By the late 1980s, only one in five marked it. Now, only one in eight does so.[9]

What could possibly explain such trends? Why are citizens drawing back from election politics? Why is the voter vanishing?

American politics has many strange aspects, but few so mysterious as the decline in electoral participation. Two decades ago, the political scientist Richard Brody observed that the declining rate was at odds with existing theories about voting behavior.[10]

One such theory held that rising education levels would spawn higher participation.[11] In 1960, college-educated Americans were 50 percent more likely to vote than those who had not finished high school. With college graduates increasing steadily in number, the future of voting in America looked bright. "Education not only tends to imbue persons with a sense of citizen duty, it also propels them into political activity," the political scientist V. O. Key wrote.[12] In 1960, half of the adult population had not finished high school and fewer than 10 percent had graduated from college. Today, 25 percent hold a college degree and another 25 percent have attended college. Yet, turnout has declined.

The voting rate of African Americans deepens the mystery. In 1960, only 29 percent of southern blacks were registered to vote.[13] An imposing array of barriers—poll taxes, rigged literacy tests, and courthouse intimidation—kept them from registering. Jim Crow laws ruled southern politics, as did segregationist appeals. Ross Barnett was elected Mississippi's governor in 1959 to the tune of a race-baiting song that included a line saying he would oppose integration with forceful intent. When George Wallace first ran for governor of Alabama, he was beaten by an out-and-out racist candidate, prompting Wallace to vow: "I'll never be outniggered again." He kept his word and won handily when he ran in 1962. Only 22,000 of Mississippi's 450,000 blacks—a mere 5 percent—were registered to vote.[14] North Carolina had the South's highest level of black registration but, even there, only 38 percent were enrolled.[15]

The force of the civil rights movement swept the registration barriers aside. The Twenty-Fourth Amendment, ratified in 1964, prohibits states from requiring citizens to pay "any poll tax or other tax" before they can vote in federal elections. The Voting Rights Act of 1965 empowered the U.S. attorney general to send federal examiners to supervise registration in the seven southern states where literacy tests had been imposed and where fewer than 50 percent of eligible adults were registered. Within half a year, black registration in the states of Alabama, Georgia, Louisiana, Mississippi, and South Carolina rose by 40 percent.[16] The Voting Rights Act also suspended the use of literacy tests, which were banned completely five years later. President Lyndon Johnson told southern officials not to resist electoral change: "To those who seek to avoid action by their National Government in their own communities, who want to and seek to maintain purely local control over elections, the answer is simple: open your polling places to all your people."[17]

Many southern blacks saw their names on polling lists for the first time in their lives. African-American registration rose to 43 percent in 1964 and to more than 60 percent by 1970.[18] In the process, black turnout in the region doubled. Southern whites reacted by also voting in larger numbers, mostly for racial conservatives.[19] In 1960, participation in the South was 30 percentage points below that of the rest of the country. Today, it is less than 5 points lower. Nationally, the voting rate of African Americans is now nearly the same as that of whites. Why, then, has the overall rate declined?

The women's vote adds to the mystery. Although women gained the right to vote in 1920, they were slow to exercise it. Even as late as 1960, turnout among women was nearly 10 percentage points below that of men.[20] American society was changing, however. The tradition-minded women born before suffrage were giving way to generations of women who never doubted that the vote belonged to them as much as it did to men. Today, women vote at the same rate as men. But the overall rate has fallen.

The relaxation of registration laws in recent years also provides reason to think that the turnout rate should have gone up, not down. Unlike Europe, where governments take responsibility to get citizens registered and where participation exceeds 80 percent, the United States places the burden of registration on the individual.[21] For a long period, this arrangement was a boon to officials who wanted to keep the poor and uneducated from voting. States devised schemes that hampered all but the stable homeowner. In most states, residents had to live at the same address for as long as a year before they were eligible to register, and had to re-register if they moved only a few doors away. Registration offices were open for limited hours and were sometimes located at inconvenient or hard-to-find places. Many states closed their rolls a year before an election. By the time people got around to thinking about going to the polls, the deadline had long since passed. Many districts were also quick to purge the rolls of nonvoters, requiring them to re-register if they wanted to exercise their right to vote.

For years, the League of Women Voters sought to persuade Congress and the states to reduce registration barriers.[22] Many scholars also believed that registration reform was the answer to the turnout problem. Studies indicated that participation among America's registered voters was nearly identical to that of European voters.[23] The political scientists Raymond Wolfinger and Steven Rosenstone estimated that eased registration requirements could boost presidential election turnout by as much as 9 percent.[24]

Registration laws have been relaxed. No state today is allowed to impose a residency requirement that exceeds thirty days for a federal election. Six states—Idaho, Maine, Minnesota, New Hampshire, Wisconsin, and Wyoming—allow residents to register at the polls on Election Day.[25] The Motor Voter Act, passed by Congress in 1993, has even shifted some of the registration burden to the states. They must offer registration to citizens who seek services at public assistance agencies, such as food stamp and Medicare offices, or who apply for driver's licenses. States can also offer registration at unemployment offices and other public facilities, such as libraries and schools. Moreover, the act requires states to allow registration by mail and prohibits them from arbitrarily purging nonvoters from the rolls.

Millions of Americans have enrolled through the Motor Voter Act. Most of them would have registered anyway under the old system, but the Federal Election Commission estimates that the legislation has added at least 10 million registrants to the rolls since 1993.[26] With so many additional registrants, why did turnout drop by 5 million voters between 1992 and 2000?

The political scientists Michael McDonald and Samuel Popkin claim that the turnout decline is a "myth." "There is no downward trend [since 1972] in the national turnout rate," they say.[27] Their argument is built on the fact that the U.S. Census Bureau bases its official turnout figures on the total adult population. This population includes individuals who are ineligible to vote, including noncitizens, prison inmates, and convicted felons.* Their numbers have increased substantially since 1960. As a result of liberalized immigration laws, the United States in recent decades has experienced its largest influx of immigrants since World War I.[28] Noncitizens were 2 percent of the adult population in 1960 and today account for 7 percent.[29] Tougher drug and sentencing laws have also increased the number of ineligible voters. The nation now has a higher percentage of its population behind bars than any other country in the world.[30] Roughly 3.5 million are disqualified from voting because they are incarcerated or a convicted felon. This is a sizeable increase from 1960, when fewer than 500,000 were ineligible to vote for these reasons.[31]

When voting rates are adjusted for ineligible adults, the picture improves. Between 1960 and 2000 turnout among eligible voters

---

*The U.S. Constitution does not prevent aliens, felons, and inmates from voting. They are barred by state laws. Indeed, although all states prohibit legal aliens from voting, some allow felons to vote. Some analysts say that the most precise turnout figure is one that includes the disbarred, since the decision to exclude them is a political one. Roughly 10 percent of Americans cannot vote, compared with, for example, only 2 percent in the United Kingdom. One out of seven black males of voting age is ineligible to vote because of a felony conviction. To ignore such differences, some analysts say, is to ignore official efforts to control the size and composition of the electorate. See Pippa Norris, *Count Every Voice: Democratic Participation Worldwide* (New York: Cambridge University Press, 2002).

declined by 9 points (from 64 to 55 percent), compared with the Census Bureau's population-based figure of 12 points (63 to 51 percent). Even by this revised estimate, however, the voting rate is disturbingly low. If turnout in 2000 had been 9 points higher, 18 million more Americans would have gone to the polls—a number equal to the combined turnout in the twenty-four states of Alaska, Arizona, Arkansas, Delaware, Hawaii, Idaho, Iowa, Kansas, Maine, Mississippi, Montana, Nebraska, Nevada, New Hampshire, New Mexico, North Dakota, Oklahoma, Rhode Island, South Carolina, South Dakota, Utah, Vermont, West Virginia, and Wyoming. By any measure, that's a lot of missing voters.

The revised figures, however, reveal a potentially significant pattern. The decline among eligible voters is concentrated between 1960 and 1972. Since then, turnout among eligible voters in both the presidential and the congressional midterm elections has fallen only slightly, leading McDonald and Popkin to conclude that the appearance of steadily declining turnout is "an illusion."[32] If they are right, concern about electoral participation is overstated. There would still be the puzzling question of why the gains in education and registration have not produced the 15–20 percent rise in turnout that voting theories would have predicted.[33] However, fears that the participation problem might worsen would seem unfounded.

Unfortunately, a closer look at turnout trends—and, as will be evident later in this chapter, other participation trends—indicates that the flight from electoral politics is not illusory. For one, disenfranchised citizens in 1960 were not limited to noncitizens, prison inmates, and convicted felons. Southern blacks may in theory have been eligible to vote, but most of them were effectively barred from participating, as were the many poor southern whites who could not afford the poll tax or pass a literacy test. Thus, the clearest picture of what's been happening with turnout in recent decades emerges from a look at nonsouthern states only. There, turnout among eligible voters exceeded 70 percent in 1960.[34] By 1972, it had dropped to 60 percent, and, in 1996, barely topped 50 percent. The non-South voting rate is now near the level of the 1820s, a time when many eligible voters could not read or write and had to travel by foot or on horseback for hours to get to the nearest polling place.[35]

Since the 1970s voting rates have also fallen in presidential primaries. Nearly 30 percent of adults in states with presidential primaries voted in these contests in 1972 and 1976.[36] Since then, the primary election turnout has fallen sharply. It was just 17 percent in the 2000 presidential primaries and 13 percent in 1996 (when only the Republicans had a contested race).

Turnout in congressional primaries has also been on a downward trajectory. It fell from 30 percent in 1970 to 20 percent in 1986. Since then, the average has been closer to 15 percent.

Voting rates for statewide and local elections are not readily available, but fragmentary evidence points to a sharp decline here as well. In Connecticut, for example, turnout in municipal elections fell from 53 to 43 percent between 1989 and 1997.[37] After surveying a number of states and cities, Jack Doppelt and Ellen Shearer concluded in 1999 that turnout had become "an embarrassment." They reported no locations where voting numbers had risen significantly and plenty where the numbers had dropped to historic lows. For example, the *combined* turnout for two statewide 1998 Texas primaries, a regular one and a runoff election, was 14 percent of *registered* voters. Only 3 percent showed up for the runoff.[38]

The first elections after the September 11, 2001, terrorist attacks did not disrupt the trend. In the two highest-profile statewide races—those for governor in Virginia and in New Jersey—turnout fell from its level four years earlier. It dropped by 5 percentage points in Virginia and by 10 points in New Jersey. Even in New York State, where residents had been urged to come out in local elections in order to show the world that democracy was stronger than ever, voting was down. Syracuse had its lowest turnout in seventy-six years, Binghamton its lowest in thirty years, and Buffalo apparently its lowest ever. Even in New York City, only 36 percent of registered voters (about 25 percent of the adult population) went to the polls.[39]

It is too early to know the impact that the World Trade Center and Pentagon attacks will have on political involvement. Americans might stage a triumphant return to the polls in upcoming elections. But any claim that their interest in voting has not flagged since the 1970s is based on incomplete evidence.

Does a diminished appetite for voting affect the health of American politics? Is society harmed when the voting rate is low or in decline? As the *Chicago Tribune* said in an editorial, it may be "humiliating" that the United States, the oldest continuous democracy, has nearly the lowest voting rate in the world.[40] But does it have any practical significance?

Some observers take comfort in low-turnout elections. They say the country is better off if less interested and less knowledgeable citizens stay home on Election Day. In a 1997 cover story in *The Atlantic Monthly*, Robert Kaplan wrote that "apathy, after all, often means that the political situation is healthy enough to be ignored. The last thing America needs is more voters—particularly badly educated and alienated ones—with a passion for politics."[41]

The gist of this age-old argument is that low turnout protects society from erratic or even dangerous shifts in public opinion. Irregular voters are not as well informed as habitual voters and are therefore more likely to get carried away by momentary passions. If these voters participate heavily, it is argued, outcomes could vary greatly from one election to the next, resulting in disruptive policy shifts. In his essay "In Defense of Nonvoting," the columnist George Will says "good government" rather than voting is "the fundamental human right." He notes that high turnout and massive vote swings contributed to the political chaos that brought down Germany's Weimar Republic, enabling the Nazis to seize power.[42] Will claims that America's declining voting rate is a healthy development.

America's voters, however, have not acted whimsically. Except for an interlude in the 1780s, when the Articles of Confederation governed the United States, erratic voting has not been a persistent source of political instability.

America's voters have typically recoiled at the prospect of radical change.[43] William Jennings Bryan's "Cross of Gold" speech enthralled the 1896 Democratic convention delegates, but his nomination prompted large numbers of swing voters to abandon the Democratic Party in fear of free coinage of silver.[44] "Thou Shalt Not Steal," blared an anti-Bryan editorial in the *Chicago Tribune*.[45] When Barry Goldwater, the Republican nominee in 1964, exclaimed that "extremism in defense of liberty is no vice," he got buried in one of the greatest landslides in presidential history. Hard-core Republicans backed him, but other voters went sharply in the other direction. Eight years later, the Democratic nominee, George McGovern, took positions on Vietnam and income security that alarmed many, and he lost both the election and the swing vote by even wider margins than Goldwater.

Small and obstinate electorates rather than large and whimsical ones have been America's affliction. During the South's Jim Crow era, low-turnout, whites-only elections helped sustain segregation. Even today, electoral dysfunction typically stems from small electorates. As turnout in recent congressional primaries declined, hard-core partisans (the "wing nuts") became an increasingly larger proportion of those voting, which contributed to the more frequent defeat of moderate candidates. In turn, Congress became a more divided and rancorous institution.

U.S. elections are hardly at a crisis point. Swing voters still decide the outcome of national elections, and the drop in turnout has not threatened the legitimacy of elected officials. Nevertheless, elections are now less adaptive. As electorates shrink, they tend to calcify. If huge shifts in the vote are antithetical to sound government, so, too, are tiny ones. They signal a polity with a reduced capacity to respond to changing needs.

Elections have also become less representative. Politics is prone to what the political scientists Sidney Verba, Kay Lehman Schlozman, and Henry Brady call "participatory distortion." Citizens of higher income, education, and age are greatly overrepresented in nearly every political activity, from contacting legislators to contributing money. Voting is the least distorted activity.[46] For a long period, in fact, election analysts claimed that turnout was irrelevant because voters and nonvoters thought alike.[47] "Most electoral outcomes," Ruy Teixeira concluded in 1992, "are not determined in any meaningful way by turnout."[48]

This argument is still heard, but the evidence for it is less convincing than it was even a decade ago.[49] Who votes does matter. As the electorate has shrunk, it has come to include proportionally more citizens who are older, who have higher incomes, or who hold intense opinions on such issues as gun control, labor rights, and abortion. On balance, these tendencies have worked slightly to the Republicans' advantage,[50] which, in close races, can tip the balance. Polls indicated that if all eligible adults had voted in 2000, the Democrats would have captured the presidency and both houses of Congress.[51] Turnout also affected the outcome of the 1994 midterm election that launched the "Republican Revolution" in Congress. Surveys showed that nonvoters preferred Democratic congressional candidates by a substantial margin.[52]

If turnout among those of lower education and income were substantially higher, the GOP would not necessarily have lost the 1994 and 2000 elections. Republican candidates would run on broader platforms if more people voted regularly. So, too, would Democratic candidates, who have increasingly directed their appeals at special interests and higher-income voters. Campaign platforms have always been tailored to those who vote.[53] As the political scientists Steven Rosenstone and John Mark Hansen note: "The idle go unheard: They do not speak up, define the agenda, frame the issues, or affect the choices leaders make."[54]

The increasing number of nonvoters could be a danger to democracy. Although high participation by itself does not trigger radical change, a flood of new voters into the electorate could possibly do it. It's difficult to imagine a crisis big and divisive enough to prompt millions of new voters to suddenly flock to the polls, especially in light of Americans' aversion to political extremism. Nevertheless, citizens who are outside the electorate are less attached to the existing system. As the sociologist Seymour Martin Lipset observed, a society of nonvoters "is potentially more explosive than one in which most citizens are *regularly* involved in activities which give them some sense of participation in decisions which affect their lives."[55]

Voting can strengthen citizenship in other ways, too.[56] When people vote, they are more attentive to politics and are better informed about issues affecting them. Voting also deepens community involvement, as the philosopher John Stuart Mill theorized a century ago.[57] Studies indicate that voters are more active in community affairs than non-voters are. Of course, this association says more about the type of person who votes as opposed to the effect of voting. But recent evidence, as Harvard University's Robert Putnam notes, "suggests that the act of voting itself encourages volunteering and other forms of good citizenship."[58]

Going to the local polling place and voting does not require a lot of time. In most locations, it takes about as long to drive to a video store and rent a couple of movies. Other forms of electoral participation, such as canvassing or paying careful attention to election news, can be far more time consuming. How involved are citizens in these more demanding forms of participation?

When it comes to joining groups or helping in campaigns, Americans have a stronger tradition of participation than Europeans.[59] Since the publication of Alexis de Tocqueville's *Democracy in America,* the United States has been admired for its political activism. "A nation of joiners" was Tocqueville's characterization of the United States. But it is losing this distinction in election campaigns. Millions still put bumper stickers on their cars, wear campaign buttons, display lawn signs, attend campaign rallies, or work on a campaign, but their numbers are falling. In 1972, 12 percent of Americans attended a campaign rally or speech and more than 6 percent worked for a party or candidate. By the 1980s, citizens were a third less likely to engage in these activities and, today, are only half as likely.[60] The number who contribute money to a candidate or party has also decreased by nearly 50 percent since the 1970s.[61]

Attention to election news has also declined. Campaign coverage has never been more plentiful, or so widely ignored. In 1960, nearly 50 percent claimed to have watched a "good many" election programs. That figure has fallen to fewer than 30 percent. Attention to newspaper coverage of campaigns has decreased even more sharply.[62]

. . .

Although they are still a major attraction, even the October presidential debates get less attention than before. Except for the Super Bowl, the Summer Olympics, and the Academy Awards, the debates are the most watched events on television. Like those other contests, the debates are, as Alan Schroeder writes, "human drama at its rawest."[63] Conflict, risk, and suspense are all elements of drama, and the debates offer them on a level unmatched by other campaign events.[64] They have regularly produced surprising performances. Ronald Reagan demonstrated an unexpected command of the issues in 1980 and, just as unexpectedly, addled his way through a 1984 debate, concluding his performance with a time-capsule anecdote to which he forgot the ending.

Although the October debates still attract tens of millions of viewers, the numbers have been falling steadily. The four Kennedy-Nixon debates each attracted roughly 60 percent of all households with television sets.[65] When debates resumed with Carter and Ford in 1976, viewers again flocked to their TVs, as they also did for the single Reagan-Carter face-off in 1980. Since then, except for the Clinton-Bush-Perot encounters in 1992, debate audiences have been declining. Only 46 percent of the country's television households watched the two Reagan-Mondale debates in 1984. Barely more than 36 percent saw the Bush-Dukakis debates in 1988. The Clinton-Dole debates in 1996 averaged 29 percent.

The debate audiences in 2000 were widely expected to exceed that level. The Bush-Gore contest was much tighter than the Clinton-Dole race, and large numbers of voters had not yet settled on a candidate. "In just thirty-five days, Americans will choose a new president," said CBS's Dan Rather on the night of the first debate. "What's about to happen . . . could have a big impact on whether it will be Democrat Al Gore or Republican George Bush. . . . [T]he race is tight."[66] Yet, the audience rating for the three Bush-Gore debates was no higher than for the three Clinton-Dole debates. The third debate in 2000 had a 26 percent rating—the lowest ever.

The audiences for primary election debates are also shrinking. Large numbers of Americans saw Robert Kennedy and Eugene McCarthy face off in 1968 and watched Hubert Humphrey and McGovern debate in 1972. The 1980 Republican debate in New Hampshire that thrust Ronald Reagan back into the lead for the GOP nomination also attracted a sizeable audience. In contrast, the two dozen primary debates in 2000 drew, on average, 1.8 million viewers— about a fifth of the audience of the typical prime-time program. None of these debates attracted even as many as 5 million viewers. If the debates had been a new television series, they would have been cancelled after the initial episode. The first Democratic debate in 2000 went head-to-head with a World Wrestling Federation match: the wrestlers had four times as many viewers as the candidates. Even then, WWF's *SmackDown!* with 7.2 million viewers was rated ninety-first among the week's television shows.[67]

The convention audience is also dwindling. At one time, Americans could hardly get their fill of the televised national party conventions. They were so popular that they became even a marketing tool. "Buy a television, watch the conventions," suggested a 1952 RCA ad. Another RCA ad said: "With the aid of television, we had what amounted to the greatest town meeting ever held. . . . Sixty million people had front-row seats and got a better picture of what was going on than any delegate or any reporter on the convention floor."[68]

In 1952, the typical television household watched 25 hours of convention coverage, often in the company of friends and neighbors.[69] Even as late as 1976, the typical household viewed the conventions for 11 hours. Since then the ratings have hit the skids. By 1996, the average had fallen to less than 4 hours. A new low was reached in 2000: 3 hours of convention viewing for the typical household. In 1976, 28 percent of television households had their sets on and tuned at any given moment to the convention coverage. Only 13 percent were watching in 2000, down from 17 percent in 1996.[70]

Throughout the 2000 campaign, as part of our Vanishing Voter Project, we monitored Americans' attention to the campaign through weekly national surveys. By the time Election Day arrived, we had conducted 80,000 interviews in fifty-two weeks, the most comprehensive study ever conducted of election interest. Our polls paint a disturbing picture of involvement in the world's foremost democracy. During the typical week, four times as many respondents said they were paying "just some," "only a little," or "no" attention to the campaign as said they were paying "a great deal" or "quite a bit" of attention.

The 2000 election was slow to engage Americans. By Thanksgiving 1999, the candidates had been campaigning nonstop for two months, and four primary debates had already been held. Nevertheless, the campaign might just as well have been taking place in Siberia. Americans sat around their holiday dinner tables talking about everything but George Bush, John McCain, Bill Bradley, and Al Gore. Only one in twenty adults reported having talked about the campaign on Thanksgiving Day—and that included conversations of any length with anybody, not just extended discussions with family members over turkey and trimmings.[71]

Interest rose during the period of the Iowa caucuses and the New Hampshire primary, and it continued to grow through early March's decisive Super Tuesday primaries, fueled in part by McCain's drawing power. The number who said they were paying close attention nearly doubled. Even then, many were tuned out. In the week after New Hampshire's GOP primary, only 47 percent could name McCain as the winner. Four percent claimed Bush had won, and 49 percent said they did not know.

After Super Tuesday, interest dropped sharply. By the end of April, three in four said they were paying almost no attention to the campaign. Americans were so uninvolved during the late-spring and early-summer months that many forgot some of what they had learned about the candidates' policy positions earlier in the campaign.[72]

Not until the August conventions did people again start to pay closer attention. The news that Gore had selected Joseph Lieberman as his running mate—the first Jewish candidate to run on a major-party ticket—was known to 66 percent of Americans within forty-eight hours of the announcement.[73] The October debates also sparked interest, as did the news four days before the election that Bush had been arrested in 1976 for driving while intoxicated. Within a day, 75 percent were aware of the incident.[74] But these were unusual moments. In only two weeks out of fifty-two did the number of adults who said they were paying "very close" or "quite a bit of" attention reach 40 percent.

An inattentive public is an uninformed one. As the 2000 campaign entered its final week, only one issue position—Gore's stand on pre-scription drugs—was familiar to a majority of Americans.* During the past half century there has been a revolution in higher education and in mass communication. Citizens have never had so much information available to them or been better equipped to handle it. Research indicates, however, that Americans today are no better informed about election politics than they were fifty years ago.[75] The high school–educated public of 1948 knew as much about Harry Truman's and Thomas Dewey's positions on price controls and the Taft-Hartley Act as the media-saturated, college-educated public of 2000 knew about Gore's and Bush's stands on prescription drugs and tax cuts.[76]

Ironically, it was not until after Election Day that the public became keenly interested in the 2000 campaign. The unfolding drama in Florida captured imaginations in a way that the campaign itself never did. Interest had peaked just before Election Day when 46 percent were paying "a great deal" or "quite a bit" of attention. During the following week, as it became clear that the Florida vote would decide the outcome, nearly 80 percent were paying close attention. For a period, a majority acted as if election politics really mattered, talking about it with interest, and absorbing each new twist in the Florida vote count.[77]

Except for the black community and some die-hard partisans, however, the Florida wrangling was cause for neither anger nor anxiety. Citizens were captivated by the story but not wedded to the result. Only 10 percent believed the situation was "a constitutional crisis" and,

---

*Based on asking respondents in the Vanishing Voter surveys whether they agreed or disagreed that a stated position was the actual position of a candidate on a dozen issues. Because respondents had a fifty-fifty chance of selecting the actual position by guessing alone, the level of knowledge for the public as a whole was measured by subtracting incorrect responses from correct ones. Gore's position on prescription drugs was the only one of the twelve on which the corrected measure reached 50 percent. On one other issue—Bush's stance on tax cuts—the uncorrected number of correct answers (52 percent) exceeded 50 percent. In this case, 11 percent guessed wrong, resulting in a corrected measure of 41 percent.

within two weeks, half said the dispute had "gone on too long already."[78] The public's response was a stark contrast to how Americans had reacted in 1876, the last time a president was chosen by post-election wheeling and dealing. Then they had taken to the streets, and more than a few fistfights broke out. Wider civil unrest was averted only when a political deal was brokered to end the Civil War Reconstruction. Nothing remotely like that was required to keep the peace in 2000. "There will be no mobs gathering to shout 'Gore or blood' or 'Bush or blood,'" the *New York Times*'s Adam Clymer wrote. "Nobody cares that much."[79]

What is going on here? Why are Americans less engaged by political campaigns today than a few decades ago? And is the situation likely to change anytime soon?

Some commentators say participation follows a natural cycle and will rise again soon, just as it did after downturns in the 1890s, 1920s, and 1940s. "Historians will almost certainly remember our time," says the *Boston Globe*'s David Shribman, "as the preface to a new period of political activism, agitation, and passion."[80]

But this argument overlooks the persistence of the current trend and the special nature of those earlier periods. Turnout dropped sharply in the 1890s before stabilizing a few elections later. That era, however, was defined by deliberate efforts to suppress voting.[81] Democratic-controlled southern legislatures used poll taxes, literacy tests, and the grandfather clause in order to prevent African Americans from registering. "The costs of voting were deliberately made so high," writes the political scientist Walter Dean Burnham, "that probably half of the white electorate was effectively disenfranchised along with almost all of the [blacks]."[82]

Turnout in the South was 65 percent in the 1880s. By the early 1900s, it had fallen to 30 percent. In the North, Republican-controlled legislatures imposed registration requirements only on big-city residents, most of whom were working-class Democrats. The ballot fraud perpetrated by urban political machines declined as a result but so did the voting rate of eligible voters.[83]

Turnout also fell sharply in the 1920s, the first decade in which women were allowed to vote. Men had long been out of arguments for keeping the vote from women. Senator Wendell Phillips had said in 1898: "One of two things is true: either woman is like man—and if she is, then a ballot based on brains belongs to her as well as to him. Or she is different, and then man does not know how to vote for her as she herself does."[84] Finally, in 1920, ratification of the Nineteenth Amendment gave women what they had been seeking for decades.

Nevertheless, women were slow to take advantage of suffrage,[85] and the overall turnout rate fell sharply. Turnout had been 62 percent in 1916.[86] It was a mere 49 percent in 1920. In Illinois, the only state where ballots for the two sexes were counted separately, women's voting rate in 1920 was 27 percentage points lower than that of men. "It was not to be expected that the adult women who suddenly find themselves in possession of the franchise should be as conscientious in its exercise as men who from childhood had been encouraged to think politically," wrote Arthur M. Schlesinger and Erik McKinley Eriksson in "The Vanishing Voter," a 1924 article in *The New Republic*.[87]

Turnout also fell sharply in 1944 and 1948, but, in this case, too, there were special circumstances: world war and its aftermath. In Britain as well as in the United States, people were so preoccupied by the war effort that partisan politics was a secondary concern. No analyst has fully explained why this had to be the case or why the wartime governing parties in both England and the United States suffered stinging defeats in postwar legislative elections. By the 1950s, voting rates in Britain and America had returned to normal. Except for 1944 and 1948, turnout was near or above 60 percent in every U.S. presidential election between 1936 and 1968.

The recent downturn in voting has lasted longer than the earlier ones and has occurred despite the upward pressure of advances in education, registration, and civil rights. The latest period does not closely resemble any past period, and there is no end clearly in sight. What might possibly explain it?

Politics has had to compete with more things for people's time and attention. Life today offers distractions on a scale unimaginable even a few decades ago, not only from cable television and the Internet but also in career and lifestyle choices. This development has been felt in European democracies as well, which have also experienced declining participation rates, although on a much smaller scale than in the United States.

The decline is also attributable in part to the march of time. The civic-minded generation raised during the Depression and the Second World War has been gradually replaced by the more private-minded X and Y generations that lived through childhood and adolescence without having experienced a great national crisis.[88] Today's young adults are less politically interested and informed than any cohort of young people on record.[89] The voting rate of adults under thirty was 50 percent in 1972. It was barely above 30 percent in 2000.

The participation decline, however, is not due entirely to generational replacement. Changes in the electoral system, political parties, the news media, and the conduct of campaigns—many of which are the consequence of deliberate policy choices—have contributed to the decrease in turnout and involvement. An explanation of these developments is the focus of this book, which will also offer a few modest suggestions on what might be done to address the problem.

For one, the electoral system needs fixing. Although the Florida debacle in 2000 revealed defects in how ballots are cast and counted, the participation problem does not reside at the tail end of the campaign. What happened to ballots in Florida and elsewhere is an inexcusable failure of election officials to safeguard the integrity of the vote. Nevertheless, because Americans were not aware of the problem until after Election Day, it cannot possibly explain why only half of them showed up at the polls or why only a sixth of them voted in the primaries or why three-fourths of them ignored daily events on the campaign trail.

The front end of the campaign is where the real participation problems start. Three decades ago, against the backdrop of the Vietnam protests, the presidential selection system was changed in order to place the voters in control of the nominating process. In its report, *Mandate for Reform,* the McGovern-Fraser Commission said: "popular participation is the way . . . for people committed to orderly political change to fulfill their needs and desires within our traditional political system." The commission might have accomplished its goal if the reformed system had been properly designed. Instead, the reform produced a presidential campaign that starts far too early and lasts far too long, that runs on big money and responds to special interests, that has sapped the national party conventions of their energy and purpose, and that wears down the public as it grinds its way month after month toward November. If ever there was an election system designed to drive an electorate into submission, the year-long system of electing presidents is it.

Although some observers place the blame for declining participation squarely on citizens—they are portrayed as lazy and indifferent to their responsibilities—that argument, as will be shown, is refuted by the adverse changes that have taken place in U.S. politics during the past four decades. Ordinary citizens have been buffeted by developments they do not control and only vaguely comprehend, and which have diminished their stake, interest, and confidence in elections.

The great tools of democracy—its electoral institutions and media organizations—have increasingly been used for private agency. Personal ambition now drives campaigns, and profit and celebrity now drive journalism. Candidates, public officials, and journalists operate in a narrow professional world that is largely of their own making and that is remote from the world of the public they serve.

To be sure, ordinary Americans share some of the blame for their lapse in participation. It's always easier to leave the work of democracy to others. But most of the fault lies elsewhere, and citizens cannot be expected to rededicate themselves merely because they are told their democracy needs them. Stronger leadership is required. Officials, candidates, and the media have failed in their responsibility to give Americans the type of politics that can excite, inform, and engage them—and that will fully and fairly reflect their will. The political scientist E. E. Schattschneider said it best: "Democracy was made for the people, not the people for Democracy."[90]

CHAPTER TWO

Parties and Candidates

Politics of the Moment

About the parties? I don't think of anything.
—thirty-three-year-old South Dakota resident[1]

I don't know enough about the parties to be able to choose which to vote for.
—thirty-three-year-old Pennsylvania resident[2]

I hate all the negativity and mudslinging.
—fifty-three-year-old North Carolina resident[3]

The candidates promise all these things and then never follow through with it.
—thirty-six-year-old Florida resident[4]

IN 1953, congressional conservatives pressured the newly inaugurated Dwight D. Eisenhower to throw the institutional weight of the presidency behind an effort to roll back Franklin Roosevelt's New Deal. They wanted to dismantle social security, curtail business regulation, and terminate labor's bargaining rights. Eisenhower had an instinctive aversion to big government but was a problem solver rather than an ideologue. He chose not to make the fight.[5]

Although not widely noted, Eisenhower's decision effectively marked the end of a lengthy political era based on visionary ideas powerful enough to define the parties and divide the public. The 1930s Great Depression had brought the struggle to a head. As unemployment rose sharply, demands for federal action increased. Philosophically

23

committed to the free market, the Republican Party rejected calls for a major federal relief program. The Democratic Party was also stymied.[6] Outwardly the party of the poor, the Democrats were also the states' rights party. Finally, more than two years into the Depression, Democrats pushed through Congress a major relief bill, which President Herbert Hoover promptly vetoed, calling it "an unexampled raid on the public Treasury."[7]

Time magazine characterized the pending showdown between the parties as "The Masses Against the Classes."[8] Although Franklin Roosevelt offered few details during the 1932 campaign, he promised to serve "the forgotten man at the bottom of the economic pyramid."[9] Once in office, he launched a series of ambitious federal programs designed to put Americans back to work. The ensuing controversy reached even into the Supreme Court, which struck down major New Deal programs, including the National Industrial Recovery Act. When the Court under pressure gave up its opposition to the New Deal in 1937—"the switch in time that saved nine"—America's public philosophy and public policies were transformed. From that moment, the government would regulate markets, protect labor's work and rights, and provide income security to the elderly, the unemployed, and the disabled.

This struggle, like all great political struggles, lingered. When Angus Campbell and his colleagues at the University of Michigan interviewed eligible voters in 1952 for the National Election Studies (NES) survey, they found that respondents had no difficulty saying what they liked and disliked about the Republican and Democratic Parties. Only 10 percent had nothing to say about either. Seventy-four percent commented about both parties. The Democrats were the party of "workers" and "common people," of "big government" and "regulation," and of "social security" and "jobs." Conversely, the GOP was the party of "big business" and "the well-to-do," of "small government" and "free markets," and of "low taxes" and "self-reliance."[10]

Two decades later, many respondents were left speechless when asked the same survey questions. Twenty-seven percent could say nothing about either party, a threefold increase from 1952. Only 54 percent in the 1972 NES survey commented about both parties. Since then Americans' ability to talk about the parties has not improved substantially. There was even a time in the 1980s when more than half had no comment about one or both parties.

With the notable exception of Martin Wattenberg's research, this development has not figured heavily in scholars' assessments of U.S. parties.[11] A leading scholar argued in the 1980s—a time when the number of citizens who could find nothing to say about the parties was at nearly its highest level ever—that the parties were stronger than ever.[12] Scholars admire the parties for how they have adjusted to campaigns based on money, media, and top-down organization. This adaptability has indeed been remarkable, but to equate it with vibrancy is to confuse resilience with vitality. Parties are always opportunistic. They do not always have a hold on the public imagination.

Politics today is candidate- rather than party-centered. In this politics of the moment, strategic advantage and targets of opportunity are paramount. Candidates cannot afford to ignore the slightest ripple of public opinion because their future is firmly rooted in the present. Unlike the party politics of old, there is no thought of using today's defeat to build toward tomorrow's victory. Indeed, there is almost no tomorrow in today's politics and sometimes not even a yesterday. In 1988, George Bush pummeled Michael Dukakis with a roughshod campaign based on taxes, race, crime, and the environment—issues that were not all that salient until Bush's pollsters identified them as his best weapons. After his election Bush brushed off his mean-spirited campaign: "That's history—that doesn't mean anything anymore." As his 1992 reelection campaign was about to begin, he said: "I'm certainly going into this as a dog-eat-dog fight, and I will do what I have to do to be re-elected."[13]

Americans have grown to dislike almost everything about modern campaigns. They offer a litany of complaints: too much money, too much theater, too much fighting, and too much deception. For some, these are reasons not to participate, as this chapter will show.

The decline of the party as an idea—something that people carry in their heads—has also reduced election participation. At one time, the party cast its messages forward in the form of large ideas, thereby linking its future to that of its supporters. Politics now is based on small and immediate promises to almost any constituency that is a source of votes. This makes it harder for people to recognize and embrace parties as instruments in which to entrust their future and that of the nation.

IN NO OTHER ERA has the outcome of presidential elections hinged so much on small issues as it has in recent decades. Examples certainly exist of astonishing twists and turns in the past. In 1884, for instance, the GOP denied its nomination to incumbent Chester A. Arthur and turned instead to James G. Blaine ("the Man from Maine"), who might even have won if he had not sat in silence on the same platform while a fellow Republican launched a bigoted attack on the Democrats as the party of "rum, Romanism, and rebellion."

Such developments, once the exception, are now commonplace. In 1976, Gerald Ford's campaign stalled when he asserted in the second presidential debate that "no Soviet dominance of Eastern Europe" existed. In 1980, Jimmy Carter and Ronald Reagan were deadlocked going into the campaign's final days when the collapse of negotiations for the release of American hostages in Iran sent voters scurrying toward Reagan. In 1988, George Bush went from 17 points down in the polls to 16 points up after launching a no-holds-barred attack on Dukakis.[14] In 1992, Bill Clinton's run for the presidency ended almost before it began when Gennifer Flowers alleged a twelve-year sexual relationship; the campaign ended with a frantic Bush calling Clinton, who at one time had trailed both him and Ross Perot in the polls, a "bozo." In 1995, Clinton looked like a one-term president until congressional Republicans' shutdown of the federal government backfired, thrusting him into a large lead he never relinquished. In 2000, Al Gore was solidifying a lead when he huffed and puffed his way through the first presidential debate, sending his campaign skidding until a late-breaking news story told of his opponent's arrest for drunken driving a quarter century earlier.

Against this backdrop, one has difficulty imagining that U.S. elections periodically were battlegrounds between parties over large ideas. These ideas stemmed from Americans' deepest hopes and fears, and had the power to cement their loyalty to a party and draw them to the polls.

America's first political parties, in fact, emerged from Thomas Jefferson's and Alexander Hamilton's competing visions of the new nation.* Hamilton saw society as divided between common people and those he called "the rich and the wellborn," who he said should have "a distinct, permanent share in the government." His vision of a stratified nation constructed on commercial wealth clashed with Jefferson's notion of an egalitarian society rooted in the interests and values of small landholders. After defeating the Federalist John Adams for the presidency, Jefferson hailed his election victory as the "Revolution of 1800." Jefferson had no clear notion of how a popular government might work in practice, but he taught ordinary Americans to look upon the national government as belonging to all, not just to the privileged few.[15]

Not until Andrew Jackson did the country have a leader determined to put popular government into practice.[16] Whereas Jefferson had organized the political party only at the leadership level, Jackson organized it from the bottom up. During the 1828 campaign the Democrats staged public rallies, parades, meetings, and barbecues, which, along with more liberal suffrage laws, contributed to a threefold increase in the number of voters.[17] After his election Jackson tried to get Congress to abolish the Electoral College. Failing that, he persuaded the states to tie their electoral votes to the popular vote, a system that is still in effect. By 1840, although some states still had property requirements, most white males could vote, and turnout among those that were eligible exceeded 70 percent. So fundamental was this empowerment of

---

*Indeed, democracy itself was born of the idea that the future could be changed. Before the Enlightenment, children expected to live the same lives as their parents. Heaven held out the hope of something different, but the passage of earthly time did not. The Enlightenment inspired the notion that the future could be altered through science and reason. The idea of alternative futures spread to politics, unleashing notions of personal rights and self-government. As democratic impulses emerged, there developed a need for organizations to serve as carriers of these aspirations. Political parties became those carriers.

the ordinary citizen that the historian James MacGregor Burns has labeled it America's "second constitution."[18] Alexis de Tocqueville expressed it in loftier terms: "The People reign in the American political world as the Deity does in the universe."[19]

The party system could not answer the slavery issue, and it collapsed in 1860 for the first and only time in the nation's history. The end of the Civil War restored the party system and presented a new issue: economic power.

The Civil War precipitated what political scientists have described as a party realignment. This concept describes the impact of an unusually powerful and divisive issue that changes the party coalitions to the lasting advantage of one party. As a result of the Civil War, the Republicans replaced the Democrats as the nation's majority party. The GOP became dominant in the larger and more populous North, while the Democratic Party had a stronghold in "the Solid South." During the next three decades the Republicans held a majority in one or both houses of Congress for all but four of those years.

The Republican Party's governing philosophy—"industrial nation building"—also prevailed.[20] Capitalists would be entrusted with fashioning a stronger country. Hamilton's notion of nation building through commerce had assigned a visible hand to government. No such role was envisioned this time. After Republican lawmakers put in place a protective tariff and a national banking system, they stepped aside to let the private sector and the hidden hand of the profit motive take over.[21] The idea of a free market seemed vaguely like the principle of self-reliance, which enabled small-town businessmen and Protestant churchgoers to embrace the Republican philosophy nearly as wholeheartedly as the Wall Street financiers did.

On the opposite side were the fodder of the U.S. industrial revolution: the western farmers exposed to unstable commodity prices, usurious credit, and exorbitant rail-shipping fees; the factory laborers subjected to low wages and harsh working conditions; and the Catholic immigrants relegated to menial jobs and city slums. An organic partisan cleavage occurred. "The center of gravity of wealth is on the

Republican side, while the center of gravity of poverty is on the Democratic side," the historian Charles Beard wrote.[22] The Democratic Party, however, was an unreliable advocate. Its patronage-minded urban machines and its conservative southern wing kept it close to the ideological center,[23] which enabled third parties like the Grangers, the Greenbackers, and the Populists to spring up on the left.* Class tensions were high, and turnout averaged 80 percent, although it responded to the issues of the moment. In the sharply defined elections of 1876 and 1888, turnout rose to 85 percent, whereas in 1872 and 1892, when passions were less strong, it fell to nearly 75 percent.

Tensions within the Democratic Party gradually reached a breaking point. The American economy was expanding rapidly, but farm prices and workers' pay were stagnant.[24] However, just as a populist groundswell was starting to pull the Democratic Party leftward, the economy crashed in 1893. As the Democrats' luck would have it, Grover Cleveland was president at the time, and people blamed him and his party for the crash.[25] When the Democrats and Populists then jointly nominated William Jennings Bryan in 1896 on a radical cheap-credit platform that spread fear in the industrial Northeast and Midwest, it triggered a party realignment from which the Republicans emerged stronger than ever.[26] For the next thirty-six years, the Republicans held the presidency except for Woodrow Wilson's two terms and had a majority in Congress for all but six years.

Party competition collapsed in the wake of the 1890s realignment. The Republicans thoroughly dominated the North and East while the Democrats continued to control the South. As competition within states fell and as they began to use registration laws as a means of restricting the vote, turnout dropped sharply.

---

*The tight hold that the party machines had on the cities was one reason virtually all of the third parties had an agrarian base. Another reason the United States, unlike the emerging European democracies, did not develop a strong and permanent socialist or labor party was, ironically, the absence of feudalism. Some analysts have claimed that the nation's natural wealth cushioned even its weakest citizens from the worst effects of capitalism. But conditions were not any better in American cities and factories than in those of Western Europe. European socialism was less a response to capitalism than to feudalism. Because European workers had to fight against hereditary aristocracies to get even the right to vote, they acquired a class consciousness that was much stronger than that of their American counterparts. "No feudalism, no socialism," is how the political scientist Walter Dean Burnham expressed it.

With the Democratic Party now more dependent than ever on its urban machines and southern wing, forward-looking leadership came from the Progressives. A belated middle-class reaction to the ills of industrialization, the Progressive movement, which was dominated by New England and midwestern Republicans, looked upon government "as an agent of human leadership."[27] The Progressives advocated a form of positive government that combined the egalitarian impulse associated with Jefferson with the governmental nationalism associated with Hamilton.[28] As the Progressives saw it, the federal government would, in the words of one observer, take "responsibility for humanizing industrialism and managing it."[29]

But would either major party accept the Progressive idea as its own? Theodore Roosevelt railed against the robber barons (even as he took their money for his 1904 campaign), but he could not break their hold on the GOP, so ingrained was its commitment to unregulated capitalism.[30] After Roosevelt failed to wrest the GOP nomination from William Howard Taft in 1912, Republican Progressives lost their influence within the GOP. Woodrow Wilson's New Freedom was a Progressive platform, and he succeeded in getting much of it adopted, but opposition from southern Democrats in Congress limited its scope. When old-guard Republicans regained the presidency in the 1920s in "the return to normalcy," the Progressive idea looked dead. The voting rate of low-income workers fell as their issues were swept aside.[31] Turnout among women, newly enfranchised, was even lower, plunging voting to a historic low.

Then came the shock of the Great Depression and Roosevelt's New Deal, which was an embodiment of the Progressive idea. It fused America's egalitarian and national impulses on a scale so large that opponents derided it as socialism.

People without money and jobs didn't care what Republicans called it. Roosevelt's work and security programs gave them the relief they sought.[32] The New Deal drew millions of new voters to the Democratic Party and, momentarily at least, erased its divisions. Although it is sometimes said that the South supported Roosevelt only because it had always voted Democratic, the region was mired in poverty and embraced the New Deal.[33] (The nation's poorest state, Mississippi, backed Roosevelt by more than 90 percent each time he ran.) Gallup polls indicated that the South was the region most supportive of Roosevelt's business regulatory policies and least inclined to believe his presidency threatened "the American way of life."[34] That the New Deal also appealed to black Americans, so much so that they abandoned their allegiance to the party of Lincoln, would only later antagonize the white South.[35]

Voter turnout among working-class Americans rose sharply in 1936, for the first time in four decades. They had not voted in large numbers in 1932 but did so after Roosevelt delivered on his promise to remember "the forgotten man."[36] Large numbers of young voters were also won over.[37] The New Deal did not completely erase the old divisions. At all income levels, Protestants were less enamored of Roosevelt and his policies than Catholics were.[38] Nevertheless, Roosevelt's election in 1932 marked the beginning of a party realignment that launched a thirty-six-year period of Democratic presidencies interrupted only by Eisenhower's two terms. During this period the Democrats also dominated Congress, losing control only in 1947–48 and 1953–54.

As the United States moved into the 1960s and then into the 1970s, election analysts were on the lookout for the next realignment. Previously, realignment had occurred every third or fourth decade, roughly the length of time required for loyalties developed in the last one to fade. According to realignment theory, the majority party can contribute to its own downfall, as Republicans under Hoover had done, by stubbornly sticking to its old policies even as new problems emerge.[39] As time ticks by, discontent grows until it boils over in response to a critical development.[40]

What many observers underestimated was the role that deep and enduring divisions play in realignments.[41] Analysts were so tightly focused on the rhythms of the realignment cycle that the root causes of past upheavals were not adequately considered. Realignments had been triggered, clearly enough, by critical issues. But what if the sources of resentment and insecurity that had fueled such issues were to dry up?

The United States had entered a new era. The New Deal resolved much of the economic and status uncertainty that fueled the realignment cycle. A safety net for the economically vulnerable now existed, as did policy mechanisms for stabilizing the economy. After the Second World War economic growth, which this time led to increased wages as well as increased profits, further alleviated Americans' economic fears. The median family income doubled between 1947 and 1973.[42] Meanwhile, the percentage of families living below the poverty line fell to a historically low 12 percent.[43]

Many poor people remained—twice as many as in some European democracies.[44] But the poor now represented a distinct minority, and the new federal food-stamp and public-housing programs met some of their needs. A majority that could be rallied by calls for economic redistribution no longer existed. Lyndon Johnson's much-heralded War on Poverty floundered after a few years for lack of congressional and popular support.[45] Even the twin pillars of Johnson's Great Society, Medicare and Medicaid, resulted as much from political opportunity as from public demand. Although support for government-provided medical care had been growing in the public and among leaders of both parties, it was not until the Kennedy assassination and Goldwater's ill-fated 1964 presidential bid swept a tide of liberal Democrats into Congress that there were enough votes to enact the programs.

The economic issue was losing its power. The Democratic Party now had a firm foothold in the middle class,[46] and Republican constituencies had accepted government's role in market regulation and income security.[47] A 1961 Gallup poll found only a 3 point difference in the opinions of managers and workers on the issue of business regulation; a 1940 Gallup poll had revealed a 35 point difference.[48] With widening affluence and a government safety net, liberals had won the public policy war. But they were losing their surefire election issue.

As the economic issue weakened during the 1960s, what Richard Scammon and Ben Wattenberg called the "social issue" emerged.[49] This set of issues included civil rights, the Vietnam War, social disorder, street crime, sexual liberation, school prayer, and welfare dependency.

Advances in technology, communication, and transportation had combined with changes in income, education, and public policy to produce rapid social change, creating aspirations and anxieties that spilled into the political system, disrupting both parties.*

The new social issues intersected the older economic division in confounding ways. Opposition to antiwar demonstrations united working-class whites and blacks but civil rights demonstrations divided them.[50] No one supported crime, but conservative Republicans and blue-collar Democrats more frequently considered jails the answer than did moderate Republicans and middle-class Democrats. Few said godlessness was good for society, but Protestant fundamentalists of both parties were most opposed to the ban on school prayer. Political, economic, and reproductive rights for women created divisions even among women. And so it went, issue after issue.

How do you create cohesive party coalitions out of that mix? The short answer is that you don't. Too many crosscutting issues existed for either party to combine them in a way that would easily satisfy its followers. By the early 1970s, the number of self-described independents had increased by 15 percentage points.

Turnout tumbled. Many people were turned off by both parties, and some chose not to vote. From a high of 63 percent in 1960, participation dropped to 54 percent in 1972, one of the sharpest declines ever, despite a surge in voting by southern blacks and whites.

Although Vietnam received more attention and contributed to a growing lack of confidence in government, civil rights had a larger impact on the party coalitions. The issue was a renewal of Americans' struggle for political equality. Would the United States live up to its creed "that all men are created equal"?[51] Against the backdrop of World War II,

---

*Before this time religion had been the major social issue. A Protestant-Catholic cleavage had characterized party politics since the 1840s. The issue virtually disappeared during the 1960s, after the election and assassination of John Kennedy, the nation's first Catholic president. In the 1960 election, turnout among Catholics (in support of Kennedy) and churchgoing Protestants (in opposition to Kennedy) increased significantly.

where black soldiers had fought to defeat fascism, that question res-
onated more powerfully than at any time since the Civil War. Even so,
not until the Democrats' northern congressional wing embraced the
cause was either party willing to accept the political risk of using federal authority to abolish Jim Crow laws. Nevertheless, the 1964 Civil
Rights Act and the 1965 Voting Rights Act were enacted with the support of most Republican lawmakers and, according to public opinion
polls, had the backing of a majority of northern Republicans and
Democrats.

Abruptly, however, the momentum behind the black civil rights
movement slowed. The Watts riot in Los Angeles in 1965, the race riots
during the long hot summer of 1966, and the fiery outbursts in U.S.
cities in 1968 after the King assassination did not help the cause of
African Americans. But the crux of the matter was that the civil rights
agenda had shifted. Although most northern whites welcomed an end
to enforced segregation, they were not enthusiastic about forced integration. Racial busing, minority set-asides, and quota-based affirmative action lacked majority support. A belief in equality had collided
with self-interest and a belief in freedom of choice.

Partisan realities had also intruded. Lower- and middle-income
white Democrats who lived in neighborhoods or worked at jobs
directly affected by busing and affirmative action were among those
most strongly opposed to the policies. In Michigan, they expressed
their displeasure with the party's direction by handing George Wallace
a 51 to 27 percent victory over George McGovern in the Democratic
presidential primary. That fall, a record number of working-class
whites voted Republican.[52]

However, the GOP had its own conundrum. Although in 1964 five
southern states voted Republican for the first time ever in a backlash
against civil rights, the GOP, until then, had not been identified with
opposition to racial change. However, as the agenda shifted toward
racial busing, affirmative action, and minority set-asides, Republicans'
small-government philosophy came to the fore. If racial discrimina-
tion was unacceptable, the use of federal authority to impose integration on schools and workplaces was problematic. This tension could be
leveraged in a way that served partisan purposes. Upon taking office in

1969, Richard Nixon launched a "southern strategy" designed to bring racial conservatives into the GOP.

The race issue brought about a partial realignment of the party system.[53] The white South gradually shifted to the Republican Party, drawing it to the right on issues such as abortion and education. Black Americans became a mainstay of the Democratic Party, moving it to the left on issues ranging from criminal justice to welfare assistance.

The civil rights movement had spurred women to assert their rights, which, in combination with their rising level of education and employment, was making them into a powerful political force. Women and men had once held nearly identical policy views, but a gender gap was developing that would go beyond questions of sexual equality. On issues such as gun control, education, health, and welfare, women were separating themselves from men, which, in the 1980s, would be reflected in the party coalitions: women leaning Democratic and men leaning Republican.

Powerful though it was, the civil rights issue had to compete for attention with a host of other concerns, including a weakening economy.[54] With so many issues in play, the electorate had a hard time finding all of their answers within one party. Ticket splitting increased accordingly. Most voters in the 1950s and early 1960s had supported a party's entire slate of candidates. By the 1970s, two-thirds cast a split ticket.[55]

In the latter part of the 1970s, with the intensity of the civil rights issue having diminished, the parties settled into a pattern that can be described as interest group politics, party style.[56] The nation had entered its post-industrial phase; it was a vastly more complex and differentiated society than it had been even as late as the Second World War. Special interests were everywhere, and each had its own lobbying group.[57] Environmentalists found ways to divide themselves into 250 organizations, each with its own specialty. Nearly every government program had a clientele group that, in turn, had its own organization, such as the Associated Milk Producers, the National Welfare Rights Organization, and the National Association of Broadcasters. Hundreds of specialized trade associations, representing nearly every conceivable type of industry or business, had materialized to lobby alongside the Chamber of Commerce and National Association of Manufacturers, which once nearly had the trade association sector to themselves.[58] Historically disadvantaged groups—women, Hispanics, gays, the disabled, and others—had formed separate political movements. When Congress changed the campaign finance laws in 1974, group-related political action committees (PACs) increased in number from 600 to 4,000 within a decade.[59]

The proportion of citizens who believed interest groups ran the government jumped from 31 percent in 1964 to 67 percent in 1988.[60] Wherever Americans had stood on the economic issue, they could claim it as their own. Now nearly every issue seemed to belong to "somebody else." Even headline issues, such as the spotted owl controversy, seemed obscure to most. The political landscape was littered with issues but not defined by any of them. Commentators employed all sorts of fancy labels—neo-liberals, neo-conservatives, the New Left, the Old Left, the Old Right, the New Right, and more—in an effort to tie groups and ideas into neat bundles. But if these distinctions made sense to the pundit, they made no sense to the ordinary citizen, who was also finding parties increasingly difficult to describe. In 1980, 34 percent, the highest proportion ever, had nothing to say when asked what they liked and disliked about the parties.[61]

Party platforms assumed the look of the menu at a Chinese restaurant. Platforms had been declarations of broad goals and principles. Now they became promissory notes to special interests. The 1948 Democratic platform was 2,800 words in length. The 1984 Democratic platform contained 47,800 words, the longest ever. The Republican platform mushroomed from 2,000 words in 1948 to 28,000 in 1984.[62]

Much of this change happened during Ronald Reagan's presidency. Although Reagan's victory in the 1980 presidential election is often attributed to his broad economic philosophy, he almost lost because of it. Reagan was the least popular candidate since the start of polling to win a presidential election.[63] Fortunately for him, Jimmy Carter was even less popular. The Iranian hostage crisis, double-digit inflation, and high unemployment had made Carter vulnerable to any Republican challenger.

Reagan's popularity was no better during his first eighteen months in office; his approval rating plunged faster than that of any president since the Gallup organization began measuring it. An economic rebound during the second half of Reagan's first term saved his presidency. Even then, on most issues of the 1984 campaign, Americans said they preferred his opponent's positions.[64] Reagan was personally popular, but public opinion on most issues changed very little during his presidency and was concentrated in the political center.[65]

Lawmakers, however, were gravitating toward the vocal groups on the extremes of their parties. The campaign and lobbying support these groups could provide, when combined with the intensity of their members' beliefs, enabled them to climb over other claimants for lawmakers' attention. Christian fundamentalists, for example, had come together around a set of "cultural issues" and had aligned themselves with the GOP.[66] Before the 1973 *Roe* v. *Wade* abortion decision, fundamentalists were less active politically than other Americans; afterwards, they were more active on several dimensions than comparable groups.[67] Opposition to abortion became a litmus test for Republican officeholders. Pro-choice groups were nearly as successful in forcing Democratic officeholders to back liberal abortion policies.

Congress was the major battleground for the contending groups of the right and the left. "Warfare among elites, waged . . . in the name of causes, not compromises," was how Harvard's Richard Neustadt described the situation.[68] As the parties became increasingly responsive to their aligned single-issue groups, Republican and Democratic lawmakers had trouble finding common ground. The number of bills on which a majority of Republicans lined up against a majority of Democrats nearly doubled between 1970 and 1986, before peaking in 1995.[69] As the congressional parties duked it out, they lost sight of the public's concerns. By the 1990s, only about 40 percent of major bills enacted by Congress were in line with what a majority of Americans said in polls they wanted government to do. Two decades earlier, majority opinion and public policy had been aligned 60 percent of the time.[70]

Late-nineteenth-century politics had been stood on its head. Then, the public had been divided while the parties' leaders clung together. Now, the public was clustered in the middle while the leaders were divided. Then, the issues were larger and officials were intent on avoiding them. Now, the issues were smaller and officials were fighting over every last detail. Would the waiting period for gun purchases be one day or three? Would the waiting period apply also to gun shows? In *Why Americans Hate Politics,* the journalist E. J. Dionne writes of a public weary of a stifling partisanship that insists on "yes/no, either/or approaches" to problems that beg for compromise.[71]

Plenty of congressional moderates were as frustrated as the press and the public by the lack of comity. "The important thing is to try to build a consensus," said Senator John C. Danforth (R-Missouri).[72] Occasionally, the political center did hold, as, for example, on the Family and Medical Leave Act, NAFTA, and the Welfare Reform Act. But in Congress, the center was weaker than at any time in the post–World War II era.

In presidential politics, however, the political center was king. Presidential campaigns are usually won or lost in the center, where the swing voters reside. By running too far to the left or the right, a candidate can expect to lose most of the moderates who make up the swing vote and, with that, can expect to lose the election. With his "third way" moderate positions on race, crime, taxes, and other issues, Bill Clinton nearly removed the "L-word" from the Republicans' lexicon. George W. Bush's "compassionate conservatism" buffered his candidacy in much the same way. These "philosophies," however, were as much about means as about ends. They offered no large vision of the nation's future.

Dozens of small- and medium-sized policies, everything from school uniforms to prescription drugs for the elderly, were the currency of presidential politics. When candidates ran short of overtures, new ones were devised.[73] Who, exactly, were the soccer moms that figured so prominently in the 1996 campaign? With the exception of Clinton's 1992 health-care and welfare-reform proposals, no presidential nominee floated truly new and ambitious policy ideas.

It would be easy to fault the candidates, but no overarching issue existed on which to base a presidential campaign. There was nothing like Vietnam or race, or even the battle between isolationists and internationalists in the period before World War II.[74] To be sure, the electorate had the look of being sharply divided. There were significant differences in the candidate preferences of men and women, whites and minorities, churchgoers and non-churchgoers, northerners and southerners, westerners and easterners, city dwellers and rural residents, lower-income and higher-income workers.[75] Partisanship was also apparent in the vote. In 2000, for example, Bush received the support of 91 percent of self-described Republicans and Gore was backed by 86 percent of self-identified Democrats.

Even so, passions did not run deep except among the issue activists. The large majority felt their lives and the country's fate would not be much different if the Democrat or the Republican won. Only about half of adults bothered even to vote in the 1988–2000 elections, despite a surge in registration after passage of the 1993 Motor Voter Act.

As the issues of politics have become smaller and more numerous, Americans have had difficulty focusing on political parties. "My mind has just gone blank," said a Florida resident in 2000 when asked to describe the parties.[76] Citizens are more highly educated today than in the 1950s, but they have a harder time talking about parties. As noted earlier, nearly three in ten have nothing to say when asked what they like and dislike about the parties.

During the 1980s and 1990s, when the battle lines between the two parties were sharply drawn over issues such as abortion and health care, the number of people who were able to talk about the parties increased somewhat. Nevertheless, there are still a lot fewer of them today than there were in the 1950s. Moreover, people's impressions of the parties today are more negative than they were in the 1950s, and are spread across a wider range of issues and concerns. The concentrated and enduring party images of the past have given way to ones that are more fleeting and more particular.

Party identification has also weakened. In the 1950s, nearly 80 percent identified themselves as Democrats or Republicans. Half of them claimed to be "strong" partisans. By 1972, strong partisans numbered only 25 percent and independents had increased to 35 percent of the adult public.[77] Ever since, independents have outnumbered strong partisans. In 2000, the number of independents reached the 40 percent mark.[78]

Scholars have offered any number of reasons for the parties' decline: ballot and civil service reforms, the development of advertising and public relations, the rise of the news media, increased levels of education, the nationalization of politics and policy, and the shift toward executive-centered government.[79] Any such listing, however, fails to distinguish the merely noteworthy from the truly important. Parties have lost their hold primarily because the issues of politics have changed.

Parties have no rival when a big, enduring, and divisive issue dominates the agenda. They are the only institution designed to organize a potential majority around such an issue.[80] But parties falter when crosscutting issues occupy the agenda. A century ago, James Bryce worried that the growing complexity of American society threatened the parties' ability to forge cohesive majorities.[81] Social complexity is now orders of magnitude greater and has clearly overtaken the parties.

Parties have never had so many communication weapons at their disposal, yet they have never found it so hard to communicate their message. As Franklin Roosevelt's voice crackled into living rooms through the vacuum-tube radio, his pledge to "the forgotten man" had a persuasive power that today's media consultants would envy. Listeners didn't have to be told what FDR had in mind or to whom he was speaking. Old-style party politics was easy to conceptualize. The issues were large, close to home, and enduring. When people said the Democrats represented the "working people" while the GOP represented "business," they spoke from experience.

Campaign messages today are strikingly different in the wide range of issues they address, the contradictions they contain, and the speed with which they turn over. Since 1972 nearly every successive presidential campaign has been run on a new set of issues. It is therefore not surprising that a lot of people have trouble expressing thoughts about the parties.*

---

*Interestingly, even today, many make sense of the parties by falling back on the old economic divisions. A substantial proportion who express likes and dislikes about the parties do so in the context of economic class. This is particularly true of older Americans. This aspect of party images is beyond the scope of this chapter, which is intended to show how party attachments, whatever their content, affect election participation.

Campaign rhetoric has adjusted to fit the new reality. Roderick Hart, a communication scholar at the University of Texas, examined changes in presidential candidates' word usage during the 1948–96 period. As time went by, candidates talked a lot more about themselves and a lot less about political parties. They spoke more about the here and now and less about the future. Declaration surrendered to ambiguity, as candidates increasingly tried to negotiate their way across the bumpy terrain of crosscutting issues.[82]

The rhetoric of presidential politics has also been scaled down. In addressing narrow and complex issues, candidates sound at times like policy analysts rather than national leaders. Statistics and technical terms pour from their mouths. During the 2000 debates Bush and Gore argued about fiscal projections, program eligibility, and performance criteria. Ironically, in the process of trying to advance their points, both candidates talked down to their audience. A computer program designed to assess the reading difficulty of school textbooks found that Kennedy and Nixon in the 1960 debates used words suited to tenth graders, but Bush's and Gore's words in 2000 were pitched to seventh and eighth graders—five levels below the national average.[83]

High-sounding arguments do not hold up well when demands are coming from every angle. When George W. Bush proposed an across-the-board tax cut ("it's your money, not their money") during the 2000 campaign, it contained echoes of Republican campaigns dating back to Hoover and McKinley. However, it did not resonate deeply, nor did Bush expect it to do so. Like Gore, he was pursuing the swing voters who now decide the outcome of presidential elections. Thus, when Gore made inroads among senior citizens with his prescription-drug plan, Bush countered with a "their money" plan of his own. The projected cost of Bush's prescription-drug benefit was $158 billion, which he heralded as a savings over the $253 billion tab for Gore's proposal.[84]

As organizations, parties have adjusted smoothly to the new politics of media and money, which, for some analysts, is proof enough that they are as meaningful as ever. But, as Robert Putnam says, to leave voters out of the equation "is to miss the whole point."[85]

As the parties have declined as objects of loyalty and thought, so has Americans' concern with election politics. Like any other emotional attachment, party loyalty heightens interest and commitment. For its part, party awareness reflects people's ability to recognize what's at stake in election politics and the options available to them.[86] Party attachments, in short, give people reason to vote. During the 1952–2000 period, partisans who had thoughts about both parties had a voting rate that was twice that of independents who could not talk about either party. Although this ratio changed very little from one election to the next, the size of the two groups has changed substantially. Since the 1960s the number of partisans with an awareness of both parties has declined by 25 percent while the number of independents with thoughts about neither party has nearly doubled.[87] In other words, the type of citizen who votes more often has been replaced by the type who votes less often.

For every category of identifier—from the strongest partisans to the purest independents—those who are unable to find words with which to describe the parties have significantly lower voting rates (Table 2.1). The difference at the extremes is very large. Strong partisans with an awareness of both parties have a voting rate 47 percentage points higher than that of pure independents with an awareness of neither party. (People's ability to talk about parties and their party identification contribute almost equally to their voting tendency. The correlation with turnout is .20 for party identification and .25 for party awareness, both of which are statistically significant at the .0001 level.)

The ability to talk about parties is also associated with day-to-day campaign involvement. Our Vanishing Voter surveys during the 2000 election revealed that citizens who did not have a mental image of the parties, at least in the sense of being able to express that image in words, were only about half as likely to talk, think, or follow news about the campaign on a daily basis. Even when age, education, and income were controlled, large and statistically significant differences existed in the campaign involvement of those who had and those who lacked images of the parties.

The findings indicate, moreover, that the so-called myth of the independent voter is only partially a myth. Scholars have noted that

TABLE 2.1

HOW VOTER TURNOUT RELATES TO PARTY
IDENTIFICATION AND PARTY AWARENESS

Turnout Rate (Self-Reported) Among Those:

	Unable to Say Anything About Either Party	Able to Say Something About One Party	Able to Say Something About Both Parties
Strong Partisan	74%	78%	88%
Weak Partisan	61%	69%	80%
Leaning Independent	58%	65%	81%
Pure Independent	41%	54%	75%

Source: American National Election Studies, 1952–2000.

most self-described independents behave like "closet partisans." Two-thirds of independents admit to "leaning" toward a party. These "leaners," moreover, tend to act like real partisans when choosing a candidate. In some elections, they are nearly as loyal as strong partisans to their preferred party—thus, the "myth" of the independent voter.

When it comes to turnout, however, there is a substantial gap between independent leaners and strong partisans. In National Election Studies surveys, independent leaners have consistently reported turnout rates below those of strong partisans and, in the surveys where reported voting has been checked against actual voting records, the difference has been roughly 10 percent. Even when education and income differences are controlled, the difference is statistically significant at the .01 level.

The gap widens further when it comes to day-to-day election involvement. Our Vanishing Voter surveys during the 2000 election

found that strong partisans were in a league of their own when it came
to talking, thinking, and following news about the campaign. They
were nearly twice as likely as pure independents, independent leaners,
and weak partisans to engage in these activities during a typical day of
the campaign. Week-to-week attention to the campaign displayed the
same pattern. Strong partisans were roughly twice as likely as the others to say they had paid "a great deal" or "quite a bit" of attention to the
campaign during the past week.

When independents go into the polling booth, most of them have a
partisan inclination that affects the choice they make. In other respects,
however, they are not at all like strong partisans. Independent leaners
attend to the campaign with much less regularity than strong partisans
and are less likely to make it to the polls. The myth of the independent
voter is only partly a myth. Independents and partisans are not the
same when it comes to participation. The rise of the independent voter
has contributed to the fall in election turnout and interest.

Political change rarely affects all groups equally, and the decline of the
party is no exception. Historically, the less privileged have gained the
most from parties. Because their strength is in their numbers rather
than in their economic or organizational resources, they have traditionally depended more heavily on parties than on lobbying activities
to achieve their policy goals. It is no accident that the interests of the
lower classes led to the formation of America's first political party and,
later, its first grassroots party. For both the Jeffersonians and the Jacksonians, the party was the means by which those with less hoped to
compete successfully against those with more.[88]

Accordingly, the decline of the party has primarily affected those of
lower income and education. Although a "class gap" in turnout has
been a persistent feature of American politics, it widened during the
1964–76 period, when voting among working-class northern whites fell
sharply. The issue they cared most about, economic security, was
shrinking in significance just as the social issue was weakening the
attachment many of them had to the Democratic Party.[89]

Political scientists have waged an inconclusive debate about whether turnout among this group continued to decline after the early 1970s.[90] Whatever the case, working-class northern whites did not reengage when single-issue groups began to dominate the agenda. Group-centered politics operates on money and communication skills, both of which are in short supply among those of lower income and education.

Party conflict during the period between the Civil War and the Great Depression had centered on working-class whites. They now inhabit the periphery of policy debates. In our Vanishing Voter survey they were about 30 percent more likely than those in the middle- or top-income groups to say the election's outcome would have little or no impact on their lives.[91]

The complexity of modern politics has also affected their interest in elections. In the 1950s, education and income were only marginally related to people's ability to identify the parties. The economic division between the parties was so robust that nearly everyone could recognize it. Class issues are what the political scientists Edward Carmines and James Stimson call "easy" issues. No real degree of political sophistication is required to understand them.

On the other hand, many current political issues are "hard" in the sense that factual information and analytical skills are required to sort them out.[92] Moreover, newer labels such as the "liberal party" or the "conservative party" are harder to grasp than traditional phrases such as the "party of working people" or the "party of big business." Not surprisingly, education has become a more important factor in the ability to recognize what the parties stand for. In 1952, only one in ten adults with a high school education or less had difficulty describing the parties. Today, one in three cannot find the words with which to describe them. This weakened capacity to recognize the options that parties offer is associated with lower voting rates. The less educated who lack an image of the parties are much less likely to vote than those who possess such an image, whether they are strong partisans, weak partisans, independent leaners, or pure independents.[93]

The class gap in American politics is extraordinary. Turnout among those at the bottom of the income and education ladders is only half that of those at the top—a pattern unheard of in Europe but found also in some less-developed democracies, including India. Moreover, our Vanishing Voter surveys indicate that day-to-day involvement levels— how much people think and talk about the campaign and follow it in the news—are just as stratified as is turnout. Even high moments in the campaign, including the October debates, do not greatly alter the pattern.

The weakened state of the party as both an idea and the object of loyalty is central to any explanation of why election participation has slipped, both generally and among the less advantaged particularly. Partisanship in both forms encourages participation. It helps people to recognize their stake in elections and gives them a side in which to entrust their political future. However, in the absence of a large issue that divides the parties on a continuing basis, or when the sheer number of choices the parties offer confounds the difference between them, people—especially those of lower education and income—may conclude that the parties differ in marginal, bewildering, or unsatisfactory ways. Any such conclusion is bound to weaken party attachments and, with that, weaken the inclination to take part in elections.

This predicament will not be solved by the emergence of a strong third party, even though some Americans like the thought. In our Vanishing Voter surveys in 2000, only 23 percent agreed that "the two-party system works fairly well." A larger number, 39 percent, agreed that "the two-party system has real problems but with improvement can still work well." For 28 percent, however, there was a feeling that "the two-party system is seriously broken and the country needs a third party." However, third parties are born of issues rather than wishes. No third-party candidate of the left since 1924 has garnered even as much as 5 percent of the vote, and Wallace's 1968 bid was the last on the right to do so. Big issues, economics and race, fueled those insurgencies. Ross Perot's 1992 candidacy shows only that there is a vacancy in the political center when the major parties drift too far apart and that it fills rapidly when they tighten up. The fact is, the same factors that have weakened the major parties—the decline of the large overarching issue, the creation of an economic safety net, and the rise of groups to satisfy particular demands—have deprived third parties of the raw material they need if they are to thrive.

Some commentators—those of the "vote for the person, not the party" persuasion—would make a virtue of the weakening of party and of partisan attachments. It is not a virtue, nor is it a fault, at least in the sense that someone is obviously to blame for the change. Party decline was inevitable when the long-term struggle over competing visions of the nation waned.

AS THE PARTIES were weakening during the 1960s, the candidates were becoming increasingly prominent. Americans were initially thrilled by the chance for a closer look at the candidates and their campaigns.[94] Theodore H. White's *The Making of the President, 1960* topped the best-seller list. Gradually, however, people came to dislike almost everything they saw.

Until the 1960s, presidential candidates based their campaigns largely on the party organizations, although, in truth, these organizations were never all that powerful. For every locale that had a party machine capable of delivering the vote, scores more had a smattering of volunteers who were doing well if they found time to knock on a few doors.[95] Nevertheless, campaigns were organized around the parties during the first half of the 1900s. Signs of what the historian Richard Jensen called the advertising campaign style—one focusing on the candidates and conducted through the media—were emerging,[96] but the communication system was not yet of a kind suited to a national campaign. Newspapers were locally based, and radio and television newscasts were too brief to provide the publicity that was needed.[97]

In the early 1960s, however, television news changed and so did presidential campaigns. The networks lengthened their evening newscasts to a half hour and began to produce news with pictures. With their national audience, they were ideally suited to the publicity needs of presidential hopefuls.[98] Candidates scheduled their events to fit the deadlines of the evening news and staged their appearances in settings suited to the networks' desire for good pictures.[99] Televised political advertising was also blossoming. Spending on ads in the 1964 election was 300 percent greater than it had been in 1960.[100]

Control over campaigns was shifting rapidly from the parties to the candidates. The presidential nominating process was no exception. Although party leaders still had the power to pick the nominees, presidential candidates were increasingly using primaries to force their hand.[101] After the 1968 campaign, party leaders lost control of nominations when a primary-based system was established.

These changes were occurring just as voters' partisan attachments were weakening. Some analysts have linked the two developments,[102] but it was as much coincidence as cause. Nevertheless, diminished partisanship—and in primaries, the absence of party labels—meant that techniques of mass persuasion could be used to greater effect, assuming the candidate knew how to use them.[103] Not all candidates did. After his 1988 campaign Michael Dukakis acknowledged "a failure to understand" the new-style politics. He had stuck stubbornly to the issues, even as his campaign fell apart around him. "I said in my acceptance speech in Atlanta that the 1988 campaign was . . . about [governing]. I was wrong. It was about phraseology. It was about 10-second sound bites. And made-for-TV backdrops. And going negative."[104]

Journalists became central players in campaigns. To get to the people, candidates would have to go through the press. This empowered the press to assess the candidates' electability and fitness for office—functions the parties had performed in the past. However, the press is not like the parties. The parties are driven by the force of their traditions and constituent interests, which is why Republican leaders in 2000 favored Bush, a predictable Republican, over John McCain, a maverick. In contrast, the press is driven by what the *New York Times*'s James Reston described as "the exhilarating search after the Now."[105] The media's thirst for novelty explains why, during the 2000 general election, Bush's arrest twenty-five years earlier for drunken driving received more election coverage than did all foreign policy issues combined.[106]

The new style of campaigning has brought out aspects of politics that had previously been downplayed. Ambition, manipulation, and peccadilloes are now as visible to the electorate as issues of policy and leadership. But politicking, like sausage making, is best viewed from a distance. Elections are supposed to bring out the issues. They are not supposed to ruin one's appetite.[107] But that is the best way to understand much of what Americans now see during a campaign and why some don't have much taste for it.

Not all aspects of the modern campaign are associated with lower levels of involvement. Our Vanishing Voter surveys found, for example, that respondents who believe "interest groups and donors" have too much influence over candidates were actually somewhat more likely than others to follow the campaign in the news and even 5 percentage points more likely to vote on Election Day. This is not to say that a concern with campaign money spurs participation; those who participate more heavily may simply be more aware of the money problem. Moreover, people don't witness the exchange of money. But they regularly see other unsavory aspects of modern politics, and it is these features that discourage participation.

"The air is thick with charges, defenses, recriminations, till the voter knows not what to believe."[108] James Bryce was describing presidential elections in the age before the air meant the airwaves. The fiery rhetoric was fed by the passions of late-nineteenth-century politics. Deepening class conflict was part of it, as was lingering bitterness over the Civil War. ("The left wing of the new Confederate army" was Treasury Secretary John Sherman's description of the Democrats.)[109]

Today, the political heat is the result of strategic calculation and is applied to the degree that it suits the candidate's purposes. One cannot mark the exact date when attack politics was devised, one can only provide examples to indicate its existence, none more clearly than the 1988 Bush campaign. When *Time* magazine's cover story "The Year of the Handlers" heralded consultants who manipulate symbols and bring "hot button" issues into play, the Bush campaign was the prototype.[110] Its symbol became a felon who not by chance was also an African-American male: Willie Horton. (He was William Horton before the spin doctors latched onto him.) A political ad by "Americans for Bush," a conservative action group, explained that Horton had brutally raped a white woman while on weekend furlough from a Massachusetts prison. The ad sent the press into a tizzy, and the Bush campaign produced a spot that exploited the newfound issue. "As governor, Michael Dukakis . . . gave weekend furloughs for first degree murderers not eligible for parole. While out, many committed other crimes like kidnapping and rape. And many are still at large." As the commercial concluded, the words "268 Escaped, Many Are Still at Large" scrolled across the television screen.

Negative advertising has become a defining feature of presidential politics. In his study, Roderick Hart found that "reactive ads," which are attacks on an opponent or defenses against such attacks, increased from 11 percent in 1960 to 43 percent in 1996.[111] Brown University's Darrell West also reported a sharp increase in negative messages, particularly in those ads that figure prominently in candidates' campaigns. About 35 percent of "prominent" campaign ads in 1972 and 1976 were negative or attack ads. That proportion jumped to 60 percent in 1980, 74 percent in 1984, and 83 percent in 1988 before dropping somewhat in 1992.[112] Other scholars documented similar trends. Three studies concluded that campaign advertising in 1996 was the most negative yet.[113] Moreover, the candidates and parties are not the only ones that run attack ads. In 2000, interest groups spent roughly $16 million on ads aimed at the presidential candidates.[114]

Journalists have contributed to the negative tone of campaign politics. Attack journalism emerged out of the Vietnam War and the Watergate scandal, and reporters have zeroed in on political candidates. Coverage of presidential candidates was 25 percent negative in 1960. By 1972, it had increased to 40 percent. It reached 50 percent in 1980 and has stayed at or above 60 percent since 1988.[115]

Negative campaigns are as old as the Jefferson-Adams race of 1800, but today's version has no historical parallel. The volume is unlike anything that has gone before. "You can't compare a nasty quote about Thomas Jefferson," says former presidential speechwriter Richard Goodwin, "with the intensity and penetration [of today's attacks]."[116]

Attack politics is sometimes designed to keep voters away from the polls. At a 1984 conference, a Republican consultant said he makes a "deliberate attempt to create the maximum amount of cross pressures on the weak [Democratic] 'Party voter' so that the voter will 'come over to us or not vote at all.'" A Democratic consultant at the same conference said, "Some of the tactics we use in political campaigns do very much suppress the vote. We call it chloroforming or deep-freezing."[117]

That these tactics work as the consultants say is disputed by scholars.[118] Although Shanto Iyengar and Stephen Ansolabehere argue from experimental evidence that negative ads suppress turnout slightly,[119] the preponderance of evidence shows no such effect.

These studies of short-term effects, however, do not speak to the question of whether negative campaigning over the long run discourages participation. What happens when negative campaigns become so commonplace that they appear to the public to be the defining feature of elections? What happens when they become so prevalent that citizens come to believe that politicians spend most of their time fighting each other?

In fact, most Americans now feel exactly that way about candidates, and it has diminished the interest of some of them in campaigns. In our 2000 Vanishing Voter survey, 75 percent of the respondents agreed with the statement "political candidates are more concerned with fighting each other than with solving the nation's problems."[120] Respondents who held this belief were on the average day 12 percent less likely to discuss the campaign and 6 percent less likely to pay attention to news of it. The differences are not large, but they occur across the course of the campaign. Day in and day out, those who believe candidates are like street fighters attend less closely to the campaign, even when levels of education and income are controlled. Negative politics appears to wear some people down to the point where they simply want less of politics.

Of course, conflict can draw people to politics, as happened with the 2000 post-election squabbling and some particular events during the campaign itself. A good fight always draws a crowd. But a sharp encounter is different than the hum of negativity that surrounds the modern campaign. In fifty-six separate surveys over the course of the 2000 campaign, we asked people how attentive they had been to the campaign in the previous week and what they thought its tone had been. The more negative people perceived the tone to be during a given week, the less likely they were to talk, think, or follow news of the campaign that week. (The aggregate-level correlation was .40, significant at the 0.1 level.)

Politics, like the marketplace, cannot function without ambition. The challenge, as the political scientist James Ceaser says, is "to discover some way to create a degree of harmony between behavior that satisfies personal ambition and behavior that promotes the public good."[121] Always a hard goal to achieve, candidate-centered politics makes this balance more elusive because the current campaign is everything. Parties once disciplined candidates because the party had to accept the consequences of an adverse campaign, but no tomorrow exists for today's candidates.

Not all candidates give in to the temptation to climb over their opponent in order to win. In 1996, some of Dole's handlers wanted him to use the "L word"—not liberal, but liar—in statements about Clinton. Dole refused to do so.[122] For many others, however, attack politics is just another instrument in the campaign tool kit, waiting there to be hauled out when needed.

Three years into Bill Clinton's first term, the Knight-Ridder news chain assembled a list of his 1992 campaign promises in order to check them against his policy record. The list contained over a hundred pledges.[123] After his 1976 campaign Jimmy Carter asked his staff to make a record of his commitments, and they prepared a booklet containing more than 150 entries.[124]

The entrepreneurial nature of candidate-centered politics forces a presidential hopeful to act like a department-store Santa Claus. Promises are handed out left and right from the first day of the season to the last. In 1984, the Democratic front-runner, Walter Mondale, was attacked by his opponents as "the captive of special interests" for the pre-primary endorsements he received from labor, women's, and civil rights groups. But each of his opponents had actively sought the very same endorsements.

Of course, candidates are not free to make any promise they might wish, and they must declare commitments they might wish to avoid. They are constrained by their alliances and by the fact that not even the U.S. Treasury is bottomless. Nevertheless, they make lots of promises.[125] For the Bush campaign in 2000, the tough decision was not whether to offer a prescription drug plan for the elderly—Gore's inroads on this issue required a response—but how to shape the proposal so that it did not sharply contradict Bush's other positions.

Reporters get suspicious when they see candidates handing out IOUs. From a journalistic perspective, the campaign is less a struggle over the direction of national policy than a match between power-hungry candidates.[126] Journalists recognize that candidates' policy positions are rooted in partisan values and social problems but see candidates as so determined to win that they are willing "to be deceitful, to engage in hypocrisies, to manipulate appearances."[127] By deduction, one cannot take candidates at their word, and it's the journalist's job to warn the public. Journalists routinely criticize politicians for shifting their positions, waffling on tough issues, posturing, or pandering to whichever group they happen to be facing.[128] Sometimes, they find a way to say outright that the candidates cannot be trusted to keep their word. "Neither Al Gore nor George W. Bush," said a source on the *NBC Nightly News* of October 3, 2000, "will be able to deliver on their promises."[129]

Most Americans now share that view. In our Vanishing Voter surveys, 81 percent agreed with the statement "most political candidates will say almost anything to get themselves elected."[130] In her study, Doris Graber found that even those who trust politicians tend to discount their promises. Whatever they say is "swallowed with the proverbial grain of salt."[131]

The belief that candidates cannot be trusted discourages some people from participating more fully. In our Vanishing Voter surveys, respondents who believed candidates say whatever it takes to get elected were 10 percentage points less likely to vote than the other respondents. They were also less likely to pay attention to the campaign, particularly if they were otherwise interested in public affairs. Among these individuals, those who were mistrusting of candidates' words were 16 percent less likely on a typical day of the 2000 election to engage in a campaign-related conversation and 26 percent less likely to recall a campaign-related news story. Their belief that candidates cannot be trusted to keep their word resulted in campaign avoidance.

The irony is that candidates actually do deliver on most of their campaign promises. Four major scholarly studies have compared what modern presidents did in office with what they said as candidates.[132] Each reached the same conclusion: Presidents attempt to fulfill their campaign promises and succeed in achieving most of them. Bill Clinton's performance was about average for postwar presidents. A year before his first term ended, he had delivered on two-thirds of his 1992 campaign promises and had pursued half of the rest only to lose out in Congress.[133]

When presidents fail to deliver on a promise, it's usually because Congress has blocked the program or because conditions have changed enough that it no longer makes sense. And why, upon reflection, would presidents choose to break their promises? Presidents seek to govern and to do so they need the support of the interests that backed them during the campaign. "Presidents do, by and large, keep their campaign promises," says the political scientist George Edwards.[134]

There is no use, however, in trying to persuade voters to take candidates at their word. With so many promises in the air and with the press deflating most of them, Americans are sure to believe otherwise. They actually get the worst of two worlds: the one they imagine and the one they get. Not only do people wind up trusting candidates less as a result of all the promises they make, the country winds up with a host of programs that exist only because the nature of the modern campaign encourages candidates to spread promises around as if they were jelly.

The difference between recent presidents and those of several decades ago is not in their fidelity to their promises but in the number they had to make in order to get to the White House. Unlike their predecessors, recent presidents were unable to campaign on broad statements of principle within the context of a dependable party coalition. Thus, the problem is not that today's presidential candidates make promises they do not intend to keep, but that they make scores of promises they ought not make but have to make and keep.

At a Labor Day event in Illinois, George W. Bush, apparently unaware that he was standing near a live microphone, leaned over to his running mate, Dick Cheney, and nodded toward a nearby reporter. "There's Adam Clymer—major league asshole—from the *New York Times,*" said Bush. "Yeah, big time," replied Cheney. The incident made the news, big time. It ran repeatedly on television and was reported in nearly every daily paper. That week, 52 percent of our Vanishing Voter survey respondents said they had seen or heard the story, and most of them had talked about it with a family member, acquaintance, or co-worker.

Candidate gaffes are now an indelible part of presidential politics. Through the 1972 election, campaign controversies ("short-term concerns about how candidates and their campaigns *should* behave")[135] did not receive even half as much news coverage as did policy issues ("enduring disputes about how government *should* behave").[136] Since 1972, they have received equal time.[137] Even a partial list indicates just how salient they have become: Ford's statement on Eastern Europe, Carter's "lust in my heart" *Playboy* interview, Ted Kennedy's bumbling interview with Roger Mudd, Reagan's Taiwan and Vietnam goofs, Geraldine Ferraro's tax returns, Jesse Jackson's "Hymietown" remark, the Donna Rice affair, Dan Quayle's assault on Murphy Brown, the Gennifer Flowers affair, Gore's Buddhist temple appearance, and Bush's "rats" ad.

Some gaffes are merely entertaining. They fit Roger Ailes's "orchestra-pit theory" of news: "If you have two guys on a stage and one guy says, 'I have a solution to the Middle East problem,' and the other guy falls in the orchestra pit, who do you think is going to be on the evening news?" Ailes's good story versus good government theory was confirmed in 1996 when Dole fell off a speaking platform in Chico, California, and landed at the top of the nightly news.

Other gaffes give reporters and opponents an opportunity to

unmask a candidate by exploiting the disparity between the impression
the candidate has been trying to create and what the incident seems to
suggest. Gore's exaggerations in the October debates had reporters
leaping at the opportunity to question his honesty, which they had
wanted to do at least since his dissembling response to their questions
four years earlier about the Buddhist temple fundraiser. In many such
cases, the opposing candidate sits on the sidelines watching the targeted candidate squirm in the media spotlight.

Gaffes tend to make news for several days running. Policy issues seldom get this treatment. A study found that more than 50 percent of
gaffes get extended news coverage (at least one story for two consecutive days) compared with 15 percent of policy stories. The television
networks were the extreme case. Their nightly newscasts gave extended
coverage to more than 65 percent of gaffes, but only 10 percent of policy issues.[138] Gaffes trigger what the political scientist Larry Sabato calls
a "feeding frenzy." "The wounds may have been self-inflicted, and the
politician may richly deserve his or her fate," observes Sabato, "but the
journalists now take center stage in the process, creating the news as
much as reporting it."[139]

Campaign controversies get people's attention. In 2000, news audiences took more notice of stories about such incidents than they did of
stories about policy-based events, such as news reports of Bush's and
Gore's speeches on military readiness at the Veterans of Foreign Wars
national convention. On average, when compared with policy-based
news stories, gaffe-based stories were more widely noted (63 versus 36
percent), more accurately recalled (84 versus 54 percent), and more
widely discussed (46 versus 29 percent).

Gaffes draw the public into the campaign. That's no small feat in the
modern age. But if nearly everybody likes a good story, people don't
necessarily like the prominence that gaffes have attained or the emphasis that the candidates themselves place on flashy imagery. In our Vanishing Voter surveys, 62 percent agreed with the statement "political
campaigns today seem more like theater or entertainment than like
something to be taken seriously." Those who held this opinion were no
less likely than others to vote on Election Day. But, on the average day,
they were 7 percent less likely to discuss the campaign, 13 percent less

likely to think about it, and 16 percent less likely to attend to news about it.* The theatrical nature of the modern campaign is a turn-on for some but a turnoff for others.

A critic once said of the comic Jerry Lewis that he would have been the funniest ever if he had known when to end a joke. So it is with news of the candidates' blunders and indiscretions. Some of this coverage enlivens the campaign and informs the voters. The rest of it sullies everyone concerned. During the last week of the 2000 campaign, when many (19 percent claimed they made their choice in its final days) were still trying to determine which candidate to support, Bush's 1976 drunken driving conviction was plastered across headlines and on newscasts across the country. The story got people's attention: 83 percent said they were aware of it. It also got them talking: 59 percent of those who knew of the incident said they had a conversation about it—the highest level of any of the news stories examined. But only 17 percent said they found the story "informative"—a new low for the stories examined. People resent the type of election coverage that makes mountains out of molehills.

The candidates also contribute to the theater-like atmosphere of the modern campaign. They shamelessly employ dramatic appeals. In 1992 Clinton bridled at reporters' questions about his personal life but posed for *People* magazine and bared secrets from his childhood at the Democratic national convention. His running mate invoked his sister's death and his son's brush with death after being hit by a car. Gore described "waiting for a second breath of life" from his son, likening it to the nation which "is lying in the gutter, waiting for us to give it a second breath of life."[140] George Bush and his running mate mimicked their performance a few weeks later at the Republican convention with tales of their childhood and family life. Four years later, Elizabeth Dole told convention delegates and a national television audience how thoroughly she loved her husband. Four years after that, Gore planted

---

*Each of these relationships is statistically significant at the .05 level and usually at the .01 level when age, education, or income is controlled. When all three are controlled, the relationships are still statistically significant. The relationships are even stronger when the correlation involves the "candidates will say anything" variable. In the case of the "candidates spent their time fighting" variable, however, control variables reduce the relationship more substantially, except among people who express a general interest in public affairs.

a long kiss on his wife, Tipper, in front of convention delegates and viewers.

But journalists are the primary source of this kind of material, just as they regularly expose the staging and backdrops of the candidates' policy statements. On the basis of her 1988 study, the sociologist Kiku Adatto concluded that "time and again reporters called attention to the politicians' use of television imagery," thereby implying that what is being promised is the real artifice of politics. "The language of political reporting [is] filled with accounts of . . . camera angles and scripts, sound bites and spin control, photo opportunities and media gurus," Adatto writes. "Political reporters . . . sound like theater critics, reporting more on the stagecraft than the substance of politics."[141]

When journalists in the 1960s began to peer into candidates' campaigns and private lives, they failed to ask how and where it should stop. Theodore White, for one, wished it had never started. His bestselling books on the inner workings of presidential politics had inspired other journalists to follow his lead. "I invented [this] method of reporting," said White, "[and] I sincerely regret it."[142]

The desultory tone and content of today's campaign discourage some Americans from participating more fully. It is not the largest barrier to greater involvement, but it is a significant one.

Of the factors that inhibit voting, as indicated by our Vanishing Voter surveys, the nature of political competition ranks at the top, as Table 2.2 shows. Those who perceive little difference between the parties or who find politics hard to understand have much lower turnout rates and are less likely than others to attend to the campaign, engage in campaign conversations, reflect on the campaign, and follow news about it. Clearly, the passing of the era of big, divisive issues—a time when there was no doubt in people's minds that there was a significant difference between the parties—has diminished the incentive to participate. The greater complexity of today's politics affects participation in a similar way. An inability to comprehend what's at stake in politics is not, in the end, all that much different from thinking there's not much at stake. In either case, the public's capacity to recognize its options is diminished.

The conduct of election politics also affects participation, though less so, as Table 2.1 indicates. For those who believe politics includes too much theater, deceit, fighting, and pandering, participation rates are

TABLE 2.2
CAMPAIGN INVOLVEMENT AND
BELIEFS ABOUT POLITICS

	Vote Intention	Talked About Campaign (Daily)	Thought About Campaign (Daily)	Recalled Campaign News Story (Daily)	Paid Attention to Campaign (Weekly)
NATURE OF POLITICAL COMPETITION					
Parties are alike	-.25*	-.07*	-.17*	-.10*	-.16*
Politics is complicated	-.14*	-.09*	-.05*	-.05*	-.15*
PERSONAL INTEREST					
Campaigns are not interesting	-.08*	-.12*	-.17*	-.18*	-.28*
Life is hectic	-.10*	-.14*	-.19*	-.18*	-.30*
CANDIDATE CONDUCT**					
Candidates say anything to get elected	-.09*	-.04*	-.07*	-.04*	-.15*
Political campaigns seem like theater	-.03	-.03	-.08*	-.03	-.18*
Candidates are more concerned with fighting	-.04	-.05*	-.03	-.05*	-.10*

*Indicates that the correlation coefficient is significant at the .05 level. A negative sign indicates that respondents who agreed with the item tended to rank lower on the respective indicator of involvement.
**When the three items in this category are combined in an index, the relationships are significant at the .001 level, except for voting, which is significant at the .01 level.

lower than for those who feel differently. The belief that candidates cannot be trusted to keep their word is particularly detrimental.

The nature of political competition is not, of course, the only barrier to participation. In 2000, about 42 percent said that campaigns are not interesting to them and 49 percent said their lives are so hectic they don't have much time for elections. Such factors are major barriers to participation, but so, too, is Americans' low opinion of the modern campaign.

The nature of the campaign, including the news coverage of it, also diminishes people's impressions of the candidates. Opinion polls in recent elections reveal a public less than fully satisfied with the candidates and, in some cases, pondering a choice between the lesser of two evils. This was not the case in the 2000 election. Polls taken during the closing days of the campaign showed that, although most people were not enthusiastic about Bush and Gore, they were satisfied with the two men and the choice they offered. But the general trend is unmistakable. The Gallup organization first asked voters about their satisfaction with the presidential candidates in 1936. Through the 1960s, the only candidate who, on balance, was perceived unfavorably was Barry Goldwater in 1964. Since then—that is, during the era of candidate-centered politics—nearly half of the presidential candidates have had an unfavorable rating.[143]

V. O. Key described the impact of elections in metaphoric terms: "The output of an echo chamber bears an inevitable and invariable relation to the input." It should occasion no surprise that as the underside of politics, through attack ads and attack journalism, has become a larger part of what people see and hear during campaigns, they would think less highly of those who seek the presidency.

ARE THERE CHANGES in the offing that will lure Americans back to elections? Will parties stage a comeback as carriers of big and competing ideas? Will candidates change the way they campaign? Will the press alter its coverage of elections? The answer in each case would seem to be no. The tendencies that have dominated recent elections are almost certain to remain.

Political parties inevitably reflect the environment in which they operate. Without a deep and persistent problem that divides society, parties cannot credibly present themselves as the carriers of large and opposing ideas. They have learned not even to try. Recent economic downturns and international crises have been addressed as problems to be solved rather than as partisan crusades. The parties have fought over means rather than ends. This is not a bad thing. Few would trade social disharmony for heightened party competition. But consensus comes at a cost. A lowering of the political stakes reduces the incentive to participate.

Even if a powerful realigning issue should surface, it is not clear that the parties would benefit mightily from it. Today people are less inclined to look to parties for answers to their problems. The decline of the party as an object of identity and thought may have progressed to the point where the party no longer has the potential to rally a majority for the long run. In the short run, no doubt, one party or the other would gain from a disruptive issue. What is harder to imagine is that the favored party could ride the crest for decades and in the process remake the political and policy landscape, as happened during the New Deal era. The fact is, people need the parties less than they once did.

Parties have become the creations of their successful leaders. In turn, candidates have become the creations of an electoral system that rewards entrepreneurship and is driven by group demands and resources. Endless self-promotion and the tireless courting of groups are hallmarks of today's politics, and there is little reason to believe that a change is imminent. Of course, marginal adjustments will occur in how candidates campaign. Even before the terrorist attacks on the World Trade Center and the Pentagon, Americans were growing impatient with partisan bickering and negativity. Accordingly, Bush and Gore toned down their advertising during the 2000 campaign. But these were tactical decisions rather than a reflection of a deep change in the nature of the modern campaign.

The modern campaign is a form of patronage politics. It is not the patronage of government jobs and contracts; it is the patronage of group-centered policies in exchange for group support, financial and otherwise. To be sure, election politics has always had this component.

But the professionalization of political office and the proliferation of groups have magnified it beyond anything in the past. This type of campaign politics is a poor substitute for party-centered politics. The great virtue of party-based competition is not that it produces the best leadership and provides a full discussion of the issues, for it sometimes fails at these things, but that it offers a steady and relatively coherent set of ideas and traditions from which the voters can choose. The discontinuous and fluid form of group politics that now prevails can at times evade the grasp of even the more attentive citizen. It is a politics of shifting standards and fleeting controversies with no easily identifiable core for the voter to fix on.

This type of campaign politics necessarily takes place through the medium of the press, which exaggerates both the appearance and the reality of a relatively chaotic process. The media have a powerful drive toward skepticism, a persistent need for novelty, and a weakness for personality. These are deeply rooted and longstanding tendencies within the media that are based on their need to attract an audience and to avoid taking sides in partisan conflict. These tendencies, however, are not the desired characteristics of an electoral intermediary. What voters need from an intermediary is enough consistency and permanence to enable them to keep their eyes on the horizon. What they get instead from the press is a version of politics that centers on incidents and interruptions. When the test of the candidates' positions is the precision of the facts and statistics that the candidates use in talking about the issues, as it was for the press during much of the 2000 campaign, politics resembles a high-stakes spelling bee rather than what it is at its best: a critical struggle over society's values.

So campaigns have come down to this: amorphous parties, aggrandizing candidates, and amoral media. The irony is that, although this type of politics has the power to sway the vote, it has very little power to move the voters in the sense of giving them compelling reasons to participate.

CHAPTER THREE

The News Media

The Politics of Anti-Politics

The news commentators come on and they act like we're totally
stupid and they have to interpret everything.
—fifty-seven-year-old Kentucky resident[1]

The press should report the news instead of making the news.
—sixty-year-old Indiana resident[2]

We need less emphasis on the sensational.
—eighty-year-old North Carolina resident[3]

ILL WORDS FOLLOWED George W. Bush as he traveled the campaign trail. On the network evening news, Bush's coverage was 63 percent negative in tone and only 37 percent positive.[4] Major newspapers gave him an equally rough ride—more than 2 to 1 percent negative coverage.[5] Everything from his interpersonal skills to the way he ran his campaign came under attack. When it was revealed that the word "rats" was embedded as a frame within a Bush campaign ad targeted at Al Gore, a voter interviewed on the *CBS Evening News* said: "When I heard that 'Rat' thing, the first thing that came to mind was Nixon and Watergate."[6]

To die-hard Republicans, Bush's negative coverage represented just another bashing by the liberal media. Ever since the writer Edith Efron charged in 1968 that the television networks had "actively opposed the Republican candidate, Richard Nixon,"[7] Republicans have believed that the media favor the Democrats. In 2000, the Republican national chair, Jim Nicholson, sent the telephone numbers of network anchors Dan Rather, Peter Jennings, and Tom Brokaw to party activists so that they could call to complain about Bush's coverage.[8]

However, if the press favors the Democrats, why did it also bash Al Gore? On the nightly news, Gore's coverage was substantially more negative (60 versus 47 percent) than Bush's during the primaries and almost as negative (60 versus 63 percent) during the general election.[9] Gore, like Bush, was raked up one side and down the other. On NBC News, a voter was heard to say: "My biggest concern is that Al Gore will say about anything he needs to say to get elected President of the United States."[10]

The news media were showing their bias, but it was not a liberal or a conservative one. It was a preference for the negative. Often, the more highly charged the subject, the more one-sided is the portrayal. A good deal of Bush's coverage during the 2000 election suggested that he was not too smart. There were nine such claims in the news for every contrary claim. Gore's coverage was dotted with suggestions he was not all that truthful. Such claims outpaced rebuttals by seventeen to one.[11]

Studies reveal that this negative tendency is not limited to presidential candidates. When a president's approval rating drops, it gets more news coverage than when it rises.[12] When policy programs fail, they receive more news attention than when they succeed.[13] When public officials misbehave, they get more coverage than when they triumph.[14] The press, said the scholar Michael Robinson, seems to have taken some motherly advice and turned it upside down: "If you don't have anything bad to say about someone, don't say anything at all."[15]

Some journalists claim it has always been that way and that Washington, Jefferson, Jackson, and Lincoln endured far worse, but this is not the case.[16] Although many early newspapers could be downright nasty, they were partisan journals that heaped on praise as they dished up criticism.[17] Rather than the claim that "they're all a bunch of bums," the partisan press was based on the premise that the bums were all on the other side. In 1896, the *San Francisco Call* devoted 1,075 column inches of glowing photographs to the Republican ticket of McKinley-Hobart and only 11 inches to the Democrats, Bryan and Sewall.[18] San

Francisco Democrats had their own bible, the Hearst-owned *Examiner*, which touted William Jennings Bryan as the savior of working men.

Partisan journalism slowly died out in the early 1900s and a more neutral form replaced it. The critical style, in turn, gradually overtook its predecessor. Political coverage started to become more negative in the 1960s, and by the 1980s attack journalism was firmly in place.[19] The tendency was interrupted by periodic bouts of patriotism. The press did an abrupt shift whenever the United States faced an international threat—for example, the Iranian hostage crisis in 1979, the bombing of the marine barracks in Lebanon in 1983, the Gulf war in 1990–91, the Balkan air wars of the 1990s, and the war against terrorism that began in 2001. Each time Americans rallied around the flag, so, too, did the press. NBC outfitted its peacock logo with stars and stripes following the World Trade Center and Pentagon attacks, and computer-generated flags festooned the other networks. Nevertheless, the long-term tendency has been decidedly negative.

The impact has been substantial. The news provides a day-to-day window on the world of politics. Not that Americans accept the press's version of reality in its entirety. Audiences filter the news through their personal needs, interests, prejudices, attitudes, and beliefs. Yet the media supply most of the raw material that goes into people's thinking about their political leaders and institutions. In this sense, politics is a secondhand experience, lived through the stories of journalists.

What people receive through that window affects how they respond to politics. If the portrayal is inviting, they will be encouraged to get involved and pay attention. But if it's disheartening, they will maintain their distance and disengage. Therein lies the significance of negative news.

The American press today is at a crossroads, as it wrestles with intense audience competition and the lessons learned from its performance before and after the World Trade Center and Pentagon attacks. Analysts differ on how they think the press will operate next year, much less five years from now. In *The News About the News*, Leonard Downie, Jr., and Robert G. Kaiser express pessimism about journalism's near future.[20] In *The Elements of Journalism*, Bill Kovach and Tom

Rosenstiel express guarded optimism.[21] But some of what lies ahead will be affected by tendencies developed in the past. The story of modern political journalism begins near the time that voting rates started to slip.

"THE AIR WAS THICK with lies, and the president was the lead liar," said the *Washington Post*'s editor, Ben Bradlee.[22] Watergate and Vietnam are now distant enough that it's easy to misjudge just how much courage and tenacity the press mustered in the face of serious government threats and abuses of power.[23] The investigation of the Watergate break-in and the publication of the secret Pentagon Papers were risky undertakings but, ultimately, journalism's finest hour. This moment also marked a turning point in the relationship between the press and politicians. Journalists believed they had let the country down by taking politicians at their word, and they vowed not to let it happen again.

Although Vietnam and Watergate altered the relationship between the press and politicians, an earlier and less heralded development also contributed to the change. This development started innocently enough, at the time the television networks decided they could make money by expanding their news programming.

During the 1950s the network newscasts were inconsequential. They were short, blatantly commercial (*The Camel* [cigarette] *News Caravan*), and consisted mainly of headline news gathered by newspapers and wire services. In 1963, however, the networks introduced the thirty-minute newscast and launched picture-centered news. They quickly discovered that the print style of reporting was poorly suited to a visual medium. Viewers didn't have to be told what they could see with their own eyes. Moreover, straightforward description seemed dull when told to a viewing audience. A livelier, more structured style of reporting built around story lines was needed.[24] Reuven Frank, executive producer of NBC's nightly news, told his correspondents: "Every news story should, without any sacrifice of probity or responsibility, display the attributes of fiction, of drama. It should have structure and conflict, problem and denouement, rising action and falling action, a beginning, a middle and an end."[25]

An interpretive style of reporting that was explanatory as well as descriptive began to emerge.[26] With the old style, the journalist's job was to transport the audience to the scene of an event and describe what had happened. The new style, however, asked the journalist also to serve as an analyst, telling the audience not just the "what" of an event but the "why." News reports became news *stories.*

Newspapers slowly followed suit.[27] Morning papers could not survive if they simply retold events that people had heard about the night before on the evening news. Print journalists would have to explain, analyze, and interpret, going deeper into events than television's time constraints allowed.

If this was all that interpretive journalism represented, it would have been an inconsequential development. But it served gradually to shift control of the news to the journalists. Newsmakers held the upper hand with the old form. The journalist's task was to describe events, which typically meant telling the audience what newsmakers had said and done. "It is my job," said an influential journalist, "to report the [newsmaker's] words, whether I agree with them or not."[28]

Interpretive journalism altered that requirement. Newsmakers' actions would still make the news and even provide many of the headlines and story leads, but the message itself would be shaped by the interpretation the journalist imposed on events.[29] Instead of simply reporting events, the raw material would be repackaged with the journalist, not the newsmaker, at the center.[30]

The change did not take place all at once. Vestiges of the old form clung for a long time, particularly in print reporting. Even as late as the 1972 presidential campaign, newspaper reporters were laboring under its constraints. "[We were] caged in by the old formulas of classic objective journalism, which dictated that each story had to make some neat point; had to start with a hard news lead based on some phony event that the candidate's staff had staged," wrote the journalist Timothy Crouse. "If the candidate spouted fulsome bullshit all day, the formula made it hard for [us] to say so."[31]

Interpretive journalism offered a way out, and television journalists were already wriggling free. Their reporting showed signs of the change that was to come. When George McGovern appeared unannounced at New York's Columbus Day parade during the 1972 campaign, for example, CBS's news story was filled with sly put-downs ("Marchers grumbled that politicians ought to go find their own fun and leave other people's parades alone") and crafty asides ("A Republican dignitary huffed and puffed about the political impropriety of turning up at parades without an invitation").[32]

The "wrap" to a story became the television correspondent's sharpest weapon. Some stories in the 1960s did not even have a wrap-up comment by the reporter. By the late 1970s, all of them did,[33] often in the form of a put-down.[34] Reporters were ten times more likely to close a story with an assertion than with a fact.[35] CBS's Bernard Goldberg, for example, concluded a 1980 election story by saying the candidate's campaign was following "the path of Skylab—the orbiting satellite that had crashed to earth."[36] Politicians were nearly powerless to affect such reporting. Interpretive journalism gave reporters the last word.

Newsmakers eventually became like Victorian children, seen but seldom heard. In 1968, when presidential candidates appeared in a television news story they were usually pictured speaking. Two decades later, when they were visible on the screen with their mouths moving, their words in most cases could not be heard; the journalists were doing the talking.[37] In 1968, the average "sound bite"—a block of uninterrupted speech by a candidate on television news—was more than 40 seconds.[38] By 1988, the average had shrunk to less than 10 seconds.[39]

For every minute that Bush and Gore spoke on the evening newscasts during the 2000 campaign, the journalists covering them spoke for 6 minutes.[40] The two candidates received only 12 percent of the election coverage. Anchors and correspondents took up three-fourths of the time, with the rest allocated to other sources, including voters, experts, and group leaders. A viewer who watched the network news every evening between Labor Day and Election Day would have heard 17 minutes each from Bush and Gore, or about 15 seconds a night.[41] When Bush appeared on CBS's David Letterman show on October 19, he received nearly as much airtime as he did on the *CBS Evening News* during the entire general election.[42]

Newspapers have also squeezed out the newsmakers. In 1960, the average continuous quote or paraphrase of a newsmaker's words in a front-page story was 20 lines. By the 1990s, the average had fallen to 7 lines, usually in paraphrased form.[43] It is now rare for a newsmaker to be quoted at length in a newspaper story.

As the first signs of this new journalism surfaced in the early 1970s, some in the profession expressed concern. The *Washington Post* editor Russell Wiggins regularly told his reporters: "Journalists belong in the audience, not on the stage."[44] But his view was eclipsed by the lessons of Vietnam and Watergate.[45] Journalists had concluded, says the scholar Michael Schudson, that "there is always a story *behind* the story, and that it is 'behind' because someone is hiding it."[46]

Although the full impact of interpretive journalism was not immediately apparent, a few observers thought it would be substantial.

The analyst Paul Weaver believed political news would be dominated by stories of strategy and infighting. Because journalists tend to see politics as a competitive struggle for power, he believed they would interpret the news primarily through that lens, which would alter the content of news. Although newsmakers think strategically, their rhetoric is aimed at public policy, which, in descriptive reporting, had placed issues at the forefront of the news. With interpretive reporting, the journalists' rhetoric—that of the "strategic game"—would take center stage. Policy issues and debates, Weaver said, would become "noteworthy only insofar as they affect, or are used by, players in pursuit of the game's rewards."[47]

In a study of television's 1972 election coverage, Robert McClure and I found that Weaver's hypothesis was more than a hunch. As reported on television, that election was a spectacular struggle: rapid followers, dramatic do-or-die battles, strategy, tactics, winners and losers. Far down the list were issues of policy and leadership. "The contest theme," our study concluded, "was carried to the campaign's very end, at the expense of the election's issues and the candidates' qualifications for office."[48]

But it was Michael Robinson, then at Catholic University and later at Georgetown, who put his finger on what would become the new journalism's major legacy: negative reporting and jaded citizens.

Writing in 1976, Robinson argued that television's preference for crisis, conflict, and drama, when combined with journalists' "negativist, contentious, or anti-institutional bias," would result in deeply skeptical reporting. Political leaders and institutions would be relentlessly criticized, fueling public disaffection. Robinson offered persuasive though inconclusive survey and experimental evidence to back up his thesis, which he labeled "videomalaise."[49]

A study of ninety-four newspapers conducted shortly thereafter by the University of Michigan's Arthur H. Miller, Edie N. Goldenberg, and Lutz Erbring indicated that print coverage might have the same effect. They found that readers exposed to newspapers which had a "higher degree of criticism directed at politicians and political institutions were more distrustful of government and [had] higher levels of cynicism."[50]

Perhaps even more so than Vietnam, Watergate made a deep impression on reporters. Watergate quickly became the prevailing myth of journalism.[51] Reporters believed that the press had saved American democracy and that it had a continuing responsibility to protect the public from lying, manipulative politicians.

The watchdog role was an old one, but Watergate gave it an urgency that changed even the basic assumptions of journalism. Politicians would no longer be taken at their word.[52] Reporting would be rooted in the assumption that officials could not be trusted.[53] If politicians were willing to lie to the media, their every word would be subject to scrutiny. Newsweek's Meg Greenfield said journalists had previously believed "the worst thing we could do . . . was [to] falsely accuse someone of wrongdoing." Now, "the worst, the most embarrassing, humiliating thing is not that you accuse someone falsely but that you . . . fail to accuse someone of something he ought to be accused of."[54]

Some journalists, including Greenfield,[55] were uncomfortable with the change and concerned about its consequences, but their view was a minority one, particularly among network correspondents. Although there had always been prominent journalists, such as Walter Lippmann and the Alsop brothers, television had a way of making celebrities of quite ordinary reporters. Network correspondents were inflated by the public's sense that anyone on television had to be important. The temptation to rise above the story was irresistible. The wall that had separated reporting and editorializing was collapsing.[56]

But how can the journalist act aggressively in the context of the humdrum of everyday public affairs? "How does one," as an aspiring investigative reporter asked a U.S. senator, "hunt people like you?"[57] Wrongdoing on the scale of Watergate is exceedingly rare, and investigative journalism in any case is slow and painstaking. It's no simple matter to uncover a politician's true motives or to verify rumors of wrongdoing. Even if one tries, the truth may be so fragile or the trail so cold that, in the end, there is no story to tell.

An everyday alternative to investigative journalism was needed, and by the late 1970s reporters had found it. When a politician did something newsworthy, they turned to his adversaries to tear it or him down. It was an old technique, but it became a constant practice.[58] The critical element was supplied, not by careful investigation of whether a politician was sincere or a proposal was sound, but by inserting a contrary opinion. "You come out of a legislative conference and there's 10 reporters standing around with their ears twitching," said U.S. Senator Alan Simpson. "They don't want to know whether anything was resolved for the betterment of the United States. They want to know who got hammered, who tricked whom. . . . They're not interested in clarity. They're interested in confusion and controversy."[59] Conflict, always an element of political coverage, became its theme. The level of conflict in congressional coverage rose sharply in the 1970s and the 1980s.[60]

By the mid-1980s, journalists often did not even bother to find someone to express the opinions they wanted to voice. They had become critics in their own right.[61] They were careful to avoid the appearance of taking sides in policy disputes over issues such as abortion and health care. But they didn't hesitate to weigh in on questions of character and competence. A study of 1988 election coverage found that television journalists spent three-fourths of their airtime "evaluating what was right, good, or desirable" and only one-fourth providing factual information.[62]

Seldom were reporters' judgments based on thorough investigation.

Many were rooted in the assumption that politicians are self-serving.[63] Sometimes, a commonplace event was made into a news story only by the "edge" that the journalist gave it.[64] When George Bush traveled in his shirtsleeves by bus through Illinois during the 1988 campaign without subjecting himself to a press conference, ABC's Brit Hume suggested that Bush's casual attire was a ruse. Bush might have appeared like "a man in tune with rural America," but his posh bus "had a microwave oven [and] a fancy restroom." Hume wrapped up his report with a second put-down: "Polls show Bush behind in Illinois and he apparently thought getting out among the people would be just the thing. Did that also mean that he would answer reporters' questions? Not today. After all, you can carry this accessibility stuff too far."[65]

Critical journalism had become like a drug. Reporters were routinely sticking needles into the nation's highest leaders. It was exhilarating and, once experienced, it was hard to stop. Vice President Dan Quayle delivered a half-hour speech on moral values that included a one-sentence criticism of the unwed television character Murphy Brown for "bearing a child alone and calling it just another 'lifestyle choice.'" The comment produced front-page stories and, in the tabloids, mocking headlines: "Quayle to Murphy Brown: 'You Tramp'" (New York Daily News). At a White House press conference called to discuss U.S.-Canada trade, journalists ignored both the trade issue and Canadian prime minister Brian Mulroney, pestering Bush about Quayle's statement, all the while implying the vice president lacked the brains to separate fact from fiction.[66]

Politicians were easy targets. The breakdown of comity in Congress made it simple for journalists to find lawmakers who were willing to say nasty things about a politician of the opposite party, and sometimes even about a member of their own party. The gridlock that sometimes tied up policy initiatives for months on end added substance to the press's claim that politicians were self-serving.

Politicians had come to distrust the press.[67] Some, like Bush, despised it. At his 1992 campaign stops, Bush drew loud cheers whenever he waved a bumper sticker that read, "Annoy the Media, Re-Elect George Bush."[68] There was, said Senator Simpson, "a total disregard and distrust by politicians of the media and a total cynicism and distrust of politicians by the media."[69] Politicians and journalists had become locked in what the ethicist Sissela Bok calls a "vicious circle."[70]

The old journalistic adage "bad news is good news" had become an imperative. Skepticism had been part of reporting since at least the turn-of-the-century muckraking period. As the Pulitzer Prize–winning journalist Frank Simonds had said in 1917: "There is but one way for a newspaper man to look at a politician, and that is down."[71] But the muckrakers had focused on systemic corruption: the taking of bribes, the exploitation of ethnic and religious prejudice, the unholy alliance between politicians and the business trusts. Modern journalists were tearing into politicians for everything from their clothing to their accessibility. There were larger issues, too, including Iran-Contra, the savings-and-loan crisis, and institutional gridlock, but attack journalism had become the domineering style.[72] In 1989, more than a thousand charges of ethical impropriety (sex was the leading category) were leveled at members of Congress on the nightly newscasts.[73] "I feel like bait rather than a senior member of Congress," said a U.S. representative.[74]

Bill Clinton did not even get the "honeymoon" that newly elected presidents had come to expect. His news coverage was 57 percent negative during his first two months on the job. Six months into his presidency, Clinton's numbers were even worse—66 percent negative.[75] According to the press, Clinton was doing almost everything wrong. A series of controversies, including the president's $200 haircut and his "gays in the military" initiative, had led reporters to speak of "amateur hour" at the White House.[76] Some of this criticism was on target, but much of it was not. Clinton's first-year achievements included a deficit-reduction program, a family-leave program, banking reform, NAFTA, a college-loan program, the Brady bill, and AmeriCorps. Since 1953, *Congressional Quarterly* has tracked congressional backing of legislation on which the president has taken a position. Congress backed Clinton on 88 percent of contested votes in 1993, a level exceeded only twice in the previous forty years—by Dwight Eisenhower in 1953 and Lyndon Johnson in 1965.[77]

Clinton's reward? Enough negative news to power a magneto. But it was no worse than the coverage Congress was getting. The 103rd Congress (1993–94) enacted a score of new programs but failed to pass health-care reform and was called "pathetically unproductive" in a *New York Times* editorial.[78] Network coverage of the Democratic-led 103rd Congress was nearly 70 percent negative in tone.[79] Network coverage of the Republican-led 104th Congress was also nearly 70 percent unfavorable, despite the historic first one hundred days in which many of the planks in the GOP's Contract with America were fulfilled. A poll during the 1994 election indicated that 97 percent of Washington journalists regarded the contract as "a campaign ploy." When it turned out to be something quite different, they criticized Republicans for trying to ram it too quickly through Congress.[80]

Coverage of national politics was so downbeat that it distorted Americans' sense of reality. A 1996 survey asked respondents whether the trend in inflation, unemployment, crime, and the federal budget deficit had been upward or downward during the past five years. There had been substantial improvement in all of these problem areas, but two-thirds of the respondents said in each case that things had gotten worse.[81] What could explain such widespread ignorance except the cumulative effect of daily news that highlighted the failings of national policy and leadership?[82]

Politicians, no doubt, also contributed mightily to the public's perception that government wasn't working. Conservative lawmakers were consciously seeking to drive down confidence in government in order to create support for their effort to roll back federal economic and social programs. For their part, liberal lawmakers found fit to attack government over issues that dealt with the regulation of personal conduct. The gap between these sides was often so wide that lawmakers in the middle had no hope of filling it, which fed the growing perception that government was bogged down in partisan bickering and policy deadlock.

But journalists also were working from a mindset that cast an unfavorable light on nearly all things political. For example, the 1996 GOP nominating race was, according to press accounts, a virtual bloodbath. NBC's Lisa Myers called Forbes "Malcolm the Mudslinger," saying, "With ads like [his], Forbes may find it tougher to persuade voters he's all that different from those career politicians [he's running against]."

Ninety-nine percent of journalists' coverage of the candidates' advertising campaigns was about their use of negative ads. Most of the sound bites aired on the evening newscasts showed one candidate attacking another. The 1996 GOP race, however, had a rather different look from ground level. The media analyst Robert Lichter examined the GOP hopefuls' television ads and stump speeches. Over half the ads (56 percent) were positive in tone, and nearly two-thirds (66 percent) of the assertions in the candidates' speeches were positive statements about what they hoped to accomplish if elected. This dimension of that campaign, however, was seldom mentioned in news reports. "Forget about the issues," ABC's Peter Jennings said of the Republican race, "there is enough mud being tossed around . . . to keep a health spa supplied for a lifetime."[83]

During the Watergate era, critical journalism had been a means by which the press could hold politicians accountable. Now it was an end in itself. Criticism was the starting point in the search for and crafting of news stories. It was also the path of advancement. Coveted appearances on network and cable talk shows were granted to journalists adept at sharp-edged commentary. The measured voices in the Washington press corps could still be heard, but cable television had created a lot more seats at the table. The nation's "fourth branch" was now as entrenched as the officials it covered. Journalists had established themselves as a counter-elite operating within the tidy confines of Washington, as insular as the politicians they criticized for having lost touch with the public they serve.

In the view of David Broder, the dean of Washington journalists, the press had spun out of control. "Cynicism is epidemic right now," he wrote. "It saps people's confidence in politics and public officials, and it erodes both the standing and standards of journalism. If the assumption is that nothing is on the level, nothing is what it seems, then citizenship becomes a game for fools, and there is no point in trying to stay informed."[84] The warning did not slow the flow of negative news, which suited some journalists just fine. Expressing her enthusiasm for a "raffish and rowdy" press, the *New York Times*'s Maureen Dowd said journalists had exposed politicians for the scoundrels they were.[85] When journalists were asked in a 1995 Freedom Forum/Roper poll whether the public's mistrust of Congress was due primarily to the press or to Congress itself, thirty-six times as many of them pointed the finger at Congress.[86]

By the early 1990s, the major barrier to the flow of political criticism was a cutback in political reporting. Public-affairs coverage was being reduced to make room for "soft news."

Soft news was a response to the competitive environment created by cable television. The number of American homes with cable had jumped from fewer than 10 percent in the 1970s to more than 50 percent by the early 1990s. In the process, the broadcast networks lost their monopoly on the dinner-hour audience. By 1995, in the face of competition from cable's entertainment programs, the evening news audience had shrunk by a third.[87] Newspaper readership was also declining, for the first time ever except during hard economic times.[88]

A historic reversal was taking place. For 150 years the news audience had expanded. Fewer than 5 percent of Americans in the early 1800s received the daily news. The invention a few decades later of the hand-cranked rotary press drove the price of a paper down from five cents to a penny and newspaper readership began to increase, propelled also by rising literacy. Near the end of the 1800s, the invention of newsprint and the steam-driven press enabled metropolitan dailies to sell as many as 100,000 copies a day. Radio news came along in the 1920s, and television news followed in the 1950s. By 1980, 75 percent of adults were partaking of daily news. But, suddenly, the trend had reversed. The news audience was shrinking.

News organizations' initial response was to cut costs. Foreign news bureaus were among the first things to go. The public presumably didn't care all that much about international news, much less about its quality.

When news audiences continued to shrink, many media outlets opted for a market-driven style of news intended to compete directly with cable entertainment programs. Commentators coined the terms "infotainment" and "news lite" to describe it. Within the news business, it was commonly called soft news to distinguish it from traditional hard news (breaking events involving top leaders, major issues, or significant disruptions to daily routines).

The market strategy was not exactly new. Jacked-up stories of crime, exotic places, celebrities, and medical breakthroughs had been prime weapons in the circulation wars that big-city newspapers waged in the early 1900s.[89] The yellow-journalism era, a newspaper historian wrote, featured "a shrieking, gaudy, sensation-loving, devil-may-care kind of [reporting that] lured the reader by any possible means."[90] Named after the Yellow Kid, a cartoon character used to attract readers, yellow journalism became synonymous with the worst kind of reporting.[91]

Yellow journalism eventually blackened the press's reputation, and some observers believed that history was repeating itself as a result of cable competition. "The networks now do news as entertainment," said former CBS anchor Walter Cronkite. "[It is] one of the greatest blots on the recent record of television news."[92] NBC's Tom Brokaw defended it, saying that the networks cannot "commit suicide."[93] He argued that soft news was an inevitable adjustment to changing news tastes and habits. "What we are doing is not being the wire service of the air anymore," Brokaw said. "We're picking four or five topics and trying to deal with them in a way that people can feel connected to."[94] Former Federal Communications Commission chairman Newton Minow had a less flattering depiction of the trend, calling it "pretty close to tabloid."[95]

The indisputable fact was that the news had softened considerably. A study by Harvard University's Shorenstein Center showed that celebrity profiles, lifestyle scenes, hard-luck tales, good-luck tales, and other human-interest stories rose from 11 percent to more than 20 percent of news coverage between 1980 and 1999. Stories about dramatic incidents—crimes and disasters—also doubled during this period. The number of news stories that contained elements of sensationalism jumped by 75 percent.[96]

As soft news took up more space, public-affairs coverage dwindled. "Public affairs used to be at the core of the news," said media analysts Robert Lichter and Jeremy Torobin. "Now it is one niche in a news agenda oriented more toward features and lifestyle issues."[97] From 1980 to 2000, public-affairs stories decreased from 70 percent of news coverage to 50 percent.[98] Nearly every area of public affairs, including national and international politics, was cut back. In 1977, one in three *Time* and *Newsweek* covers had featured national and international leaders. By 1997 that proportion was one in ten. Meanwhile, covers that featured sex or a sexy celebrity rose from one in six to one in three.[99]

Political scandal posed the one exception because it fused hard news with soft. With roots in money, sex, power, intrigue, and wrongdoing, scandals provided a basis for both attack and titillation. According to one study, scandal coverage in major news outlets jumped from 2 percent of the news in 1977 to 13 percent in 1997.[100]

President Clinton became the main focus. Most Americans' first real awareness of him came on January 23, 1992, when Gennifer Flowers claimed a twelve-year relationship with the Arkansas governor. Some journalists later said they didn't want to carry the story, but a hundred showed up at a Clinton campaign stop that first day to question him about her.[101] The next day, five hundred turned out for a Flowers press conference at the Waldorf-Astoria Hotel.[102]

But the Flowers story was just a tease. In the aftermath of the Monica Lewinsky affair, which was real enough, it is easy to overlook just how fully Clinton's earlier coverage was driven by alleged wrongdoing. Most of these scandals were what Michael Robinson calls "medialities"—press-driven controversies of little merit.[103] White House counsel Vince Foster's death in the end was what police said it was from the start, a suicide. Nevertheless, it prompted hundreds of insinuating stories. "Filegate" and "Travelgate," which were in and out of the news for seven years, were also much ado about not all that much. "Troopergate" had a basis, but the allegations were so confounded by their right-wing sponsorship that fact and mischief were at times hard to distinguish. The Arlington National Cemetery scandal, in which grave plots were reportedly traded for campaign donations, was the nation's top story until it was shown to have no basis. The Whitewater affair was, of course, the granddaddy of them all. Compared to Watergate in a *New York Times* feature article in 1994,[104] it had an eight-year run in the news before being dismissed in 2000 by the Special Prosecutor's Office. When Whitewater surfaced early in the Clinton presidency, it received three times as much news coverage as the leading policy issue of the time, health-care reform.[105]

So much has been written about the Lewinsky coverage that little needs to be said here except to note how fully it embodied what Marvin Kalb calls "the new news."[106] When the Lewinsky story broke, facts and rumors merged. In *Warp Speed*, the journalists Bill Kovach and Tom Rosenstiel report that only 26 percent of the allegations were attributed to named sources as opposed to anonymous or unnamed sources. Only 1 percent of the charges were based on two or more named sources.[107] Some allegations proved to be accurate (for example, the claim of a semen-stained dress) and some did not (for example, the claim that a White House steward had witnessed a sexual liaison). Truth and speculation were tossed together in what was surely the decade's biggest political story, but what, in its reporting standards, was sadly ordinary. Kovach and Rosenstiel said ABC News, which broke the blue dress story, was lucky rather than good in its scoop because it had no firm confirmation of the allegation's accuracy.[108]

The Lewinsky story resembled the Watergate story but was rooted in a different brand of journalism. The *Washington Post* was more than fifty stories deep into its Watergate coverage before it made a substantial allegation that turned out to be factually wrong. The *Post*'s Ben Bradlee insisted that any allegation had to be confirmed by at least two independent sources before going to print. "We could not afford *any* mistakes," he said.[109] That standard had evaporated long before the Lewinsky story broke. Early in the Whitewater story, the *Wall Street Journal* had urged reporters to throw caution to the wind, saying the benefits would outweigh the costs of false allegations.[110]

A variation of Parkinson's Law was at work. Allegations large and small were inflated to fill available news time. Round-the-clock cable news had accelerated the news cycle and increased the demand for controversy. In the intensely competitive media environment, the pressure of running a story had eclipsed the old standard of getting the story right.

DURING THE LAST three decades of the twentieth century, the news was relentlessly negative, carrying public opinion along with it. The Vietnam and Watergate period was not the high mark of critical reporting and public mistrust but, instead, the point of departure for an increasingly assertive press and an increasingly jaded public.

Five presidents in a row after Nixon received reams of bad press.[111] Clinton's coverage was the most negative, but even the president who fared best, Gerald Ford, did not fare well. Reporters joked that Ford (a gridiron star at the University of Michigan) had played too many football games without a helmet and reveled in showing him tripping on stairs or falling on ski slopes—metaphors for their belief that he was overmatched by the demands of his office.

Congress fared no better.[112] Press coverage of the institution was steadily negative after the early 1970s, regardless of which party controlled it or how much or little was accomplished.[113] In the 1972–92 period, allegations of personal impropriety (financial dealings, sexual antics, and the like) rose from 4 percent of congressional coverage to 17 percent—one in every six stories.[114] "Over the years," concluded the scholar Mark Rozell, "press coverage of Congress has moved from healthy skepticism to outright cynicism."[115]

News of the presidency and Congress, however, was rosy compared with that of federal agencies. A study of news coverage in the early 1990s, for example, found that every high-profile agency except the Department of Defense had received more negative than positive coverage. The State Department's coverage was only 13 percent positive, and the Justice Department's was just 10 percent favorable.[116]

Public mistrust and dissatisfaction accompanied the flow of negative news. In 1964, 76 percent had said they trusted the national government to do the right thing "most of the time"; in 1994, only 21 percent held this opinion, the lowest level ever recorded.[117] The "Harris Confidence Index," based on people's confidence in leaders of the nation's major institutions, fell by more than half between 1966 and 1997, when it hit its lowest level ever.[118]

It was not a coincidence that, as the news soured during the post-Watergate period, Americans' beliefs about their leaders and institutions also soured. The decline in public confidence was not solely attributable to attack journalism, but the tone of the news was too negative for too long not to have made an impression. By choosing to present politicians as scoundrels who do not deserve the public's trust, the press helped bring about that very opinion.[119]

Studies documented the connection. One found that negative images of presidential candidates increased in lockstep with the increase in negative coverage of these candidates during the 1960–92 period.[120] Another study showed a close relationship between presidential approval ratings and the tone of presidential press coverage.[121] Still other studies documented a linkage between negative news and negative impressions of Congress and other institutions.[122]

These findings were supported by the results of experimental research.[123] In the most comprehensive of these studies, the University of Pennsylvania's Joseph Cappella and Kathleen Hall Jamieson demonstrated that messages cast in the media's primary frames—conflict, strategy, and ambition—bring out feelings of mistrust.[124] The message as opposed to the medium is the critical element. "The effect," Cappella and Jamieson write, "occurs for broadcast as well as print news, and when the two are combined, the combination is additive."[125] Negative news, they conclude, generates "cynical responses to politicians, politics, governance, campaigns, and policy formation."[126]

Critical journalism did not by itself drive down public trust in the post-Watergate period.* Scandals, policy failures, and Washington

---

*There is no reliable way to measure the separate impact on public attitudes of the various contributing influences. The explanatory problem can be likened to that for global warming, where a decades-long stream of particulate matter has had a cumulative effect but no one is quite sure how much of the change is attributable to each cause. As with the global warming issue, there are even a handful of scholars who contest the media malaise thesis. They need not be identified by name here, but it is useful to consider their arguments. One is that public malaise was a hangover from the Vietnam and Watergate eras. This contention requires the improbable assumption that mistrust is a normal condition and simply lingers on. It also requires one to overlook the many indicators (some of which were mentioned) that show a rising level of mistrust after the early 1970s. Even if mistrust in some abstract sense had not increased, it had broadened and deepened, affecting nearly every institution and leadership position. A second argument is based on the tendency of heavier news consumers to have higher levels of political commitment and interest than lighter consumers. When would this ever not be the case? It's like saying that a lousy ball team could not be the reason for low season attendance because the fans still in the seats are those with higher levels of commitment and interest in the team. What proponents of this thesis ignored was that the level of political trust among heavier news consumers was only slightly higher than lighter consumers, whereas it was once substantially higher. The sensible conclusion about attentive citizens would have been that they continued to follow the news even though they, too, had become increasingly mistrustful and dissatisfied. Moreover, news effects are not confined to heavier consumers. It is not as if more attentive citizens consume all the news and everyone dwells in Plato's cave.

infighting also contributed. Although the period was generally marked by peace, prosperity, and racial and gender progress, major setbacks occurred, including double-digit inflation, the Iranian hostage crisis, Iran-Contra, the savings-and-loan debacle, and the Lewinsky affair.[127] Social disruption was also a factor. Changing lifestyles and mores contributed to a decline in personal trust and respect for authority,[128] which affected how Americans saw all institutions, including political ones.[129] The number who believed "most people can be trusted" fell from 58 percent in 1960 to 37 percent in 1993.[130]

But journalism, too, was part of the problem. For years on end, journalists chose to tell their audience that their leaders were self-interested, dishonest, and dismissive of the public good.[131] It was a one-sided story that had a predictably negative effect on Americans' beliefs about their leaders and institutions.

This one-sided, negative story also had a corrosive interest on voter participation. The mistrust it bred has contributed to the decline in turnout. A hint of that influence surfaced in our Vanishing Voter surveys as Election Day neared. We asked nonregistrants and likely nonvoters to respond to a list of possible reasons for why they would not vote. Included on the list were such standard items as "because I've been so busy that I probably won't have time," "because I don't have any way to get there," "because I moved and haven't registered at my new location," "because I'm not a U.S. citizen," "because I'm not very interested in politics," and "because I don't like any of this year's presidential candidates." Also included on the list was an item that measured political dissatisfaction: "because I'm disgusted with politics and don't want to be involved."

"Disgusted with politics" came out at the top of the nonregistrant list and second on the nonvoter list. Thirty-eight percent of nonregistrants said that disgust with politics was a reason they were not enrolled, which ranked ahead of being busy (34 percent), not being interested (31 percent), and not being satisfied with the candidates (27 percent). Among registered voters who said they intended to sit out the election, 37 percent claimed political dissatisfaction as a reason, which ranked behind a lack of interest (46 percent) but ahead of being busy (28 percent) and not being satisfied with the candidates (29 percent).

Without doubt, these responses reflect a degree of rationalization. People who do not intend to register or to vote for other reasons may use disgust with politics as an excuse to hide those reasons. But analysts who say that all such responses are rationalizations would have to make the implausible argument that campaigns are different from all else in life. Any time an activity disgusts or discourages people, some recoil. That's true of employment, religion, family relations, schooling, and other areas. Why is voting a special case? An indication that it is not a special case is apparent in the responses of those in our pre-election surveys who said they "might not vote." They, too, could have blamed it on dissatisfaction with politics. However, only 8 percent did so. Much higher on their list was the claim that they might be too busy to turn out. That's a reasonable response from someone still weighing the decision to vote, just as it's reasonable that political dissatisfaction could underlie a firm decision not to vote.

Nevertheless, a more precise test of the relationship between political dissatisfaction and voting was also conducted. Respondents were asked a strongly worded survey question ("Do you agree or disagree that most politicians are liars or crooks?") that was designed to identify those with a high level of mistrust. The fact that nearly as many respondents (44 percent versus 56 percent) agreed that "most politicians are liars or crooks" was itself indicative of just how far political dissatisfaction had spread. But was this attitude related to turnout? Did those who expressed mistrust participate at a substantially lower rate in the 2000 election than the others? In fact, they did. They were 13 percentage points less likely to vote. The difference is statistically significant even when income, education, or age is taken into account.* Let there be no mistaking the finding: mistrust undermines the desire to vote.

---

*The simple correlation between the mistrust measure ("most politicians are liars or crooks") and voting (as measured by intention in the pre-election surveys and reported voting in the post-election survey) was .139, which is significant at the .001 level. When income is controlled, the correlation is .111, also significant at the .001 level. The control for education produced coefficients identical to those for income. When age is controlled, the correlation increases to .143, also significant at the .001 level.

Some of the respondents who claimed politicians are not trust-worthy fit the profile of the alienated citizen. They are, as the *Washington Post*'s Richard Morin and Claudia Deane describe them, "the angry men and women of U.S. politics.[132] But most of the respondents who expressed mistrust did not fit the profile. They are disenchanted rather than alienated. They are not fuming mad at government, and, unlike the alienated, they tend to believe that government has an interest in their opinions and their welfare. But they are disenchanted with how politics is conducted. If the alienated are angry, the disenchanted are weary. They express dismay at the bickering they associate with Washington politics, at the flow of special-interest money, at the scandals that seem to routinely envelop those in power, at the strategic maneuvering that often appears to win out over the public good, and at the spin that journalists and politicians put on issues and events. Said one of our survey respondents: "I'm just disgusted with politics in general these past years."[133] Politics itself is not their gripe. It is the practice of politics to which they object, and it discourages some of them from voting.[134]

These people are a new type of nonvoter. Traditionally, nonvoters have divided into three types. One is the alienated: those who are politically angry or bitter. A second type is the apathetic: those who have little interest in politics. They were and still are the largest nonvoting group. They find politics to be dull and boring, and most of them admit to not understanding it very well. They are not particularly mistrustful of politics and politicians; in fact, they are about as trusting as those who do vote. What keeps the apathetic from participating is that they don't care much for politics or know much about it. Many of the apathetic nonvoters have low levels of education and income. The third traditional type of nonvoter is the disconnected: those who are unable to participate because of advanced age, disability, or temporary ineligibility for reasons such as a recent change of address.

There is now an identifiable fourth type, the disenchanted. They are the nonvoters who have been spawned by the political gamesmanship and negative news that dominated late-twentieth-century politics. Many of them express interest in public affairs, talk occasionally about politics, and keep up with the news. In fact, the Vanishing Voter surveys show they do not differ greatly from voters in these respects. Nor do they differ significantly from voters in terms of years of education. Where they differ is in their disgust with the way that politics in the United States is conducted, which leads some of them to stay away from the polls on Election Day.

The political mistrust that emerged from the discouraging tone of news and politics in recent decades has mainly affected young and middle-aged adults. Among our respondents thirty-four years of age and younger, those who agreed that "most politicians are liars or crooks" were 17 percentage points less likely to vote in 2000 than those who disagreed. Among adults between the ages of thirty-five and fifty-four, the difference was 12 points. Among those fifty-five and over, it was only 7 points. For this last group, moreover, the relationship dwindled to insignificance when education or income was controlled, whereas it remained statistically significant among middle-aged and young adults.*

These differences help to explain a contradictory conclusion from studies based on elections in the 1980s and earlier. Although rising political cynicism, as one of these earlier analysts said, seemed "tailor-made for explaining declining voter turnout,"[135] research failed to show a clear connection between the two.[136] On the basis of their analysis of the 1952–88 presidential elections, Steven Rosenstone and Mark Hansen concluded: "Neither feelings of trust in government nor beliefs about government responsiveness have any effect whatsoever on the likelihood that citizens will vote or will take part in any form of campaign politics."[137]

---

*For the 18–34 age group, the mistrust-voting correlation was .173, significant at the .001 level. The correlation was .146 and .149 controlling for income and education, respectively (both significant at the .001 level). For the 35–54 group, the mistrust-voting correlation was .137, significant at the .001 level. The correlation was .114 and .101 controlling for income and education, respectively (both significant at the .001 level). For the 55 and older group, the mistrust-voting correlation was .091, significant at the .001 level. The correlation was .056 and .067 controlling for income and education, respectively (neither of which reached the .05 significance level).

Our 2000 Vanishing Voter surveys, however, provide evidence of the linkage.* Why the difference? Why should political dissatisfaction have contributed to lower turnout in 2000 when it did not appear to do so even as late as 1988? The answer lies in part in the cumulative effect of political mistrust. It ordinarily takes time for a change in people's attitudes to produce a change in their behavior. And even if behavior is altered, the initial response is often tentative, which can go undetected by the relatively crude measures and methods available to electoral analysts. Adjustments were undoubtedly occurring in citizens' participation patterns as a result of rising levels of mistrust in the 1970s and 1980s, but they were not yet robust enough to be easily detected. More to the point, by 2000 Americans had been exposed to additional years in which their already battered trust in politics was battered further by a seemingly unending string of scandals and the deafening crescendo of attack journalism. If some of them were not ready to retreat to the sidelines by the 1970s and 1980s, they had gone that way a decade or two later.

The answer also lies, as it often does in such cases, in what people experienced as children and young adults rather than what they experienced later in adulthood.[138] By the time people are in their thirties, many political inclinations have taken root and do not change much later on. Voting is one of these inclinations, at least for most. Although people often vote with greater frequency as they age, the inclination to vote—and typically, the first actual vote—occurs within the first decade or so of eligibility.[139] Most individuals who are committed to the process by then participate with some regularity throughout their adult lives, regardless of ensuing developments.

The point of vulnerability is childhood and early adulthood, before

---

*Rosenstone and Hansen overstated the case somewhat in claiming that political dissatisfaction had no "effect whatsoever" on turnout. They distinguish political dissatisfaction—the feeling that officials are not trustworthy—from a lack of political efficacy—a sense of personal powerlessness to affect political outcomes. Their research indicated that a lack of efficacy diminishes turnout but dissatisfaction does not. However, although efficacy and trust can be distinguished analytically, they are part of a syndrome in the real world. They and other attitudes decline in tandem when people believe leaders and institutions are performing badly. To say that one but not the other affects participation is, to some degree, to confuse causes with consequences. Moreover, in the first election after completion of the Rosenstone and Hansen study, turnout jumped by 5 percent, partly from a surge to the polls of ex-voters and first-time voters. Martin Wattenberg's study indicates that Perot's insurgent candidacy, which appealed particularly to citizens who believed government could not be trusted and was unresponsive, accounted for about three-fifths of the upswing.

a voting inclination has been established. A boost or disruption at this stage can tip the individual toward or away from a lifetime of voting. The early experiences of the two most recent generations of adults—the newest one and the baby boomers who preceded them—were much different, and much less favorable to the development of a voting habit, than the childhood experiences of the World War II generation that came before them.

Consider first the formative years of the World War II generation. Although many never completed high school, the war and its aftermath gave them an unrivaled civic education. News, as they recall it, did not play a large part in childhood, but political discussion and a drummed-in sense of civic duty did.[140] By midlife, roughly three in four voted regularly, and they have continued to participate at high rates. Vietnam and Watergate disillusioned some, but, with the possible exception of the 1972 election, these developments did not diminish their interest in voting.[141]

By comparison, the baby boomers—the oldest of whom came of voting age in the late 1960s—had a bittersweet political youth. As children, they knew a nation where the public trusted and admired political leaders. Many baby boomers also recall a childhood where news and political discussion were an everyday part of home life. But they also experienced the Kennedy and King assassinations and Vietnam. The war disillusioned many of them, and they were then blindsided by Watergate, which was followed by the era of attack journalism.

The most recent generation, those under thirty-five at the time of the 2000 election, grew up in homes where interest in news and politics was waning. They had no defining issue on the order of the Depression, World War II, the civil rights movement, or Vietnam. There was no military draft to embrace or avoid and no protest march to join or jeer. The top issues of their childhood were fleeting and remote from their daily lives: the Iranian hostage crisis, Iran-Contra, the Gulf war, and the Lewinsky affair. Even the defining event of this generation—terrorist attacks on the World Trade Center and the Pentagon—was experienced through television and came late in their formative years. Their youth was steeped in political scandal and attack journalism.

Unlike the World War II generation, the most recent generation and the baby boomers did not have deeply positive experiences to cushion the impact. Negative messages rained down on them as young adults and, in the case of the most recent generation, even in childhood, which contributed to their dissatisfaction with politics. Older Americans were not oblivious to the change in the tone of news and the conduct of politics. They, too, grew increasingly dissatisfied. But their participation pattern was largely set. Not so for the baby boomers and, even more, those of the most recent generation. Some of them gave in to their mistrust, turning away from the voting act. As one of our Vanishing Voter survey respondents said: "Politics is just not something that interests me. . . . That's pretty much true of the people I went to school with. None of us votes."[142]

Earlier studies did not detect the link between voting and dissatisfaction because they stopped with the elections of the 1980s, just as the cumulative effect of changing demographics and chronic mistrust was beginning to mount. There is today a measurable difference between the voting rates of those young and middle-aged Americans who are less trusting of politics and those who are more trusting, and it persists even when education and income differences are taken into account. These nonparticipants are a reason that turnout has stagnated or declined despite the rising level of education, which should have boosted it. Heightened mistrust has worked to hold down the voting rate.

Other influences, too, have served to weaken participation among younger adults, and scholars are divided on the degree to which the long-term voting trend is attributable to generational replacement. The political scientists Warren Miller and Merrill Shanks claim it has been the driving force in the downward trend,[143] a view shared by Robert Putnam.[144] Other scholars claim the generational effect is smaller. Wayne State University's Thomas Jankowski and Charles Elder, for example, argue that age may have had less influence on the decline than institutional changes have had.[145] What most scholars do agree upon is that since the 1970s succeeding groups of first-time eligible voters have voted at a lower rate than the preceding group.*

---

*According to U.S. Census Bureau figures, turnout among eighteen-to-twenty-four-year-olds was 50, 42, 40, 41, 34, 41, 32, and 31 percent, respectively, in the eight elections between 1972 and 2000.

What our research demonstrates is that political mistrust has contributed to this development.* Young and middle-aged adults are not necessarily more mistrustful than older ones, but unlike them, their mistrust has translated into a reduced tendency to vote.

SOFT NEWS also diminishes politics. This type of news, as the writer Paul Weaver notes, is so irrelevant to our public life that it gives the public little reason to get involved.[146]

The press has a responsibility to provide a view of the world that does not lead people to think they are in the Land of Oz when they are traveling through Kansas. News that highlights unusual incidents is disorienting, even to the point of warping one's sense of reality. Few developments illustrate this issue more than the public's response to the "if it bleeds, it leads" reporting of the early 1990s. Crime news tripled in 1992 and 1993. On network television, it accounted for 12 percent of the coverage, overshadowing all other issues, including the economy, health care, and the Bosnian crisis.[147] The focus continued into 1994. The nightly newscasts aired more stories on crime than on the economy, health-care reform, and midterm elections combined.[148] "Lock 'Em Up and Throw Away the Key: Outrage Over Crime Has America Talking Tough" was *Time* magazine's cover story of February 7, 1994.

The coverage had a dramatic impact on public opinion. At no time in the previous decade had even as many as 8 percent named crime as the nation's most important problem. In 1994, however, an astonishing 39 percent said it was the country's most pressing problem.[149] Unfortunately, the public was responding to media portrayal rather than to reality. Justice Department statistics show that the level of crime, including violent crime, had been dropping for three years. Public opinion was being driven by news images and was, in turn, driving public policy. Responding to growing concern with crime, state and

---

*Other reasons include the weakening of family and neighborhood ties and the spread of materialistic values. The weakening of civic education in the schools, as some have claimed, may also be a reason, although research on this effect is sparse.

federal officials enacted tough new sentencing laws and began building prisons at the fastest rate in the nation's history. Six years later, the United States had a larger portion of its population behind bars than any other country in the world.

Public discourse is also impoverished by soft news. Much of what people talk about when their thoughts turn to public affairs is based on what they have just seen or read in the news. As the journalist Theodore H. White noted: "The power of the press is a primordial one. It determines what people will think and talk about."[150] If people are steeped in entertainment and distracted by news of remote or titillating incidents, civic life suffers. The media theorist Neil Postman asserts that, as a public, we risk "amusing ourselves to death."[151]

The diminution of political news itself signals that politics is a marginal activity, as even election coverage indicates. In 1992, the nightly newscasts carried 728 campaign stories during the general elections. The networks averaged 8.2 minutes of coverage per night. In 1996, the number of election stories fell to 483. The coverage dropped again in 2000, to 462 stories, even though the campaign was more competitive than the one in 1996. The networks averaged only 4.2 minutes of coverage a night.[152] The decline was even sharper in the nominating stage. Although both parties held contested races in 2000 (only the GOP had one in 1996), network coverage in the pre-convention period was down by 33 percent.[153] During one stretch the custody fight over Elián González garnered the Cuban boy twice as much airtime on the evening newscasts as was received by front-runners Bush and Gore combined.[154]

The decline in election coverage had the effect of reducing Americans' involvement in the 2000 campaign. As election coverage rises and falls, so, too, does the level of campaign interest. Our Vanishing Voter surveys reveal a close association between the ups and down in the amount of coverage and the ups and downs in involvement (Figure 3.1). As coverage rises, people increasingly think and talk about the campaign. As would be expected, they also are more likely to report having seen, read, or heard election news stories. Of course, the public's attention and the media's coverage are responsive to many of the same developments in the campaign. The October debates, for ex-

FIGURE 3.1

CITIZEN INVOLVEMENT AND ELECTION NEWS

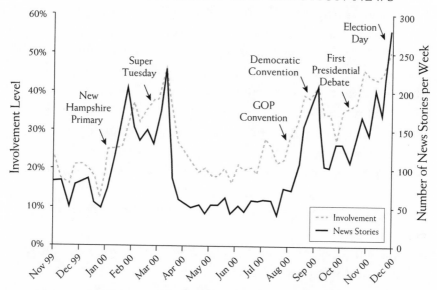

The heavier the election coverage, the more involved people are in the campaign, as measured by how much they talk, think, and attend to news about it. (See Appendix for information on how citizen involvement during the campaign was measured.)

ample, provoke heightened discussion even apart from the heavy coverage they receive. But even during quieter moments of the campaign, heavier coverage stimulates interest. If the coverage in 2000 had been as heavy as it was in 1992, people would have talked and thought more about the campaign. As a result, they also would have been better informed about the candidates and issues.[155] Turnout might also have been marginally higher in 2000 if news coverage had been heavier. Our Vanishing Voter surveys indicate that, as campaign involvement increases, the number of people who say they intend to vote also increases.

THE EXCESSES of post-Watergate journalism may have exhausted themselves with the feeding frenzy that was the Gary Condit story. For nearly four months in 2001, it dominated our national news, a distinction earned not by Representative Condit's stature—he was a back-bench member of the House—or by new developments—the known facts changed hardly at all during the story's run. The story's prominence owed to its ingredients—power, sex, and mystery. Even though the D.C. police repeatedly told reporters, on the record and off, that Condit was not a suspect in Chandra Levy's disappearance,[156] the odd chance that he could resolve the mystery kept the story alive.

Condit was the subject of hundreds of news reports and talk-show programs before his story abruptly disappeared. It was not that charges against him had been dropped; they had never been filed. It was not as if Levy had been found; she was still missing. Reality had intruded. The Condit frenzy stopped at precisely 8:46 a.m. on September 11, 2001, the moment that the first hijacked airplane hit the World Trade Center in New York City.

This time, the press rose to the occasion. At a cost of hundreds of millions in direct expenses and lost advertising revenues, the media made a supreme effort to get abreast of the story. In the weeks and months that followed, Americans received information they had never heard before about Islam, Afghanistan, the Taliban, Pakistan, global terrorism, Al Qaeda, and homeland security.

A troubling question was why the press had not awakened earlier. Several months before the terrorist attacks, the U.S. Commission on National Security, which was headed by former senators Warren Rudman and Gary Hart, issued a comprehensive report predicting a "catastrophic attack" by international terrorists and urging the creation of a homeland security agency. CIA director George Tenet had also issued a warning, saying at a Senate hearing that Osama bin Laden's "global network" was the "most immediate and serious" threat facing the country.[157] Except for a few publications, such statements were considered too boring or remote to deserve attention. In the year preceding the World Trade Center and Pentagon attacks, the Al Qaeda terrorist network was mentioned by name only once on the network evening newscasts.

International coverage had been pruned to make room for soft news. A study of ten daily newspapers found that foreign news had declined to 3 percent of total coverage in the period before the terrorist attacks.[158] Even the networks and most major newspapers had cut foreign news by a third or more.[159] Former U.N. ambassador Richard Holbrooke said, "The media's role in the last decade was grossly irresponsible, because the stories mattered."[160]

The closing of foreign news bureaus had also left the media unprepared to report accurately on the terrorist threat. Virtually no U.S. journalists were stationed in Afghanistan or neighboring Pakistan when the attack occurred. "From our flag-decorated TV screens," wrote the *New York Times's* Frank Rich two weeks after the bombings, "you would hardly know that the Taliban's internal opposition and our would-be fellow freedom fighters, the ragtag Northern Alliance, is anathema to Pakistan, our other frail new ally. Or that Pakistan and its military, with its dozens of nuclear weapons, are riddled with bin Laden sympathizers."[161] Gradually, the press gained control of the international aspects of the story, but it was a rocky start.

Although it is unreasonable to expect the press to shoulder the full burden of an informed public, it is reasonable to expect the press to provide a window on the world of politics that is clear enough to illuminate that world. Therein lies a major failing of journalism in recent decades. It misled Americans about the nature of political reality, both at home and abroad.

The mainstream press is at a crossroads that will decide its future and affect the quality of the nation's civic life. The press must decide whether to proceed along the negative and soft news paths it has tread so heavily or to take a newer and more constructive road, such as the one so earnestly pursued in the aftermath of the September 11 attacks.

False choices can blind journalists to their options. Should the media defer to or attack those in power? When the issue is framed this way, any self-respecting journalist has only one choice: attack.

However, it is the wrong choice because it is the wrong question. Knee-jerk criticism only weakens the press's watchdog capacity. When the press condemns everything and everyone, audiences will shun the messenger. Such was their response to the Clinton-Lewinsky scandal. Even though the press suggested that the president would have to resign ("his presidency is numbered in days," said ABC's Sam

Donaldson),[162] the public wasn't buying. The news coverage was so sensational and so deeply rooted in hearsay that most Americans supported Clinton, though not his behavior. Having barked too loud for too long, the watchdog had lost its bite.

In effect, the press had squandered its moral authority. During the Watergate period the press was one of the nation's most trusted institutions. Two decades later it was one of the least trusted. A 1998 Pew Research Center poll indicated that 63 percent of Americans believed that the press "gets in the way of society solving its problems." A 1998 Gallup poll found that journalists' reputation for honesty was as low as that of the politicians they covered and just above that of lawyers and building contractors. A 2000 National Public Radio (NPR) survey found that only one in five citizens had "quite a lot" of confidence in the news media. Without moral authority, the press cannot be an effective watchdog. What Alexander Hamilton said of the judiciary's power—"it has only judgment"—applies also to the press.

The proper exercise of that judgment would benefit the press in more ways than one. An irony of attack journalism is that, as it erodes the foundation of political involvement, it also eats away at the foundation of news consumption. As politics becomes less attractive to people, so, too, does the news. Individuals who have a weak interest in politics are five times less likely (15 percent to 84 percent) to regularly follow the news than those with a strong interest.[163]

Critical reporting needs to give way to a more constructive form. Journalists should not ignore official wrongdoing, nor should they turn their agenda over to the newsmakers. But they should give proper voice to the newsmakers, pay sufficient attention to what government does well, and assess politicians' failings by reasonable standards. The challenge is to strike the proper balance. Before Watergate and Vietnam, newsmakers had far too much control over the news, contributing to an arrogance of power that had tragic consequences. But the pendulum then swung too far in the journalists' direction.

A second false choice is that between informing and entertaining the news audience. Should the press give its audience what they want or should it give them what they need? This question assumes that audience wants and needs are opposites. The public could not have realized before September 11 that it needed to know more about the global terrorist threat. Had it known more, it might well have wanted more. "This business of giving people what they want is a dope pusher's argument," said Reuven Frank, former president of NBC News. "News is something that people don't know they're interested in until they hear about it. The job of the journalist is to take what's important and make it interesting."[164]

Catering to what people want also assumes that what they want initially is what they will want in the end as well. Although marketing studies indicate that soft news has appeal, what is not known is whether it can hold an audience over the long run.[165] A 2000 study by Harvard University's Shorenstein Center found that soft news can alienate the hard-news consumers who are the core audience.[166] The recent experience of NPR also suggests that a soft-news strategy might be shortsighted. With a 300 percent increase in audience in the past decade, NPR has defied the downward trend.[167] Although NPR relies on features as well as hard news, its features tend to be interpretive of hard-news events. NPR has become a haven for hard-news consumers dissatisfied with other broadcast outlets.[168]

The picture, admittedly, is not as clear-cut as the NPR case might suggest. *The NewsHour with Jim Lehrer* on PBS has lost a significant part of its audience during the past decade. Moreover, some soft-news television stations have risen to the top of their local markets. On the other hand, the Project for Excellence in Journalism, which tracks the content and audience ratings of 146 local television news programs, has found that hard-news formulas currently seem to work best. Nearly two-thirds of the highest-quality news programs have had a ratings increase in recent years, a higher percentage than any other type of news program, including those that load up on sensational stories of crimes, fires, and accidents.

It is still too early to conclude with certainty that soft news is a weak base upon which to build a loyal audience. Nevertheless, if people are looking primarily for entertainment, they ultimately can, and likely will, find something more amusing than news, however soft it might be. Heavy doses of soft news may even wear out an audience, just as the best sitcoms eventually lose theirs. A NewsLab study of former or less frequent viewers of local TV news found that many of them had simply tired of the soft-news formula: "too much crime" and "too many fluff stories" were among the top reasons respondents gave for paying less attention.[169]

In contrast, hard news is an ongoing public-affairs story affecting all of us. For more than a century, it has been the reason that millions each day choose to invest some of their time following the news. Hard news, by illuminating today's events, builds interest in tomorrow's. Of course, even ardent hard-news consumers enjoy the occasional amusing or shocking story, but that is different from placing such stories at the center of news coverage.

The attacks on the World Trade Center and the Pentagon in 2001 resurrected news and politics in the nation. Within a few weeks, confidence in journalists and political leaders reached heights not seen in decades. It also awakened many in the news business and in politics to their civic responsibility. But will the new spirit last? Six months after September 11, many news outlets had reverted to their soft-news and hard-ball formulas.[170]

One should not underestimate the difficulty of reforming institutions as large and complex as the press. A century ago, the press faced a comparable challenge when it confronted the excesses of yellow journalism. Two decades lapsed before journalists figured out how to juggle the quest for profits with their public responsibility. If a major transformation of today's media lies ahead, it will not occur overnight.

Yellow journalism was quieted in part by the demise of enough daily newspapers to relieve the competitive pressures that were driving it. Today, with digital television entering the media market, competitive pressures can be expected to intensify, which will severely test any attempt to develop a more responsible form of journalism. A case in point is ABC's attempt to dump Ted Koppel's *Nightline* in favor of the *Late Show with David Letterman,* even though the change would not have greatly increased the network's audience.

Audience competition will also intensify because of young adults' declining interest in news. About half of them pay little or no attention, and no more than a fourth regularly attend to news coverage. Unlike the baby-boom generation that preceded them, they did not grow up in the era when television sets across America were routinely tuned to the evening newscasts at the dinner hour. Entertainment programming was available at all hours, and it dominated their after-school viewing. Few children have an interest in news, but, if exposed to it regularly from an early age, they may develop one. Without this type of exposure, they are only half as likely by adulthood to have acquired an interest in news.[171] With no change in sight in children's viewing habits, the news media will find themselves fighting over fewer and fewer customers.

That will be a blow to politics as well as to news. The news is a day-to-day instrument of democracy. Unless people partake of it regularly, they are unlikely to be politically aware or interested. There is something worse than exposure to persistently negative news, and that's no news exposure at all.

Many journalists are determined to change the situation. The Committee of Concerned Journalists, for example, includes more than a thousand reporters and editors from around the country who are committed to restoring traditional news values. They will need help in achieving their goal. Most news organizations today are embedded in huge corporations that are driven by the bottom line. As the *Washington Post*'s Leonard Downie, Jr., and Robert G. Kaiser note, news departments are under enormous pressure to keep the earnings coming.[172] Owners who recognize that the news is more than just another commodity are needed. Audience demand must also change. However much Americans may complain about the news, they do not always show a preference for quality reporting. Schools should be encouraged to promote a news habit as a duty and a pleasure, so that the demand for better news will grow in the years ahead.[173]

But journalists, too, will have to rethink how they define themselves. The Washington press corps particularly has developed values and interests that do not coincide with those of their readers and viewers. In many newsrooms, journalists are admired for being tough on politicians and are considered wimps if they are not. Audiences can be wooed momentarily by disdain and inside dope, but these also contain the seeds of discontent. The journalist's voice is heard above even that of the newsmaker, and put-down, not purpose, is too often the order of the day. Elections seem to bring out the worst of it. "I know a lot of people who are thinking about this election the same way they think about the Iran-Iraq war," wrote Meg Greenfield in 1980.[174] "They desperately want it to be over, but they don't want anyone to win." George Will said much the same thing in 1992: "The congestion of debates may keep these guys off the streets for a few days. When they emerge from the debates, November—suddenly the loveliest word in the language—will be just around the corner."[175] Shortly before Election Day in 1996, Tom Brokaw opened his newscast by remarking: "If this campaign has an unofficial motto, it is this—wake me when it's over."[176]

What are citizens to do? Cast as voyeurs in a world distant from their own, they have backed away from politics and from news. In the long run, this doesn't serve anyone's interest, as the Columbia School of Journalism's James Carey so pointedly says:

> Journalism and democracy share a common fate. Without the institutions or spirit of democracy, journalists are reduced to propagandists or entertainers. When journalists measure their success solely by the size of their readership or audience, by the profits of their companies, or by their incomes, status, and visibility, they have caved into the temptation of false gods, of selling their heritage for a potage. . . .[177]

CHAPTER FOUR

The Long Campaign
The Politics of Tedium

It seems like it goes on for umpteen months.
—sixty-nine-year-old Wyoming resident[1]

There's too much attention to people whose primaries go first.
—thirty-six-year-old Washington State resident[2]

The convention is all staged for the TV. It is no fun anymore. I don't want to watch celebrities introducing one another. It's a big joke now.
—forty-six-year-old Texas resident[3]

SIXTY-YEAR-OLD Pennsylvania resident Bill Pelligrini* seemed almost surprised to be asked during the Christmas season how much attention he'd been paying to the presidential campaign. "Not much," he told the interviewer. "The election's too far away."

Two months later, Bill was drawn to the campaign by John McCain's candidacy. "McCain seems willing," said Bill, "to say what needs to be said even if it hurts his chances." Bill made a point of watching the election returns on Super Tuesday and was disappointed that Bush and Gore won nearly every state, effectively bringing the nominating races to an end. When the Pennsylvania primary was held a month later, Bill

---

*Bill Pelligrini is a composite. For the Vanishing Voter surveys, a new national sample was chosen each week. Thus, no respondent was interviewed weekly throughout the campaign. However, the composite is based on actual interview responses and reflects what many Americans were doing and thinking at each stage of the 2000 campaign.

shrugged it off. "Didn't vote," he said. "The choice was already made. No competition anymore."

During the next several months Bill took almost no notice of the campaign, although a June news story did catch his attention. "Gore wants to create a new type of retirement account," said Bill, who is nearing retirement and found Gore's plan intriguing. In August, Bill turned on his television set to watch Bush's acceptance speech at the Republican National Convention. "I thought Bush's speech was positive," he observed. He also saw part of the Democratic convention two weeks later. "I think Al Gore presented himself well," Bill said. "I also liked Lieberman's moral character."

As he has done in every presidential election, Bill watched the October debates. "Bush sounded better than I thought he would," he said. "Gore has a better understanding of the policies, though." As Election Day neared, Bill began for the first time in the campaign to follow the news closely. He had a mixed reaction to the story about Bush's drunken driving arrest in 1976, saying it was "kind of interesting" but "not important."

Bill voted on Election Day. He liked Bush and Gore well enough, saying he was "fairly satisfied" with the candidates. However, he described the campaign itself as "depressing, not nearly as good as it should be." He added: "The campaign is too damn long."

The long presidential campaign has been criticized for disrupting the policy process—every four years, Washington slows to a crawl awaiting the election of the next president. But the long campaign has been praised for its capacity to inform the voters' judgment. "That year-long test of endurance . . . reduces the risk that voters will make a rash decision they will come to regret not too much later," says the journalist Robert Friedman.[4]

The long campaign would seem to offer everything that a citizen would need to cast an informed vote. Unlike European national elections, which are crammed into a few weeks, the U.S. presidential contest spans a full year and includes a score of televised events, including the primary debates, the October debates, and the national party conventions. Moreover, unlike Europeans, Americans get two chances—once in the primaries and again in the general election—to cast a vote.

But time by itself does not create an informed electorate. Having the time and taking the time are two different things, as students who put off their homework until the last minute know only too well. This point may seem so obvious that it hardly requires emphasis. What makes the point relevant, however, is that too much time can actually work to the detriment of an informed electorate.[5] That's one of the problems with today's campaign. It is not delightfully long. It is numbingly long.

The long campaign dulls citizens' interest and taxes their attention. Although the campaign is filled with events, many of them are so devoid of meaning or so remote from Election Day that they get little attention. Rather than stimulating interest, the long campaign blunts it. The campaign chugs along at the start, accelerates during the early primaries, idles when they are over, revs up for the conventions, creeps along in September, and races to the finish in late October and early November. If, after each stage, people simply took off from where they had stopped, not much would be lost. But that is not how citizens behave. They tend to forget where they were heading and need a push to get going again.

How early is too early? Most Americans think that a campaign that includes Halloween, Thanksgiving, and Christmas is one that starts too early. Yet the holiday season is now part of the campaign. By Christmas 1999, the candidates had been on the hustings every day for three months. Nine televised debates had been held. Several candidates, including Elizabeth Dole, Dan Quayle, and Lamar Alexander, had already quit the race. More than $50 million had been spent, and hundreds of news stories had been filed.

Few cared. During the average week only one in seven was following the election with any degree of regularity. The average citizen didn't say anything at all about the campaign to anyone more than once a week.[6] When Elizabeth Dole withdrew from the GOP race in the fall, it made news without making a splash. A lot of people were unaware she had dropped out because they did not know she was running. When asked in our Vanishing Voter survey in late 1999 why they were not following the campaign more closely, more than half the respondents indicated "it's simply too early in the campaign."

Before the first primaries are held, candidate debates are the main attraction. They do not get as much fanfare as the October election debates, but they are the biggest challenge that the candidates face until actual votes are cast, and they get reporters' attention.[7] "George W. Bush [is] being put to the test tonight, alongside his five rivals for the GOP presidential nomination. Bush is heading into his first debate of the 2000 campaign, mindful of what he has to prove, and what his opponents hope to gain," chimed CNN anchor Bernard Shaw.[8]

However, the Republican debate drew only 1.6 million viewers—a fifth of the audience of the average prime-time broadcast.[9] The first Democratic debate a few days later fared no better. The two dozen primary debates in 2000 drew 36 million viewers, less than the number who watch a single October debate.

Even for the interested few, the primary debates gradually lost their appeal. Cable networks carried fourteen prior to the Iowa caucuses. The first seven attracted 1.7 million viewers on average. The last seven averaged only 675,000. Only 200,000 saw a January debate in Iowa that was carried on MSNBC and C-SPAN. "I'm tired of hearing the same answers over and over again," said one citizen in explaining why she quit watching after only a few minutes.

Debate audiences would have been larger if the major broadcast networks had participated more fully. They carried only two debates, neither in prime time. Even so, these debates had the biggest audiences. A December encounter on ABC's *Nightline* attracted 4.5 million viewers. A week later, 4.7 million tuned in a debate on NBC's *Meet the Press*. Of the twenty-odd debates carried exclusively on cable, the Bush-McCain-Keyes encounter on CNN's *Larry King Live* just before South Carolina's GOP primary was the biggest draw: 3 million viewers. CBS News ran a poll on its Web site that asked: "Tired of all these presidential debates?" Viewers could not have been tired if their channel selector had been locked onto CBS. The network that gave us Edward R. Murrow and Walter Cronkite did not air a single primary debate.[10]

Nevertheless, a lack of interest more than anything else explains the small debate audiences. Half who came across a primary debate while watching television quickly switched to another channel. "I had little interest, so I turned it off," said one such viewer.

Robert Dole once compared the U.S. Senate to a wet noodle: "If it doesn't want to move, it's not going to move."[11] The same can be said of the American electorate. Not much can be done to persuade people to take an interest in a presidential campaign before they are ready to do so. Citizens care about the election of the president, but they have other demands on their time.

Why are the candidates and the voters on such completely different timetables? What compels candidates to be on the campaign trail months before most citizens are willing to pay attention?

There is no fixed starting date to a presidential campaign, only the certainty that it will begin in earnest several months before the first contests in Iowa and New Hampshire. Even an odds-on favorite has no choice but to start early and to run hard. In 1980, Ronald Reagan discovered the risks of the waiting game. He had a four-to-one lead for the Republican nomination in national polls and decided not to participate in a televised debate in Iowa. Hawkeye State voters did not take kindly to the snub. After his loss there, Reagan's 30-point lead in New Hampshire polls shrank almost to nothing.[12] If he had not staged a dramatic confrontation in a New Hampshire debate—"I'm paying for this microphone"—Reagan might be a footnote to presidential history.

Active campaigning far in advance of the first primary is attributable to a change three decades ago in the nominating process. Before then, primary elections were held in a third of the states, but most of the national convention delegates were selected through party caucuses controlled by party leaders. In 1952, for example, Senator Estes Kefauver of Tennessee defeated President Harry S Truman by a 55–45 margin in New Hampshire's opening primary. Kefauver then won all but one of the other twelve primaries he entered and was the favorite of rank-and-file Democrats in the final Gallup poll before the party's national convention. Yet Democratic leaders rejected the maverick

Kefauver and chose instead Illinois governor Adlai Stevenson, a traditional New Dealer, who was not even a declared presidential candidate.[13] When asked about the significance of the primaries, Stevenson replied: "All [they do] is destroy some candidates."[14]

The bitter 1968 presidential election shattered the party-centered nominating system. The country was mired in Vietnam, and Robert Kennedy and Eugene McCarthy challenged Lyndon Johnson's bid for a second term. Their strong showing led Johnson to make a surprise announcement on national television: "I shall not seek, and I will not accept, the nomination of my party for another term as your president." Kennedy's assassination in Los Angeles on the night of the California primary left the field to McCarthy. But McCarthy had lost a string of primaries to Kennedy and had infuriated party leaders. On the first ballot, they nominated Johnson's vice president, Hubert Humphrey, who had not contested a single primary. Insurgent Democrats were outraged, and after Humphrey narrowly lost the general election, they engineered a change in the nominating process.

Through its McGovern-Fraser Commission, the Democratic Party adopted rules designed to put the voters in charge of the nominating process. State parties were directed to choose their convention delegates through either a primary election or a caucus open to all registered party voters.[15] The commission anticipated that the caucus states would reform their traditional method, but several switched immediately to the primary system and more followed thereafter. The state legislatures that authorized these primaries applied them also to the GOP, thus binding the Republicans to the change.[16]

By placing nominations in voters' hands, the reform system dictated how candidates would campaign. To gain nomination, they would have to aggressively court the public. Some candidates learned this lesson the hard way. Humphrey dallied in 1972, hoping that a draft at the Democratic convention would bring him the nomination. Senator Henry Jackson skipped New Hampshire in 1976, expecting that his labor support and a strong showing in selected primaries would carry him to nomination. That year California's Jerry Brown jumped into the race two months after the first contest but, although he defeated Jimmy Carter in their four head-to-head encounters, he had entered too late to derail Carter's nomination. After that campaign the lesson was clear. No candidate could hope to win nomination except through the primaries, and no candidate could risk a slow start.

Candidates must begin early, but citizens are not forced to do so. Their natural impulse is to ignore the early phase of the campaign, unless they revel in election politics, which only a few now do.

As a result, Americans do not learn all that much about the candidates and issues in the months before the Iowa caucuses. In 2000, some of them were blithely misinformed. When asked in a December survey what first came to mind when they thought about the Republican candidate George W. Bush, 11 percent of the respondents said he was the former president. Only 1 percent referred to a Bush policy proposal. Respondents' comments about Bill Bradley were also sparse. Half said they had never heard of him and, of those who had, many described him as a former basketball player. Fewer than 1 percent made reference to a Bradley policy proposal, despite the emphasis he was placing on his health-care plan.[17]

Information is fleeting unless people are interested enough to try to pin it down. Within an hour of a newscast, most have difficulty recalling anything they saw, unless a story was on a subject of keen interest.[18] Candidate stories a year in advance of Election Day are not of that order. When asked in December whether George Bush "favors or opposes the registration of all guns," 73 percent said they had no idea where he stood. Only 16 percent said he opposed the policy and 11 percent wrongly said (a sure sign that many of the correct responses were also mere guesses) that he favored universal gun registration.[19]

Most Americans had given so little thought to the 2000 campaign that they didn't even have a candidate in mind, despite media polls that suggested otherwise. The media's trial heats force respondents into a choice by reading them a list of candidates and asking them which one they like best. Our Vanishing Voter surveys posed the question differently: "Which candidate do you support at this time, or haven't you picked a candidate yet?" Shortly before the Iowa caucuses, the landslide winner with 66 percent was "no candidate yet." Lagging far behind were Bush (15 percent), Gore (10 percent), and McCain and Bradley (3 percent each).[20]

THE NEW HAMPSHIRE primary accomplished in 2000 what months of campaigning had failed to do. It got people interested in the election. In academic studies, scholars often treat the campaign as a seamless flow of messages and decisions. But campaigns are not seamless. They are punctuated by key moments when citizens sit up, take notice, and more actively listen and learn.

Interest rose sharply at the time of the New Hampshire February 1 primary. John McCain's surprising victory over George W. Bush was a major reason, but so, too, was the fact that votes were now being cast and counted.* Respondents in our surveys had been saying for weeks that the campaign was "discouraging" and "uninformative." Now they were calling it "encouraging" and "informative."[21]

Interest continued upward as the March 7 Super Tuesday primaries neared. At peak, shortly after Super Tuesday, more than a third said they were paying quite a bit of attention to the campaign. Nearly half could recall an election story they had seen, read, or heard in the past day, and two-fifths said they had engaged in campaign-related conversation within the past day. Not everyone, of course, was caught up in the excitement of the primaries. At least half of the public had no real interest in the nominating races even during this intensely competitive period. Nevertheless, interest had increased sharply from its pre-primary level and was still on the rise when the Super Tuesday primaries were held.

After Super Tuesday, however, interest had nowhere to go but down. Americans could hardly have thought at the time of the Iowa and New Hampshire contests that they would have only a month or so to engage the campaign and make a choice. But that is all the time they would

---

*More so than the Iowa caucuses, the New Hampshire primary draws the public to the campaign, in part because of the enormous media buildup it receives. It typically garners a fourth or more of all primary coverage, which inflates public opinion of New Hampshire's role. Although the New Hampshire primary selects only about 1 percent of the national convention delegates, Americans think the total is much higher. When asked in our Vanishing Voter survey whether New Hampshire selects 25, 10, 5, or 1 percent of the delegates, only one in seven respondents picked 1 percent. One in seven also claimed that New Hampshire selects 25 percent.

get. Super Tuesday brought the nominating races to a screeching halt, just as it had in 1996.

The time that voters had was inadequate to their task. Nominating elections provide the most difficult choice that voters face.[22] They can't rely on party labels to make their choice: the candidates are all Democrats or all Republicans. Nominating races also typically attract a half dozen or so contenders, most of them relative newcomers to presidential politics. Of the eight Republican contenders in 1996, for example, only Dole and Pat Buchanan had national reputations. In 1988, the Democratic contenders had such low recognition levels they were dubbed "the seven dwarfs." In 1976, the six active contenders for the Democratic nomination were also relative unknowns. Carter's recognition level before the New Hampshire primary was similar to that of his opponents. Most said they knew him only by name. Of the 20 percent who claimed to know more, about the best many of them could muster was that he was a peanut farmer or was from Georgia.[23]

The 2000 campaign fit the pattern. By Super Tuesday, only one in five could say, even by guessing, where the candidates stood on specific issues.[24] Of course, primary voters were not completely in the dark on Super Tuesday when they chose Bush and Gore as the party nominees. They recognized that Bush and Gore were the established candidates and that McCain and Bradley were the upstarts. Bush's support, for example, came mainly from registered Republicans, while McCain's was disproportionately from independents and crossover Democrats.[25] Nevertheless, Bush, like Gore, was nominated as much by ascription as by informed judgment.

Voters are plenty smart and, as the political scientist Samuel Popkin found, can reason effectively with small amounts of information.[26] But they are not hobbyists who fill their time cataloguing presidential hopefuls. They will make a choice, of course. Primaries are held, ballots get cast, and someone wins. But what kind of choice has been made?

Today's nominating contests end abruptly because of "front-loading"—the bunching of state contests early in the nominating process. In 2000, fifteen states held their primaries on Super Tuesday.

In that kind of contest, opponents did not stand a chance against Bush's and Gore's superior name recognition, financing, and organization. Bradley quit the race the next day. McCain retreated to his Arizona home and, two days later, announced he was dropping out. The 1996 nominating campaign also ended abruptly. When Robert Dole dominated the six Junior Tuesday contests on March 5 and the seven Super Tuesday contests a week later, his chief rivals—Lamar Alexander, Richard Lugar, and Steve Forbes—quit the race.

Before front-loading became the norm, the campaign unfolded slowly, either one state at a time or in small groups, which gave voters more time to listen and decide. Even then, voters sometimes had trouble sorting out the candidates.[27] In 1976, Democrats never did get a handle on Carter. They thought he was a decent man, which, in the aftermath of Watergate, seemed qualification enough to many of them. But even after he secured the nomination, most Democrats could not provide specifics when asked what Carter would do if elected.[28]

Nevertheless, time was the voters' ally in the 1970s.[29] The contested races went nearly to the wire before being decided. The halfway point in the selection of delegates did not occur until May, and every contested race lasted until nearly the last day of primaries. By 1988, with the advent of front-loading, the halfway point was reached in April, and the races were ending sooner. In 1996 and 2000, the races were over in early March, a relatively short time after Iowa and New Hampshire had awakened Americans to the fact they had a choice to make.

In theory, the McGovern-Fraser reform created a system in which the states are unequal only in that larger states select proportionately more delegates than smaller states. Theory and practice, however, have been quite different. The reformed system loaded the dice in favor of states with early contests. As the journalist Jules Witcover said in 1977: "The fact is that the reality in the early going of a presidential campaign is not the delegate count at all. The reality at the beginning stage is the psychological impact of the results—the perception by press, public, and contending politicians of what has happened."[30]

The smart folks in Iowa were the first ones to figure out the new system. They placed their caucuses just ahead of the New Hampshire primary and, by 1976, were basking in the national limelight. "With 88 percent of Iowa's caucuses in, no amount of bad-mouthing by the others can lessen the importance of Jimmy Carter's finish," said CBS correspondent Roger Mudd. "He was the clear winner in this psychologically crucial test." CBS then singled Carter out for extra coverage. "So the candidate with the highly prized political momentum tonight is Jimmy Carter, covered now by Ed Rabel in New Hampshire."[31]

Other states continued to operate by the old rules. They scheduled their primaries for open dates, seeking a Tuesday when they would have the national spotlight all to themselves. When Carter won the hard-fought 1976 Democratic race, for example, the primaries started in New Hampshire (February 24), went on to Massachusetts and Vermont (March 2), then on to Florida (March 9), and from there to Illinois (March 16), North Carolina (March 23), New York and Wisconsin (April 6), Pennsylvania (April 27), and Texas (May 1). Not until early May did state contests begin to clump together. The schedule was backloaded.

After Carter's unexpected victory, however, the new dynamic was apparent to all. The initial contests winnowed the field of candidates and bestowed momentum on the top finishers. To prevent an all-out fight over the opening positions, the Democratic Party reserved the initial spots for Iowa and New Hampshire and created "a window" for the other states. They would be allowed to hold their contests anytime between the second Tuesday in March (later changed to the first Tuesday) and the second Tuesday in June. The GOP followed a similar policy.*

The stage was set for front-loading. Although Iowa and New Hampshire had a lock on the starting positions, there was nothing to prevent other states from moving to the front of the window. By 1988, two dozen had elbowed their way into March. All southern states except South Carolina, along with seven others, staged their primaries and

---

*Until 2000 the GOP had no formal rule but generally conducted its primaries in accordance with the Democratic timetable. In 2000 the GOP established parameters: its window began with the first Monday in February, which enabled South Carolina, Michigan, Arizona, and Delaware, along with New Hampshire, to hold their primaries before Super Tuesday.

caucuses on the same March day. It was the first bona fide "Super Tuesday."

Some states stayed away from the front of the schedule to avoid the expense of a second primary later in the year to select their statewide, congressional, and local nominees. But the action was clearly at the front end of the process. Traditionally, California's primary was on the final day of the nominating calendar. Until 1976 it was often a decisive encounter. McGovern's victory in 1972 enabled him to secure the Democratic nomination, just as Goldwater's in 1964 gave him the Republican nod. After 1976, however, the race in *every* case was over by the time it reached California. In 1996, the state moved its primary to March 26, three weeks after the first allowable date. Even that position was too far back to enable delegate-rich California to exert its muscle. For 2000, the state moved its primary to the first Tuesday in March, the earliest allowable date. "California voters are finally going to have some clout in deciding who the major parties nominate for president," said Governor Pete Wilson at the bill-signing ceremony.[32]

California joined a crowded field. In 2000, twenty-nine states held contests in March—half of them on Super Tuesday. Sixty-three percent of the delegates were chosen by mid-March. In 1980, only 21 percent had been selected by then.

In effect, the nominees are now picked in a de facto national primary that takes place on Super Tuesday. No rule says the nominations must be decided then, and in some circumstances they might not. But the odds are they will. Whichever candidate has the most money, strongest organization, and deepest party support—like Bush and Gore in 2000, and Dole and Clinton in 1996—is likely to win big on Super Tuesday and bring the race to a sudden halt.

Although front-loading has advantages for the victorious candidates, it has no commensurate benefits for citizens. An abbreviated campaign discounts their involvement, learning, and even votes. The thousands of Florida voters disenfranchised on Election Day 2000 were for a time the most talked-about people in the nation. Almost no one commented, however, on the millions of voters in the roughly thirty states who, six months earlier, were effectively disenfranchised when Bush's and Gore's victories on March 7 completely devalued their yet-to-be-held presidential primaries and caucuses.

Front-loading explains why the overall turnout rate in presidential primaries has fallen from nearly 30 to 17 percent since the 1970s.* Turnout has become schizophrenic—respectable in states with early contests and embarrassing in those with later contests. In 2000, the voting rate averaged 21 percent in primaries held on or before Super Tuesday and only 14 percent thereafter. Since the advent of front-loading, turnout has been half again as high in contested primaries as in those held after the races were decided. Were it not for the primaries for other offices also being held in the late-scheduled states, almost no one would bother to vote.

Residents of the early states are also more likely to follow the campaign in the news and to discuss it with others. During the five-month nominating period in 2000, New Hampshire residents talked about the campaign several times a week on average, compared with less than once a week for Wyoming residents, who also were only half as likely to pay attention to election news. New Hampshire and Wyoming residents were extreme cases, but residents of contested states were more heavily involved in the nominating stage of the campaign than were residents of states with meaningless primaries and caucuses (Figure 4.1).

Even in the contested states, the attention given to a state by the candidates and the media affected involvement levels. Residents of the states where the heaviest campaigning occurred or where the media's attention was concentrated followed the election more closely than did residents of the other contested states.[33]

---

*As the 2000 Republican race demonstrated, a hard-fought nominating campaign can still draw voters to the polls. According to Curtis Gans of the Committee for the Study of the American Electorate, thirteen GOP primaries had record numbers of voters, largely because of McCain's ability to attract the support of independents and crossover Democrats. McCain appealed to many who otherwise would not have voted or would have participated in the Democratic race. In fact, he siphoned off enough Democrats that turnout in their party's primaries was the second lowest in forty years. Only in 1996, when Bill Clinton ran unopposed, was the turnout lower. McCain's candidacy also attracted additional Republican voters, many of whom came out to vote against him.

FIGURE 4.1

CAMPAIGN INVOLVEMENT IN THE WEEK
PRECEDING A STATE'S NOMINATING CONTEST
AND THE SCHEDULING OF THAT CONTEST

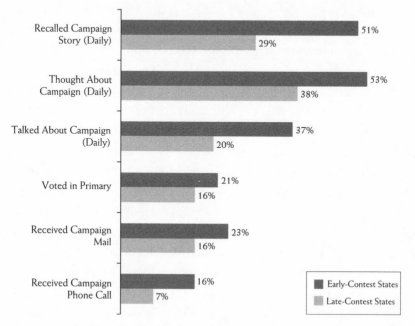

Residents of states that held their nominating contests on or before March 7 were more involved in the campaign during the week before their contests than were residents of other states during the week before their contests.

Information levels were also affected by the attention a state received. According to an Annenberg Center study of the 2000 campaign, residents of heavily contested primary states were 30 percent more likely to have particular knowledge of the candidates and issues. "What we are seeing," concluded Annenberg director Kathleen Hall Jamieson, "is a primary season of haves and have-nots—those states that have primaries with aggressive campaigning have more understanding of candidates and their positions."[34]

The presidential nominating campaign is now only in principle a national system. The sequence of primaries affects one's ability to engage and influence the campaign. There are now two different nominating electorates, one formed by residents of early-contest states and one consisting of residents of late-contest states. The first electorate chooses the nominees and is the more heavily involved.

Front-loading produces a Silent Spring that affects all Americans, whatever their state of residence. Once the nominations are settled, the campaign loses its appeal. The conventions are still months away, but the races are over, and people retreat to the sidelines.

Within a month of Super Tuesday in 2000, the number paying close attention to the campaign had been sliced in half. Bush and Gore kept on campaigning, but citizens were only slightly more attentive than they had been in the period before the New Hampshire primary. This had also happened in 1996. Election interest declined sharply after Dole's win on Super Tuesday and did not rise again until the national party conventions in August.

In 2000, there was not a single state in which involvement during the late spring was as high as it was in even the lowest-involvement state during the contested period. In most states, involvement averaged only a third of its previous level. During the contested phase, for example, more than three in ten New Yorkers said that they had given thought to the campaign within the past day. In the late spring, barely one in ten did so. And so it went, state after state. During the contested phase, there had been large differences between the states. Now, there were few differences between them. Americans everywhere had tuned out the campaign.

As involvement declined, learning slowed to a crawl. A month after Super Tuesday in 2000, Americans were actually less informed about some of Gore's and Bush's issue positions than they had been earlier in the campaign. For example, only 13 percent in April could accurately identify Bush's stand on gun control compared with 24 percent in February.[35] Issue awareness would rise slightly during the next several months as the campaign worked its way toward the summer conventions. By and large, however, the post–Super Tuesday period was a time when issue awareness languished. Candidate support also slipped.

Fewer in June said they had picked a candidate than had said so in March.

In the 1970s, when the nominating races ended later, citizens remained interested for a longer period. In 1976, for example, interest rose month by month as the campaign moved toward the final early June contests in California, Ohio, and New Jersey.[36] Today's front-loaded nominating system has a different dynamic. The nominating races end quickly, and the national party conventions are still months away. What is a public to do? Americans do what good sense dictates. They turn their attention elsewhere.

Reform Democrats could hardly have envisioned today's nominating system when they attempted after the 1968 election to create a system that would empower rank-and-file voters. Instead, they constructed a system that has become ever more responsive to other influences, including money.

Super Tuesday is tailor-made for well-funded candidates. Presidential hopefuls need to raise a lot of cash up front to compete in today's front-loaded system.[37] Money does not guarantee success, as Steve Forbes discovered the hard way, twice. But money is to a candidacy what gas is to a car. It can go a lot farther if it is running on full. An underfunded candidate can sometimes survive Iowa and New Hampshire, but, after that, person-to-person campaigning gives way to a multi-state effort based on televised political ads, which cost huge sums. McGovern and Carter were the last poorly funded candidates to win nomination.

In 2000, John McCain looked for a time as if he might beat the odds. Outspent two to one,[38] McCain still managed to stun Bush in New Hampshire and Michigan. Nevertheless, even if he had not been a party maverick, McCain had little chance of victory on Super Tuesday with its dozen or so primaries. After New Hampshire he had only five weeks to build enough voter and financial support to stop Bush's juggernaut. Iowa and New Hampshire still bestow momentum, but front-loading tips the balance toward candidates who have deep pockets and start high in the polls.

Since 1984 the candidate who has raised the most money in advance of the opening contests has won *every* nominating race.[39] Of course, money flows to candidates, like Bush and Gore, who already have substantial support. The frontrunners in pre-election national polls have won three-fourths of the contested nominating races.[40] But whatever the exact influence of money, factors firmly in place before the first contests—that is, before a single vote is cast—now go a long way toward determining the winners.

The public has taken notice. When asked at the end of the 2000 primaries whether the current method of nominating presidential candidates gives more say to "the voters" or to "the party leaders and the people who contribute money to the candidates," only 15 percent said the voters have the larger voice.[41]

Election reform is a tricky business, as illustrated by the campaign finance laws passed in 1974 in reaction to the Watergate scandal. The legislation curbed some problems but spawned others, including political action committees (PACs) and soft money. So it has been with the McGovern-Fraser reform. The commission did not intend to create an interminably long, money-driven system that strips the late-scheduled primaries of their significance, but that's what has happened.

In the process, Americans have grown dissatisfied with the way presidential nominees are chosen. In 1980, before the advent of front-loading, only 22 percent felt "the present system of state primaries and caucuses is too long and drawn out."[42] The public no longer holds that opinion. Five times during the 2000 campaign, our Vanishing Voter weekly survey asked respondents whether they liked "the long presidential campaign because it gives [you] a better chance to get to know the candidates" or whether they disliked it because it is "so long that [you] don't have time to pay attention except now and then." Each time, a majority complained about the campaign's length. In November 1999, 64 percent expressed displeasure with the long campaign. A year later, as the campaign was finally drawing to a close, 61 percent objected to the timetable.

Respondents also said they would prefer any of the major alternatives to the current nominating system. In our Vanishing Voter survey, a national primary was at the top of their list (64–36 percent), but a narrow plurality (44–42 percent) even claimed they would prefer the old convention system where party activists select the nominees.[43]

THE NATIONAL PARTY conventions were once rollicking affairs, few more so than the Democratic gathering in 1924. In the wake of the Teapot Dome scandal that had rocked the Republican administration of Warren G. Harding, the Democrats had thought that they could recapture the White House. But they had a tempest of their own brewing. The northern wing wanted New York governor Al Smith, a Catholic who despised the Ku Klux Klan and promised to end Prohibition. The Klan-tolerating, Prohibition-favoring southern wing preferred the more conservative William G. McAdoo, son-in-law of Woodrow Wilson. For nine days, sometimes with fisticuffs, the two sides battled on the convention floor with neither candidate able to muster the required two-thirds majority. After an exhausting 103 ballots, Smith and McAdoo released their delegates, and the convention turned to John W. Davis, a little-known Wall Street lawyer. The renowned journalist H. L. Mencken likened Davis's nomination to "France and Germany fighting for centuries over Alsace-Lorraine, and then deciding to give it to England."[44] In any event, the voters had seen enough of the Democrats. They elected Calvin Coolidge by a landslide.

Some of the excitement went out of convention politics when the Democrats dropped the two-thirds rule in 1936 in favor of a simple-majority rule, which the GOP had always used. That change was of small consequence, however, compared with the McGovern-Fraser reform, which stripped the conventions of their nominating power. The formal authority is still there, but the real power resides in the primary and caucus process.

Some observers say the conventions were in irreversible decline before the change in 1972.[45] No convention in the previous two decades had gone past the first ballot, and primaries had grown increasingly important. In 1960, John F. Kennedy had to show Democratic leaders that his youth and Roman Catholicism would not ruin the party's chances in the fall election, and he did so with victories in the Wisconsin and West Virginia primaries.

Nevertheless, conventions were open and tumultuous affairs. Front-runners always worried that a riveting speech, late revelation, new face, or strategic maneuver might derail their nomination. Even if they held on, there were platform fights to settle, when they could be settled. Supporters of Barry Goldwater shouted down his chief rival, Nelson Rockefeller, when he appeared on the podium at the 1964 Republican convention. Humphrey and McCarthy were each booed lustily, but from different quarters, at the 1968 Democratic convention. The delegates controlled the conventions, and every four years the electorate had the chance to see them in action.

Today, the nominees control the conventions. No viewer has witnessed anything even remotely resembling an open convention since 1984, when Gary Hart carried the delegate fight to the floor—the last candidate to do so. Jesse Jackson in 1988 and Pat Buchanan in 1992 took policy disputes into the convention, but even that form of dissent might be a thing of the past. Both parties in 1996 and 2000 presented tightly choreographed gatherings that kept any sign of division off the convention floor. "Boring is good," said the Democratic consultant James Carville as the Democrats gathered for their 1996 convention.[46]

The McGovern-Fraser Commission did not seek to eviscerate the convention. "Purged of its structural and procedural inadequacies," the commission said, "the national convention [is] well worth preserving." Brokered conventions were expected to occur periodically. Under the new rules, states were required to divide their delegates among the candidates according to the proportion of votes they received, which, in the commission's view, could prevent a candidate from acquiring the delegate majority required for nomination.*

The first nominations decided under the new rules were, indeed, tightly contested. Although none of the conventions from 1972 to 1984 went past the first ballot, the delegates were often at odds, as in the 1972 McGovern-Humphrey race, the 1976 Ford-Reagan race, the 1980

---

*This worry was substantial enough that the Democratic Party later created "superdelegates," who are chosen by the state party organizations. The change was a way to ensure that the party's top elected and organizational officials would not be kept out of the convention, but it was also intended as a mechanism for breaking deadlocks that might result when no candidate won an outright majority of the delegates selected through the primaries and caucuses.

Carter-Kennedy race, and the 1984 Mondale-Hart race. Front-loading eliminated such conventions because it produces an early and conclusive end to the contests. The convention has become a four-day testimonial designed to cast the winner in the strongest possible light. A recent Republican convention was so expertly choreographed that one wag described it as "GOP-TV."[47]

Today's conventions are akin to coronation events, a fact that riles the press to no end. Midway through the 1996 GOP convention in San Diego, Ted Koppel of ABC's *Nightline* left in a huff, saying that he was returning to New York in search of real news. Koppel's departure prompted one commentator to remark: "The smoke-filled rooms are gone, but the spectacle that remains is as barren as a pond hit by acid rain: crystal clear, utterly beautiful, and utterly dead."[48]

In earlier times, the press could hardly get its fill of the conventions. The buildup was intense. Each day brought the latest speculation about delegate counts and possible deals. In the run-up to the 1960 Democratic convention, for example, the news was filled with analysis of Stevenson, Johnson, and Stuart Symington's chances of blocking Kennedy's first-ballot bid for the nomination. Today, with the outcome known in advance, the convention is no longer eagerly anticipated by the press, or by the voters. A week before the 2000 Republican national convention, only 19 percent of the public knew it was only days away. Seventy-five percent said they had no idea of when it was scheduled and 6 percent placed it a month or more in the future.[49]

Convention audiences have fallen sharply. Even as late as 1976, 28 percent of American households at the average moment had their TV sets on and tuned to the convention. By 1988, convention ratings had slipped to 19 percent. In 2000, only 13 percent of TV households were tuned in during the average prime-time minute, which was below even that of 1996, when the race was one-sided and the nominees better known.[50]

When our survey respondents were asked in 2000 why the conventions were getting so little of their attention, the leading response—

aside from the customary ones, "I'm too busy" or "I don't care for politics"—was that the nominees had already been selected.[51]

Cutbacks in broadcast coverage have also contributed to the declining convention audience. In 1976, each of the major networks—ABC, CBS, and NBC—broadcast 25 hours of coverage of each convention. By 1984, that average had fallen to 12 hours. It was a mere 5 hours in 2000.

Although cable outlets provide gavel-to-gavel coverage, they are no substitute for the networks. A fourth of U.S. households do not have satellite or cable service. Moreover, most TV viewers routinely monitor only selected channels, which usually include the major networks. An event that appears simultaneously on the three networks is more likely to attract viewers' attention. Fully half the audience for the 2000 conventions consisted of inadvertent viewers—those who sat down in front of their television sets, discovered the convention was on, and decided to watch some of it. Three times as many of these viewers were captured through a broadcast channel as through a cable channel. But they cannot be corraled if ABC, CBS, and NBC are all televising something else.[52]

The eclipse of the convention as a deliberative forum and television sensation has reduced campaign involvement. In the heyday of the televised conventions—the 1950s through the 1970s—the average American household watched ten to twenty hours of coverage. Voters learned more about the candidates and issues during the conventions than at any other single period in the campaign. The convention was quite an education, even for children and adolescents. Just as the World Series served to awaken them to major league baseball, the summer conventions introduced them to party politics.

Conventions still do all this, only on a smaller scale. They remain a key moment in terms of their ability to draw people into the campaign. Their audience, though diminished, is not minuscule. In our Vanishing Voter surveys, roughly a fourth of the respondents said they had watched "all" or "most" of the previous night's coverage. Nearly 15 million were tuned in during the average prime-time minute. Four of five who watched said they liked what they saw.[53]

Conventions also stimulate interest in the campaign. In 2000, interest rose by 50 percent during the convention period, nearly reaching the level of the contested primary period. On the average day, one in three claimed to have talked about the campaign and one in two followed news about it. With increased interest came accelerated learning. Above all, the conventions afforded citizens a chance to find out more about the candidates. "People want to know more about Bush and Gore—what they are really like," said Republican consultant Bob Teeter. "Conventions are still important [in helping] people get that information."[54] In fact, awareness of Bush's and Gore's issue positions rose by 17 percent during this period.[55]

Many Americans also picked their candidate during the 2000 conventions. The number who said they had not yet decided on a candidate fell from 55 to 41 percent, the sharpest drop of the campaign. Although the October debates are usually portrayed as the major showdown of the campaign, far more votes are decided during the conventions. More voters are undecided about their candidate choice at this stage of the campaign, and the conventions give the nominees a nearly unobstructed opportunity to make their pitch. In an era of ten-second sound bites and thirty-second political ads, conventions are a throwback to the time when lengthy speeches were the main form of address. Even with fewer viewers, the conventions provide by far the largest audiences the candidates have to themselves during the entire campaign. As the *Washington Post*'s Howard Kurtz said of the 1992 Democratic convention: "A remarkable thing happened [last night]. Bill Clinton was allowed to address the nation for 53 minutes without being interrupted by Rather, Brokaw, or Jennings."[56]

The audience for the nominees' acceptance speeches is a receptive one. If Americans' attention span, as some have claimed, can now be measured in seconds, the acceptance speeches are an exception. They are the most anticipated part of today's conventions, and the most favorably received.[57]

Conventions have a final noteworthy effect: They lift the voters' spirits. They are upbeat events during which candidates get their most favorable news coverage.[58] During the 2000 convention period, the public saw the campaign as positive, not negative (49–22 percent), and encouraging, not discouraging (41–27 percent). Both were election-year highs.[59]

These contributions are not small ones in a campaign process that often dulls interest, learning, and trust. But they are small by comparison with the impact these quadrennial summer events once had.

NEARLY A HALF million people turned out on Labor Day in Detroit in 1936 to see and hear presidential candidate Franklin D. Roosevelt. The crowd was so deep that it extended like fingers into the streets spreading out from Cadillac Square.[60] It was the height of the Depression and Roosevelt was a hero to America's working class. By comparison, when Al Gore and Joseph Lieberman spoke at an outdoor rally in Pittsburgh on Labor Day 2000, only 10,000 showed up.

Labor Day speeches are the traditional kickoff to the fall campaign. They once served as coming-out parties for the newly chosen party nominees. The candidates were fresh news and so were their pronouncements. Today, the candidates are such old news by Labor Day that, as far as most people are concerned, it might as well be Ground-hog Day. During Labor Day week in 2000, Americans were actually less attentive to the presidential campaign than in the preceding or the following week.[61]

September was once a highlight of the campaign. As the candidates toured the nation, speaking in city squares, they packed in the crowds and laid out their positions. It was in September, for example, when Hubert Humphrey broke with Lyndon Johnson's Vietnam policy in a speech at Salt Lake City's Tabernacle on Temple Square. But September is now just another month on the long road to November. Because of front-loading, the general election campaign effectively begins in early March and has been under way for nearly half a year. The candidates are familiar faces and are running out of new things to say.

The voters, too, are worn out. In 2000, public involvement dropped during September. Unlike the post–Super Tuesday period, Americans did not flee the campaign. But they talked and thought about it less often and followed it less closely than they had during the convention period. As they pulled back, they forgot some of the information acquired earlier.[62] Issue awareness dropped by 22 percent during the month after the convention period. The optimism of that period had also dissipated. A majority now claimed that the campaign was boring and uninformative.[63]

Presidential elections might seem interminable if the October televised debates had not been resurrected in 1976. The first such debates had been held in 1960 and, for a time, they looked to be the last. After 1960 the candidate who was ahead in the polls refused each time to participate, shielded by a restriction on free broadcast time. Nixon had gone into the 1960 debates as the favorite to win the election. He emerged in second place and was narrowly defeated by Kennedy—a lesson not lost on subsequent front-runners.

An administrative ruling and two public-minded nominees, Gerald Ford and Jimmy Carter, revived the debates. In 1960, Congress had temporarily suspended the federal law that prohibits broadcasters from giving free airtime without granting it to all candidates for the same office. In 1975, however, the Federal Communications Commission reinterpreted the federal statute to say that debates could be treated as bona fide news events rather than a free-time opportunity if sponsored by an independent organization. A year later, Carter, who was leading in the polls, accepted President Ford's challenge to meet in debates sponsored by the League of Women Voters. October debates have been held ever since.

However, the malaise that has depressed other election activities has also affected the debates. More than half of television households had their sets on and tuned to debates in 1976 and again in 1980.[64] The number fell to 46 percent in 1984, 36 percent in 1988, and 29 percent in 1996. Although the 2000 Gore-Bush debate ratings were expected to top the 1996 figure because of the tight race, they did not rise, and the rating for the third debate was the lowest ever (26 percent).

Nevertheless, no development has done more to enliven the modern campaign than the October debates—the nearest things to national town meetings. That tens of millions gather at the same time to listen to presidential candidates is remarkable. More remarkable still is that a majority of viewers watch the bulk of the ninety-minute telecasts.

It is an audience that listens and learns. Although the press often complains that the debates raise no new issues (a "wind-festival" is how CBS's Dan Rather characterized the first Bush-Gore debate),[65] much of what is said is new to the viewers. Studies indicate that the October debates, without exception, have increased the public's understanding of the candidates and issues.[66] In 2000, Americans' ability to recognize Bush's and Gore's positions on key issues rose by 25 percent during the debate period.[67]

Debates give the electorate an opportunity to view the candidates through something other than the negative lens of journalism, and, nearly always, they end up liking what they see. In a few cases— Kennedy in 1960, Reagan in 1980, and Perot in 1992—their image of a candidate improved substantially. Before the first 1992 debate, for example, 23 percent said they liked Perot and 45 percent said they disliked him. After the last debate, 47 percent said they liked him and 25 percent said they disliked him.[68]

Few key moments spur public involvement as fully as the October debates. People do not just watch. They talk about what they have seen. On the day after the first Bush-Gore debate in 2000, 47 percent—twice the number on an average day—discussed the campaign. The second and third debates sparked nearly as much discussion. Debates also widen the circle of conversation. Most campaign-related discussions take place between family members, but friends and co-workers are frequently drawn into debate conversations. In 2000, half of debate-related conversations took place outside the family.[69]

The October debates can energize the campaign. Although the 1996 Clinton-Dole debates failed to revive interest in a sagging campaign, the 1992 Bush-Clinton-Perot debates helped to revitalize that contest. September polls revealed a public whose election interest was teetering. Some analysts predicted that turnout would not exceed the 50 percent level of 1988 and might even be lower. Instead, the three-way debates gave new life to the campaign, which carried through to Election Day.[70] Turnout increased 5 percentage points in 1992, the first significant jump in three decades.

The 2000 debates had a less dramatic impact. Nevertheless, citizen involvement—the extent to which Americans were following the campaign and thinking and talking about it—doubled during the two-and-a-half-week period when the debates were taking place. One in four said they were more interested in following the campaign in the news as a result of the debates.[71] And the number who felt the campaign was exciting, informative, and encouraging rose significantly.[72]

The debates are a springboard to the final days of the campaign, when the pace picks up and voters pay closer attention (Figure 4.2). Soon after the last debate in 2000, interest increased as the campaign moved toward Election Day. During the final week, involvement

FIGURE 4.2

KEY MOMENTS AND INVOLVEMENT IN THE 2000 PRESIDENTIAL CAMPAIGN

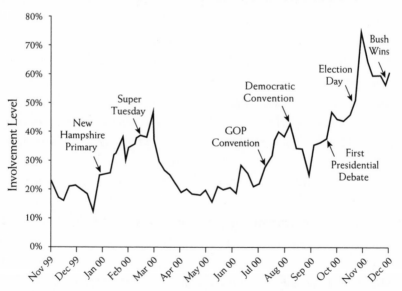

During most weeks of the 2000 campaign, the majority of Americans were paying almost no attention. Interest was high only around key moments—the contested primaries, the conventions, the October debates, and Election Day. Involvement rose dramatically during the post-election period when the election's outcome was at issue. (See Appendix for information on how citizen involvement during the campaign was measured.)

reached one of its highest levels of the entire campaign—34 percent said they were paying close attention.[73] Citizens were more involved in other ways, too. On the average day, 49 percent reported having talked about the election—the highest level at any time during the campaign.[74] Intense news coverage in the campaign's closing days contributed to the rise in interest. Although the news media have cut back on their election coverage in recent elections, the final days are still heavily reported. In the last week of the 2000 campaign, roughly half of Americans each day reported having read, seen, or heard an election story. This level, too, was a campaign high.[75]

Although interest peaked at the end, its full potential had not been tapped, as the post-election period revealed. During the five weeks that the outcome of the 2000 election rested on the results of the Florida recount, citizen involvement—as measured by people's thoughts, conversations, and news exposure—averaged 61 percent, far higher than was registered at any time during the campaign. The Florida wrangling captured public attention in a way the campaign itself did not.

As voters went to the polls after having had twelve months to scrutinize Bush and Gore, some of them were still mulling over their decision. If a long campaign, as some have claimed, helps voters to understand their choices, they should have been flush with information. In fact, they were anything but highly informed. Our Vanishing Voter poll just before Election Day asked respondents to agree or disagree with twelve issue statements—six that addressed Gore's positions and six that concerned Bush's. On the average issue, 38 percent correctly identified the candidate's position, 16 percent incorrectly identified it (an indicator that a third or more of the correct responses were also mere guesses), and 46 percent said they did not know it.

On only one issue did a majority accurately identify Gore's position. Fifty-eight percent said he favored free prescription drugs for the elderly and only 8 percent said he did not. Awareness of Bush's positions was highest on his top issue, tax cuts. Fifty-two percent said he advocated "a large cut in personal income taxes" and 11 percent believed he opposed it.

On all other issues, less than half could correctly identify the candidates' positions, and many guessed wrong. The extreme case was Bush's stand on campaign finance reform. When asked whether he favored or opposed "a ban on very large contributions to political candidates," only one in ten said he opposed such a ban, which was his actual position. Two in ten believed he favored a ban and seven in ten said that they didn't know his position. Campaign finance reform had been a leading issue in the GOP nominating race eight months earlier, but as time passed, even most of those who had known Bush's position forgot it.

Issue awareness in 2000 may have been the lowest in modern times. Comparisons with past elections are risky because research methods have varied across the years. Nevertheless, no past election study found a level of issue awareness as low as what our Vanishing Voter surveys recorded. Even the 1948 and 1976 campaigns, which were conducted on issues of roughly the same salience as those of the 2000 campaign, did not produce electorates that knew so little about the issues. Using a generous estimate,* only 25 percent of adults in 2000 could correctly identify three-fourths or more of the candidates' positions. In 1976, 33 percent identified at least three-fourths of the candidates' positions on major issues.[76] In 1948, in a survey conducted two months before Election Day, 37 percent knew three-fourths or more of the candidates' positions on major issues.[77]

Whatever the benefits might be, and it is unclear from the 2000 campaign that there are any, today's long campaign does not guarantee that citizens will accumulate mounds of information. The notion that time alone can create an informed electorate is wrong.

Of course, not every presidential campaign will spawn a well-informed electorate. A campaign's issues may be too bland or too numerous to stick in people's minds. The issues of the 2000 campaign might well have been of this nature. But no presidential campaign should be designed in a way that flattens learning. The long vacant

---

*As previously stated, we measured awareness on twelve policy positions. For the estimate we have dropped the four positions on which awareness was the lowest and have not corrected for guessing. The 1948 and 1976 figures are also not corrected for guessing.

stretches during the 2000 contest had this effect. Roughly 80 percent of what was learned about the issues during the year-long 2000 campaign was packed into the weeks of the contested primaries, the conventions, and the debates.

Moreover, no presidential campaign should leave citizens with a disheartened feeling. In the concluding week of the 2000 campaign, when asked whether the campaign had been "rather depressing, that it hasn't been nearly as good as a campaign should be" or whether it had been "uplifting, that it made [you] feel better about elections," respondents by more than two to one judged it "depressing."[78]

Election structures have consequences. They can foster public involvement or discourage it. The long campaign of today runs in spurts, taxes people's attention, and dulls their sensibilities. It serves to frustrate learning, just as it dampens interest and, in the nominating period, the inclination to vote.

Major moments, such as the New Hampshire primary, Super Tuesday, the conventions, the October debates, and Election Day, have the capacity to engage and inform the public. They are the key to an involved electorate; they bring people into the campaign. But when these moments are widely spread out, their capacity is diminished. Time—in this case, too much time—invites the public to disengage.

The problems of the modern campaign, to abuse the title of an old Cole Porter song, "begin [at] the begin." A campaign that starts a full year before Election Day may seem to offer everything citizens could possibly want or need. Instead, it sends them forth on a mind-numbing trek. If the election system is to be made fit for the American people, a place to start is its length: shorten it.

CHAPTER FIVE

Election Day

The Politics of Inequity

It was too late to register and I didn't know it was too late.
—nineteen-year-old Illinois resident[1]

*The form was nine miles long when I got my driver's license
so I said forget it, I just won't vote.*
—fifty-six-year-old Georgia resident[2]

The Electoral College doesn't seem fair to me.
—twenty-four-year-old Florida resident[3]

ON ELECTION DAY, officials unfailingly urge Americans "to get out and vote." Some of these officials are not to be taken seriously. On the whole, U.S. elections are conducted fairly and openly with the support of tens of thousands of public-minded officials and volunteer poll watchers. Lurking in the shadows, however, are official actions that serve to depress the vote.

The post-election period in 2000 exposed a number of them. Several thousand eligible Floridians lost their chance to vote because registrars had crudely purged the registration rolls. In their rush to exclude ineligibles, mainly African Americans with felony convictions, state officials knowingly used purge lists that were riddled with errors. Thousands of other Florida voters had their ballots thrown out because of machine failure, poor ballot design, and procedural error.

Florida was the tip of the iceberg. An estimated 2 to 3 percent of all ballots cast nationwide in the 2000 presidential election—somewhere between 2 million and 3 million votes—were invalidated. No one would expect every ballot in a presidential election to be properly cast and counted. But the spoilage rate in 2000 was far too high to attribute it entirely to the individual acts of inattentive or unskilled voters. The concentration of outdated voting devices and inaccurate registration rolls in poor and minority neighborhoods suggests that official mischief was also involved.[4]

Although officials in Florida and elsewhere professed ignorance of these problems, they were forewarned. Evidence had been accumulating for years that certain voting machines were "prone to jamming"[5] or otherwise given to inaccurate counts.[6] Massachusetts and other states had already banned the votomatic punch card machines that produced Florida's hanging "chads." In a 1988 *New Yorker* article, Ronnie Dugger urged Congress to take action: "Given the crucial role of public confidence in the integrity of the ballot, common sense suggests that the [problem] should be resolved definitively."[7] No congressional action was taken at the time or in the following decade.

However, Congress wasted no time in scheduling hearings to pillory the television networks for their mistakes on Election Night 2000. Shortly before 8 p.m., the networks, on the basis of exit polls, had projected Al Gore as the winner of Florida's electoral votes. Two hours later, the networks retracted the call. Then, just after 2 a.m., the networks named Bush the winner in Florida, declaring him to be the president-elect. Hearing that, Gore phoned Bush to concede defeat. Meanwhile, the network anchors were telling their audiences to stay tuned. "We haven't heard yet from either Al Gore or the triumphant Governor Bush," said CBS's Dan Rather. "We do expect to hear from them in the forthcoming minutes." Forty-five minutes later, Rather reported that Gore had withdrawn his concession. "Nobody knows for a fact who has won Florida," Rather told his audience. At 4 a.m., CBS and the other networks retracted their claim that Bush had won Florida's electoral votes.[8]

The networks' performance—"We don't just have egg on our face, we have an omelet all over our suits," said NBC's Tom Brokaw—contributed to the post-election confusion. It also renewed the long-standing complaint that the networks' Election Night projections discourage participation in states where the polls are still open. The networks' first projections aired in 1964, and Republicans complained loudly when Lyndon Johnson was declared the winner shortly after 9 p.m. EST. Their response was mild, however, compared with how Democrats reacted in 1980 when, shortly after 8 p.m. EST, nearly three hours before West Coast polls had closed, the networks declared Reagan the winner. Democrats claimed the early call cost them at least two House seats and perhaps a Senate seat or two.

These claims, however, are not supported by evidence. Studies indicate that network projections have little or no influence on turnout.[9] The 1980 election is the only one where West Coast participation clearly sagged after networks called the race. In this case, however, the analysis is confounded by Jimmy Carter's unprecedented concession speech, which, to the chagrin of other Democratic candidates, was delivered a full two hours before West Coast polls closed.[10]

Whatever the exact influence on turnout of network projections, it is small compared with other factors that lie within the control of public officials. Scholars are in full agreement that the more "costs" placed on the potential voter, the lower the participation rate.[11] These costs range from registration burdens to institutional arrangements that discount the value of the vote. "Where institutions generate disincentives to vote, turnout suffers," Robert Jackson concluded on the basis of a comparison of nineteen democracies.[12] In the American case, unfortunately, the disincentives are substantial.

ON ELECTION NIGHT 2000, the television networks were criticized for calling Florida for Gore before polls had closed in the Panhandle, which, unlike the rest of the state, is in the central time zone. One commentator claimed that 10,000 Panhandle Republicans had remained home after hearing the projection, an unlikely scenario given that the call was made only ten minutes before polls there closed.[13]

No analyst thought to ask, however, why polls throughout Florida closed at 7 p.m. local time. Why did they shut down so early? Why the rush? Florida is one of twenty-six states that require citizens to vote by 7:30 p.m. local time or earlier. The others are Alabama, Arizona, Arkansas, Colorado, Georgia, Hawaii, Illinois, Indiana, Kansas, Kentucky, Mississippi, Missouri, Nevada, New Hampshire, New Mexico, North Carolina, Ohio, Oklahoma, South Carolina, Tennessee, Texas, Vermont, Virginia, West Virginia, and Wyoming. In the 2000 presidential election, turnout in these states was 3 percentage points lower on average than in states that did not close their polls until 8 p.m. or later.

Limits on polling hours go back decades and have been a convenient way to discourage the participation of lower-income workers who are stuck at their jobs during the day and do not get home in time to cast a ballot. States with limited polling hours are concentrated in the South, which has a history of policies aimed at holding down the vote. Nevertheless, in every state that closes its polls early, some people don't vote because they are unable to get to their local polling station in time.[14]

Turnout is also reduced by registration requirements. When registration began in the later 1800s, advocates claimed it would eliminate ballot fraud. No longer would party machines be able to send their workers from one neighborhood polling place to the next, casting as many votes as time and foot speed allowed. However, registration turned out to be a double-edged sword. Fraud was reduced, but so was legitimate participation. Southern legislatures, which were controlled by white Democrats, devised almost every sort of registration barrier imaginable—from courthouse intimidation to the grandfather clause—to keep blacks from voting. Northern legislatures, which were dominated by Republicans, were only somewhat less imaginative. They enacted registration restrictions that applied only to Democratic-controlled cities.

Discriminatory registration laws are now largely a thing of the past as a result of federal laws and court rulings. Nevertheless, registration remains an obstacle to participation. For some, registration is as easy as filling out a form when applying for a vehicle license. For millions of others, however, registration requires a special effort. They may not have been registered previously or their registration may have lapsed because, for example, they have moved recently. In such cases, registration can require a trip to a registrar's office during its limited hours of operation and at a time not widely publicized or easily convenient. Further, most people are unaware of registration procedures, locations, and timetables. In our Vanishing Voter surveys during the 2000 election, five of six nonregistrants were unfamiliar with their state's registration deadline.[15]

Of course, many nonregistrants have little or no interest in voting. For this reason, eased registration requirements are not by themselves a solution to the turnout problem, as the 1993 Motor Voter Act illustrates. Although the legislation has resulted in a large increase in the number of registered voters, turnout has actually fallen since the bill was enacted.[16] Evidence indicates that the decline would have been steeper without the Motor Voter Act,[17] but the legislation has not been the magic bullet that its optimistic supporters expected it to be.

The relationship between registration and voting has been weakening. Over the past four decades, the percentage of registered citizens who vote in presidential elections has fallen by 20 points—from roughly 85 to roughly 65 percent. One reason for the drop is the eased registration requirements; some of those who have been persuaded to put their names on the rolls have little interest in voting. The turnout rate of Motor Voter registrants is roughly 10 points less than that of other registrants.[18] Even before the Motor Voter Act, however, turnout among registered citizens had dropped by nearly 15 points, a sure sign of waning interest in voting, even apart from the registration issue.[19]

Nevertheless, registration is a significant barrier to voter participation. The United States is a mobile society, and every year about one in six Americans moves to a new address.[20] Even if movers relocate to the house next door, some states require them to re-register. Many are unaware that they must re-register if they move or, if they are aware of it, don't get around to doing it in time to vote. In our 2000 Vanishing Voter survey, a fifth of nonvoters (21 percent) indicated that a change of address was a reason they weren't registered. Even noncitizenship was mentioned less often (15 percent).

The registration restriction that affects turnout the most is the so-called closing date.[21] Federal law prohibits states from closing their registration rolls sooner than thirty days before a presidential election; within that limit, states are free to choose their closing date.

In the 1950s, 90 percent of Americans lived in states that closed their registration rolls two or more weeks in advance of the election.[22] This situation has barely improved. Today, 87 percent live in states that shut down registration two or more weeks before Election Day.[23] Last-minute registration, even if that is defined as a week before the election, is not available to most Americans.

However, six states (Idaho, Maine, Minnesota, New Hampshire, Wisconsin, and Wyoming) have same-day registration, which allows eligible citizens to register at their neighborhood polling station on Election Day. North Dakota has no registration requirement, in effect making it a same-day registration state. In 2000, turnout in these seven states was 15 percentage points higher than in other states.

Same-day registration in all states would be the single most important step that lawmakers could take to increase turnout.[24] On the basis of a study of the 1960–92 period, Mark Fenster concluded it would boost participation by 5 percent nationally. Since Minnesota went to same-day registration in the 1970s, its turnout rate has led the nation. (Minnesota's voting rate was 69 percent in 2000.) Maine and Wisconsin, which also adopted same-day registration in the 1970s, have also moved into the top tier since the policy was implemented.[25]

Our Vanishing Voter surveys during the 2000 election provide new evidence for the effectiveness of Election Day registration. Its advantage lies not only in the fact that it gives nonregistrants the opportunity to wait until the last minute to enroll. The deadline date is easier for them to remember, which makes it less likely they will miss it. Registration deadlines receive little fanfare from the press or from officials, and most people (84 percent) are unable to identify their state's closing date. Some people seem almost oblivious to the requirement. In our survey during the final week of the 2000 campaign, many nonregistrants who lived in states where the rolls had already closed said they still had time to register.

Nonregistrants in states with same-day registration were in a class by themselves when it came to knowing registration deadlines. They were two-and-a-half times more likely than others to know when enrollment closed in their states (see Figure 5.1). The only possible explanation for the difference is the ease of recalling the deadline when

FIGURE 5.1

AWARENESS OF REGISTRATION CLOSING DATE

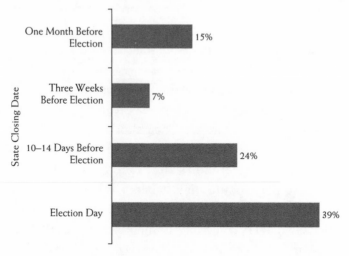

In states with same-day (Election Day) registration, residents are more aware of the date that registration closes.

it coincides with Election Day as opposed to a week or two weeks or four weeks beforehand.

A same-day policy also increases the likelihood that citizens will know how and where to register. For those who vote regularly, the process is hardly mysterious. But a third of nonregistered citizens claim they do not know how to get themselves enrolled.[26] In the case of same-day registration, it is easy. People do not have to locate an obscure government office that may be open for limited hours only. All they have to do is show up at their neighborhood polling station on Election Day.

Conventional wisdom holds that simplified registration works to the advantage of those with less income and education. They are less informed about registration requirements and less likely to have the wherewithal to take the matter into their own hands. "The rich have the capacity to participate with or without assistance," the political scientist Benjamin Ginsberg writes. "When assistance is given, it is primarily the poor who benefit."[27] This argument is typically made through comparison with European democracies that, unlike the United States, have automatic registration systems and where income and education differences in turnout are very small.

Fear that eased registration would flood the polls with lower-income voters—mostly Democrats—has led Republican lawmakers to oppose such changes. In *Who Voted?* (1982), Paul Kleppner explains how the GOP for nearly a century followed a strategy of selective disenfranchisement.[28] That strategy continued into the fight over the 1993 Motor Voter Act. Initially, Republican lawmakers blocked the bill out of concern it would swell the ranks of Democratic voters. Senator Phil Gramm (R-Texas) asked from the floor of the Senate, "Why are you helping the people in the wagon, and not the people pulling the wagon?"[29] Congressional Republicans finally agreed to support the legislation if an automatic-registration provision was deleted. Even then, Republican governors in seven states, including California, Illinois, and South Carolina, refused to put the law into effect until forced to do so by judicial or administrative action.

To Republicans' surprise, Motor Voter registration has not produced a Democratic windfall. Although more Democrats than Republicans have registered under the law, the Republican registrants have voted at a higher rate. As a result, the new voters have divided almost evenly between the two parties. In fact, on a state-by-state basis, the GOP has had the advantage. There are more states in which Republicans have improved their registration position since the change than there are states where Democrats have improved their position.[30]

Election Day registration would have a similar effect.[31] Although nonregistered citizens include more self-described Democrats, they have lower income and education levels on average and are less likely to make use of simplified registration. Moreover, the curse of modern life—"so much work, so little time"—affects affluent Americans as much as anybody else. Any measure that helps busy or mobile people to register and vote is likely to help Republicans at least as much as it helps Democrats.[32]

Simplified registration procedures would not result in a legion of lower-income voters. At this moment in American history, many of them do not see much reason to participate. They see the party system as biased toward moneyed interests. As Curtis Gans of the Committee for the Study of the American Electorate notes, "the root of the turnout problem is motivational and not procedural."[33]

FLORIDA IS AMONG the thirty-nine states that hold their governors' races in nonpresidential years. At one time, these races coincided with the presidential contest. During Franklin D. Roosevelt's four terms as president, Republicans in several states, including New York and Connecticut, in an effort to prevent other Democrats from riding into office on his coattails, spearheaded constitutional amendments that required gubernatorial races to be held in nonpresidential years. Several Democratic-controlled legislatures took the same step in the 1950s, when the popular Republican Dwight D. Eisenhower was president.

Between 1952 and 1988, nineteen states moved their gubernatorial elections out of the presidential election year.[34] Today, only ten states (Delaware, Indiana, Missouri, Montana, New Hampshire, North Carolina, North Dakota, Utah, Vermont, Washington, and West Virginia)* hold governors' races in the presidential year. When citizens do not have a contested race for governor at the same time as the presidential campaign, they are less likely to vote.[35] From their study, Steven Rosenstone and Mark Hansen estimated the turnout difference at 5 percentage points.[36]

The frequency with which Americans are asked to vote also holds down turnout. No other democracy elects the lower chamber of its national legislature (the equivalent of the House of Representatives) as often as every two years. In addition, elections for municipal officials are held in odd-numbered years in about 60 percent of U.S. cities.[37] Frequent elections reduce turnout by increasing the effort required to participate in all of them. Most European nations have fewer elections, and the voting obligation is thereby less burdensome. Many European

---

*New Hampshire and Vermont elect their governors every two years, which means their contests are held in both presidential and nonpresidential years.

countries also schedule their elections on Sundays or declare Election Day to be a national holiday, thus making it more convenient for working people to vote. The United States has traditionally voted on Tuesdays, which requires most people to vote before or after work.

The contrast with European practice is most obvious in the case of primary elections. The United States is the only major Western democracy in which party nominees are routinely chosen by voters through primary elections rather than by party leaders. Many Americans skip the primaries, preferring to vote just in the general election. Some analysts have suggested that primary elections might even contribute to turnout decline in the general election because they sap the resources of state and local party organizations and discourage voters who supported a losing candidate in the primary. Our Vanishing Voter surveys fail to confirm this argument, at least in the context of the 2000 presidential election. Nevertheless, as Harvard University's Pippa Norris notes, "voter fatigue" is a by-product of frequent elections.[38]

Frequent elections are not the only institutional structure that discourages participation. So, too, does the Electoral College. In states that are not part of the candidates' Electoral College strategies, citizens can have less reason to vote.

The Electoral College was created out of deadlock at the Constitutional Convention of 1787 over the issue of how to choose the president. Early in the debate, some delegates argued for direct election by the citizenry, but the proposal was quickly dismissed. The delegates feared that popular election would create an all-powerful presidency. The convention almost entrusted presidential selection to the Congress, but the proposal was rejected because it would have upset the separation of executive and legislative powers. The delegates also considered bestowing the choice on state legislatures, but that method would have weakened the strong central government they were determined to create.

The Electoral College was a compromise built on the lack of a better alternative. Each state would have electors equal in number to its representatives in the House and Senate, and the electors would choose the president and vice president. The compromise satisfied most of the objections to the alternatives. Although the electors would be chosen by the state legislatures, federal officeholders would be ineligible for appointment. It was assumed the electors would act independently. Even then, the framers of the Constitution thought electors would only occasionally cast the deciding vote. After the election of George Washington, which was accepted as a near certainty, it was expected that electors would normally divide their votes among several candidates, thereby denying any of them the majority required for election. In this case, the election would devolve to the House of Representatives, where each state would have one vote. This scenario was upset when political parties began to nominate presidential candidates, thus reducing the likelihood that the electoral vote would be so thoroughly divided that no candidate would get the necessary majority.[39]

The Electoral College was an artful eighteenth-century compromise that no longer makes much sense. Indeed, it has been an object of criticism for nearly two centuries. Andrew Jackson saw it as a device for withholding power from the people and tried to abolish it. Jackson received the most popular votes in 1824 but failed to win an electoral majority, and he was incensed when the House of Representatives selected John Quincy Adams. Upon winning the presidency in 1828, Jackson pressured Congress to initiate an amendment that would provide for direct presidential election. Failing that, he settled for the present indirect system in which the states tie their electoral votes to their popular vote.

The Electoral College has been a source of considerable mischief. Why should the presidency ever be handed to a candidate who loses the popular vote but is lucky enough to win in enough states to cobble together an Electoral College majority? The principle of "one person, one vote" now governs all federal and state elections, save that of the president. Every close presidential election is a game of Russian roulette; 2000 was more dramatic than most because, for the first time since 1888, the bullet was in the chamber. In what other democracy in the world would a margin of 537 votes in one state be worth more than a nationwide margin of 537,179 votes?[40]

The Electoral College survives for one reason only. Enough members of Congress to block a constitutional initiative believe that it helps their state. Small-state representatives think they gain from the electoral votes they get from their Senate members and large-state representatives think they gain from casting all their electoral votes as a unit. Electoral history indicates that these assumptions are mistaken. The Electoral College works to the advantage of a mere handful of competitive states, which change from one election to the next. These states drive the candidates' strategies in the final phase of a closely contested campaign. In the 2000 election, Florida and Pennsylvania were in the driver's seat. In 1960, Illinois had the upper hand. In 1968, New Jersey and Missouri were pivotal. In 1976, Ohio was the key. In practice, the bias introduced by the Electoral College is more nearly random than systematic. Lawmakers mislead themselves in assessing the Electoral College through the prism of their individual states.

Some analysts justify the Electoral College by saying that Senate apportionment is also based on the states and that both institutions are part of a system of representation that gives weight to things other than people. However, the fact that the American system is built on concurrent majorities selected by different rules does not justify all such rules. If that were so, we would still be using the state legislatures to choose U.S. senators. If the framers of the Constitution were doing their work today, it is easy to imagine they would devise a legislature of two popularly elected chambers, one apportioned by population and the other by state. This is a sensible arrangement for a political system based on popular sovereignty and federalism. It is inconceivable, however, that the framers, if acting today, would concoct anything as bizarre as the Electoral College as the method of selecting presidents. As the scholar Walter Berns notes, the Electoral College was created "for a reason that no longer obtains."[41]

When the Electoral College has come into play, it has tarnished other institutions of government and the winner's claim to leadership. The 1876 election was stolen when a Republican-dominated commission awarded the electoral votes of three contested states to Rutherford B. Hayes, even though in one state, Louisiana, Democrat Samuel Tilden had a 4 percent edge in the popular vote. To pacify angry Democrats, the Republicans agreed to end southern Reconstruction, which destroyed any chance that blacks might have had to keep their newly granted civil rights.

Vote swapping might have been absent in 2000, but courtroom dealing was abundantly evident. Just before the Supreme Court settled the election in Bush's favor, only a third of Gore's supporters believed a Bush win would be legitimate and only a fourth of Bush's supporters thought a Gore victory would be.[42] Our Vanishing Voter survey indicated that only 25 percent of Americans felt Bush was "very deserving" of the presidency; even among Republicans, only half held this opinion.

Some analysts argue that the Electoral College reduces the inevitable dispute in a close election to a single state or at most to a few states. A national recount, they say, "would be a nightmare."[43] This argument ignores the mathematical improbability of the need for a national recount. No presidential election in more than a century has been decided by fewer than 100,000 votes nationally. Some nineteenth-century elections were closer, but the electorate was much smaller. It is the Electoral College that creates the possibility of a recount nightmare. Whenever the electoral vote is close, the popular-vote margin is always small in a few states. Five elections in the twentieth century (1916, 1948, 1960, 1968, and 1976) were decided by a small number of votes in one or a few states. In the closest one, a shift of only 2,000 votes in California would have ruined Woodrow Wilson's bid for a second term, even though he led Charles Evans Hughes by a half-million votes nationwide. In the otherwise most lopsided of these elections, Harry Truman had a 2.1 million popular vote lead, but a shift of 30,000 votes in three states would have given the presidency to Thomas Dewey. In another close call, a shift of 9,300 votes in Ohio and Hawaii would have given Ford an Electoral College majority in 1976, even though Carter had 1.6 million more popular votes.[44]

Americans' respect for the Constitution enabled the losing side in 2000 to accept the outcome. But to say, therefore, that "the system works" is to judge the soundness of an institution by the public's willingness to tolerate its distortions. As the Supreme Court's ruling in *Bush* v. *Gore* was about to be handed down, the *New York Times*'s editors wrote: "Any wise observer—domestic, foreign or interplanetary—

has to conclude that Americans' final verdict on this mess will be that theirs is a country in need of new voting machines, not a new electoral system."[45] There is ample reason to believe, however, that Americans are in need of both.

About the best argument that proponents can muster for the Electoral College is that it only infrequently distorts the voice of the people. But even this claim does not stand up to close scrutiny. The Electoral College creates a two-tiered electorate whenever an election is close, and sometimes when it's not.

Because all states except Maine and Nebraska give their electoral votes as a unit to the candidate who wins the popular vote, the only states that truly count in a close election are those that either candidate could win. In 1960, 1968, 1976, 1980, and 2000, the candidates poured nearly every available resource into the toss-up states. Even campaign issues were shaped to suit the interests of their residents. In the 2000 general election, with Florida and Pennsylvania hanging in the balance, Gore virtually ignored the issue of gun control, knowing it would hurt him with rural residents in these states.

The Bush and Gore campaigns spent more than $100 million for televised ads targeted at only a score of states. Michigan was one, and the Detroit market saw more than $2.5 million in ad buys by mid-September.[46] Other markets were commercial-free. Of the top seventy-five media markets, nearly half had no Bush or Gore campaign commercials during the entire general election. As *New York Times* reporter Peter Marks described it, the nation was "divided into electronic haves and have-nots."[47]

News coverage was also pegged to the electoral vote. Reporters virtually ignored the noncontested states. On the nightly newscasts, there were almost no stories on these states during the final month, compared with more than thirty on the battleground states.[48] "The process effectively takes half the country and says, 'You're just spectators,'" notes the University of Pennsylvania's Kathleen Hall Jamieson.[49]

The nation's spectator states have equal access to the televised presidential debates, but they receive no candidate visits and see no candidate ads. Unless there is a hard-fought statewide or local race, they also are unlikely to see much in the way of grassroots activity. "You wouldn't hardly know that there's a presidential campaign on," said Gerald Schmitt, the mayor of Dodge City, Kansas, in the closing days of the 2000 campaign. "Nobody asks us what we think. We sit here and observe what's happening, but there's nothing we can do."[50] (It was not the first time Kansas had been left out in the cold. In 1968, a Nixon advisor said, "If you have to worry about Kansas, you don't have a campaign anyway.")[51]

In a close election, candidates have little choice but to concentrate on the toss-up states. In 1976, the Carter campaign allocated its resources through a point system that included even the candidates and their families. (Carter was worth 7 points, his running mate Mondale was worth 5, and eight-year-old Amy Carter was worth 1.) The battleground states naturally got the lion's share of the "points."[52]

Even when the election is not close, the Electoral College can drive strategy. Clinton emerged from the 1992 conventions with an almost insurmountable lead but nonetheless pursued a fail-safe strategy. States were divided into four categories: those firmly for Clinton, those firmly for Bush, those leaning clearly toward Bush, and those that were toss-ups or leaning toward Clinton. The eighteen states in the last group were the campaign's focus. Candidate visits, ad buys, and canvassing efforts were targeted at these states. Media markets, for example, were "ranked in terms of the number of persuadable voters . . . weighted by the Electoral College votes and the perceived strategic importance of the states reached in that market." Clinton carried all but one of the targeted states.[53]

If candidates are no fools in how they allocate their time and attention, neither are citizens. They participate at lower rates when their state is ignored. Although the nationwide turnout in 2000 was 2 percentage points higher than in 1996, there was a decline in nine noncompetitive states. On the other hand, turnout rose by 3.4 percent in the closely contested states, which included Florida, Pennsylvania, and Wisconsin.[54] Aggressive advertising campaigns were waged in these states, which were also the target of get-out-the-vote drives. During the campaign's final week, Bush and Gore devoted three-fourths of their visits to the larger toss-up states.[55]

The candidates' electoral strategies also affected the public's day-to-day involvement in the campaign. Stimulated by the higher level of campaign activity, residents of battleground states were more likely than residents of other states to follow the campaign in the news and to talk and think about the election (Figure 5.2).

Residents of South Dakota, which had no candidate visits during the general election, ranked dead last in involvement. Residents of

FIGURE 5.2

STATE OF RESIDENCE AND INVOLVEMENT DURING FINAL FOUR WEEKS OF 2000 CAMPAIGN

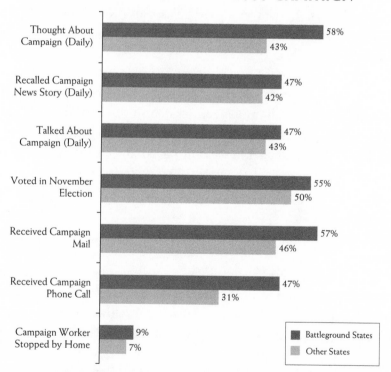

Residents of battleground states received more attention from the candidates and were more involved in the campaign during the closing month than residents of other states.

Florida, which had thirty-seven visits, were 50 percent more likely than South Dakotans to talk, think, and follow news about the campaign. As for residents of Kansas, they ranked thirty-fifth in involvement, deriving some benefit from spillover from the Kansas City, Missouri, media market. Missouri was a battleground state and, unlike Kansas, which had no candidate advertising and no candidate visits during the general election (or the primary period for that matter), was subject to heavy televised advertising and twenty candidate visits.

Information levels, too, were affected. Residents of the most heavily contested states were 13 percent more likely to have particular knowledge of the candidates' issue positions.[56] Some of this difference can be attributed to their exposure to the candidates' ads, which, as noted previously, were shown only in media markets that coincided with the battleground states. "We decry the ads, we whine about the attack advertising," says the University of Wisconsin's Ken Goldstein, "but study after study shows that people exposed to it hold more knowledgeable opinions."[57]

To paraphrase George Orwell, citizens of all states are equal participants but some are more equal than others. There are now two different electorates in the fall campaign. Residents of competitive states are exposed to a vigorous campaign, and their votes decide the outcome. Residents of other states get to see only part of the campaign, and their votes are discounted, which diminishes their interest in going to the polls, following election news, and talking with others about the campaign.

ALTHOUGH THERE are many things to celebrate about the American political system, its handling of the vote is not among them. It is not simply that voting rates here are substantially lower than in nearly every other democracy. America's electoral history is replete with examples of public policies designed to deny or suppress the vote. The fact that most of these policies were enacted by state legislatures and are no longer in force lessens the blight. Nevertheless, some are still on the books, and others have a lingering effect. Voting has been treated as a privilege rather than as an inalienable right, something to be earned (or, in some cases, arbitrarily withheld) rather than something so intrinsic to citizenship that government makes every reasonable effort to promote its exercise.

With their emphasis on individualism, Americans would vote at lower rates than Europeans even if U.S. election laws were as liberal as those in Europe. Nevertheless, the gap would be smaller if qualification barriers were lowered in the United States.

A sizeable number of American nonvoters fit the profile of those who do vote. They pay at least some attention to election news, and they periodically talk and think about the election. Some of them are quite active in community-based organizations. There are more of them than might be expected. Our Vanishing Voter surveys indicate that roughly a third of nonvoters resemble voters in their outlook.[58] They are not enchanted with the way election campaigns are conducted, but they are not deeply alienated either. Unlike other nonvoters, most of them do not describe politicians as "liars and crooks" or say they have no interest in voting.[59] Come Election Day, however, they are nowhere to be found.

When asked whether they might vote if it was easier to do so, many of them said they would. Compared with other nonvoters, they were two-and-a-half times more likely, for example, to favor same-day registration and to say it would increase the likelihood of their participation.

If officials were to take seriously their Election Day mantra "get out and vote," they would take the steps necessary to make it easier to do so. Although citizens stay away from the polls mostly for personal reasons, election laws make a difference. When officials raise barriers or fail to remove impediments, lower turnout results.[60]

CHAPTER SIX

A Model Campaign

The Politics of Participation

They ought to make campaigns a hell of a lot shorter.
—seventy-eight-year-old D.C. resident[1]

*I'd like to see more debates and more open forums. [I want to see] more
appearances by the candidates.*
—forty-year-old Illinois resident[2]

They need to get rid of the electoral votes and let the people vote for themselves.
—thirty-nine-year-old Louisiana resident[3]

AFTER EVERY presidential campaign scholars and pundits say the
election would have been better if candidates had been more forthcoming, if journalists had been more judicious, and if the citizens had
been more conscientious. True though these conclusions may be, they
should provide the start of the analysis, not its end. Why do the participants regularly fail to meet expectations? Why don't they act more
responsibly?

When all the participants disappoint, there are usually deeper
causes. Although some blame the desultory nature of recent campaigns
on events and personalities particular to each election, the persistent
problem is the electoral system itself. The campaign burdens its princi-
pals—the candidates, the journalists, and the voters—with responsibilities they cannot meet or that magnify their shortcomings.

Voters are especially vulnerable to a faulty system. It is not that they
are somehow less intelligent or less flexible than candidates or journal-

ists. Voters simply have less reason to adapt to insensible demands. Candidates enter the campaign in the hope of acquiring the extraordinary prize of the presidency. They'll compete vigorously regardless of how the process is designed. Journalists cover the campaign because they get paid to do so and because they pride themselves on good stories (and run risks from filing too many bad ones). They, too, will find a way to meet the demands of their job.

Citizens are in a different position. Though they care about the choice of a president, they do not individually suffer hardship by not participating. The polity suffers when tens of millions of them back away from the campaign, but like a dot in a pointillist painting, the individual citizen has no discernible influence on the whole. Why, then, engage in a process that starts way too early and lasts far too long, that provides too many dull stretches and too few high points, and that holds out opportunities that often turn out empty?

What can be expected from most citizens in the next election? Will they pay close attention to the candidates a year in advance of Election Day? Will they vote if they live in states that hold primaries after the races are decided? Will they mark their calendars so that they don't miss the start of the summer conventions? In all likelihood, they will behave exactly as they did in 2000 and other recent elections. They will drift along as the campaign runs its course, dipping in here and there, yet never immersing themselves fully, except perhaps at the very end.

In order to encourage Americans to act differently, the election system must be redesigned to suit their needs. Other considerations should also be weighed. The political parties require a system that ensures fair competition, and journalists require a system transparent enough to enable them to depict the election accurately. But if we seek to revitalize the campaign, we must give citizens an election system built with their needs and interests in mind.

MAJOR REFORM should not be undertaken lightly.[4] A need for order and predictability is a recommendation against frequent change. James Madison warned that if the nation undertook institutional change in response to every perceived defect in government, the only predictable result would be chaos. Many scholars share this view. "Electoral reform," Everett Carll Ladd writes, "should be approached from a perspective that recognizes how important it is in this area to settle on something and stick with it."[5]

Sweeping reform in response to a single episode runs the risk that the cure will be worse than the ailment. The convention-based nominating system cast aside by the McGovern-Fraser Commission after it went haywire in 1968 had regularly produced strong leaders. Introduced by Progressive reformers in the early 1900s, it had led to the nomination and election of the two Roosevelts, Wilson, Truman, Eisenhower, Kennedy, and Johnson—all ranked by historians as good or great presidents. (It also elected Warren G. Harding, who's at the bottom of historians' lists.) Although party leaders controlled the process, the inclusion of more than a dozen primaries gave voters a voice.[6] Party leaders wanted to win and so they listened. Every nominee but one (Adlai Stevenson in 1952) between 1936 and 1968 was the people's choice in the final opinion poll before the convention.[7]

The convention system answered many of the problems that afflict today's primaries-based system. It produced a shorter and less money-driven campaign, placed the burden of the nominating decisions on the party's most informed members, allowed for deliberation and negotiation in the process of selecting the nominees, and gave purpose to the summer conventions. These substantial advantages have led some observers to recommend a return to the old system. "Let's abolish the primaries," says the political scientist Charles Jones. "They mistakenly assume that voters are prepared to participate at a very early stage in the nominating process. Turnout is low, candidates race around the country insulting one another, the sequencing is irrational, and it is all too expensive. Let's get political parties back into the process by having caucuses and party conventions select delegates to the national convention. Why not? They work perfectly well in those states [for example, Iowa] that use this process."[8]

Nevertheless, the public sees primaries as the legitimate method of picking nominees, and the parties have shown no real interest in reviving the old system. "That issue is gone," said a Democratic Party official in 1999.[9] However, many leaders within both parties recognize a need for change. "The current system," a party official said in 2000, "may not be totally broken, but if it's not totally broken, it's on its way."[10]

In 1999 and 2000, the Republicans' Brock Commission and the Democratic National Committee's Rules and Bylaws Committee held separate hearings on the issue of campaign reform. "Today, too many people in too many states have no voice in the election of our major party nominees," said Bill Brock, chair of the GOP commission. "Today, too many fine potential candidates are unable to launch effective campaigns in a system which is basically driven so much by media and money. Surely, this can't be in the best interests of our country or our party. The time to fix it is now, and that is what we intend to do."[11]

Neither party, however, changed its nominating system. The Republicans developed an alternative system, but George W. Bush withdrew the proposal from consideration before the 2000 GOP convention could vote on it. The Democrats also delayed a decision. Competing interests and the lack of a sound proposal stymied the parties.

Nevertheless, the parties need to find a solution. The failings of the current system are endemic, and they are eroding interest and confidence in presidential elections. Our Vanishing Voter survey found that Americans would prefer virtually any alternative to the current system, including an old-style convention. When asked what they disliked most about the current system, 52 percent said it was too long, 32 percent claimed it was too costly, and 11 percent described it as unfair.

For a nominating system to be attractive to the public, it needs to have appropriate length, pace, timing, and balance.

The campaign should have a sensible starting time. Halloween is far too early for the voters, as is the December holiday season. As our Vanishing Voter surveys revealed, the vast majority do not have a nagging lust for campaign politics a year in advance of Election Day. Nothing would breathe more life into the campaign than shortening it substantially. Some analysts say the long campaign gives candidates the education they need to prepare for the presidency. Even if this dubious claim were somehow true, why squander the time of 200 million adults in the process? In our candidate-centered elections, presidential hopefuls begin running for the office almost as soon as the last election is over. The "permanent campaign" requires them to travel the country, speak with groups, meet with leaders, solicit money, and think about public issues and policies. They will get their presidential education whatever the length of the formal campaign.

For many reasons, the U.S. presidential campaign cannot mimic the month-long campaign of European democracies. Those contests center on political parties that in turn select the national leadership. American presidential races take place in a system where parties are weak, states have a role, and citizens pick the nominees and then vote again in the general election. Such a campaign cannot be completed in a month or two, but it need not last a year.*

The parties ought to examine the timing of all stages of the campaign. Although the starting date of the primaries is the key to any shortening, why must the conventions be held in summer? Why not in early September? The summertime tradition dates to the 1830s, when travel was slow and the fall was harvest season. In earlier periods, the timing also made sense because the nominees were not very active until after the conventions. Now, they've been campaigning daily for nine months by the time of nomination. Are three more months really necessary?

Second, the parties need to design the nominating system to unfold more slowly. Most voters do not pay close attention until the first contests, at which point they need additional time to evaluate the candidates. The voters' role in a nominating race is a difficult one.[12] They can't rely on party or other labels to guide their judgment, and the issue differences between the candidates are often symbolic or murky. The task is compounded by front-loading, which can enable a candidate with money, name recognition, and organizational support to force the voters into a hasty decision. If voters are to be in control, they

---

*A shorter campaign would have a secondary benefit. Every four years the policy process comes to a virtual standstill while Washington awaits the election of the new president. Programs are put on hold, judicial appointments are held up, legislation is delayed, diplomacy is slowed. The interruption may not have been all that important in a slower age but it is a disadvantage today.

require a process that draws them in, yet buys them enough time to inform their judgment.

As the campaign unfolds, it should narrow the field so that voters can concentrate on two or three candidates instead of a half dozen or more. Multi-candidate races place imposing information and calculation demands on voters. A poll of New Hampshire voters in 1976, for example, indicated that when the six Democratic candidates were evaluated in pairs, Jimmy Carter fared poorly. One-on-one, voters preferred rival candidates.[13] Yet Carter won the Granite State's primary. Its voters divided their support among his more liberal opponents, enabling Carter to finish first with 28 percent of the vote.

Third, the nominating system should be designed so that the races do not end until shortly before the conventions. The excitement of the contested primaries should carry over to the conventions rather than being frittered away, as is now the case. Voters lose interest when the drama of the race disappears. Americans were in such a stupor by the first convention in 2000 that 81 percent had no idea it was about to begin.[14] The quick end to the nominating races also dulled the fall campaign. The Bush-Gore contest began when the two candidates sealed the nominations in March. Their race was old news by September.

Fourth, the nominating process should be open and fair. The playing field ought not tilt so severely that a well-known candidate with lots of money is a cinch for nomination, depriving voters of a real choice.[15] Further, Americans everywhere should have a chance to cast a vote that counts. The current system divides us into campaign "haves" and "have-nots."[16] Early contests expose residents of the states holding these primaries to a vigorous campaign and give them an opportunity to select the nominees. Residents of other states have no say in the nominations and respond accordingly. Record low turnouts occurred in many of these states in 1996 and 2000.[17]

In short, the ideal nominating system would allow everyone to participate, enable voters to scrutinize the candidates by providing more time for decision, contribute to a shorter campaign overall, and hold public attention by moving promptly from one stage to the next.

The current system does not satisfy these requirements. The commonly discussed alternatives are also inadequate to the task. These alternatives—a national primary, regional primaries, and population-based primaries—vary in their suitability, but none fully deals with the requirements.

However, an alternative does exist that meets the criteria. It has the further benefit of being a modification of the current system and therefore is unlikely to introduce unanticipated problems. To understand its merits, an assessment of the three other options will be helpful.

The public has long favored a national primary. A 1952 Gallup poll indicated that three-fourths preferred a national primary to the existing party convention system.[18] A 1972 Harris poll showed that a national primary was favored by two to one over the newly installed state-by-state primary system.[19] Our 2000 Vanishing Voter survey revealed a national primary was preferred to any alternative, past or present.[20]

A national primary would have several advantages. With everyone voting on the same day, the campaign would consume less time while giving voters in all states a chance to participate. Moreover, if scheduled close enough to the conventions, the excitement it generated would carry over to these events.

A national primary, however, has crippling disadvantages. First, many would cast an impulsive vote. If Americans on Super Tuesday in 2000 were still struggling to understand the candidates, after having been drawn into the campaign by the Iowa, New Hampshire, Delaware, South Carolina, Arizona, and Michigan contests, how informed would their judgment have been if the first opportunity had been a candidate-crowded national primary? The election would be a cakewalk for a well-known, well-funded candidate backed by party leaders. Money and name recognition, already important, would become decisive. Less-established hopefuls like John McCain and Bill Bradley would stand no chance against candidates like George Bush and Al Gore in a contest where all fifty states were at stake on the same day. A system that favors front-runners is not necessarily the worst kind imaginable, but, as the political scientist William Mayer notes, there is something wrong if they win every time.[21]

In races without a well-established national figure, such as the Democrats experienced in 1972, 1976, 1988, and 1992, the advantage might rest with an ideologically based candidate (in 1972, George Wallace, who, until he was nearly assassinated, had accumulated more popular votes than George McGovern).[22] Or it might favor a regionally identified candidate (in 1976, Jimmy Carter, who did win the nomination), a constituency-based candidate (in 1988, Jesse Jackson, who carried more states on Super Tuesday than Michael Dukakis), or the best-known candidate (in 1992, Jerry Brown, who held the pre-primary lead in opinion polls). Such candidates could gain a plurality in a crowded race.

The winner might even be a candidate whose name popped into voters' heads on election morning. A *New York Times* poll conducted just before the balloting on "Junior Tuesday" in 1992 found that 50 to 75 percent of likely primary voters in Colorado, Georgia, Maryland, and Utah had "no opinion" about the five Democratic hopefuls even though Iowa and New Hampshire had awakened them to the campaign.[23]

Neither major party has shown an interest in a national primary.[24] They fear it would diminish their role and that of the states. Media markets rather than states would be the geographic center of the campaign, and presidential hopefuls could be judged as much by their name recognition and ability to raise funds as by the strength of their ideas and allegiance to party. The parties would certainly never consent to a national primary that did not have a second-chance provision in the case of a plurality winner. A freakish outcome (for example, a Wallace victory in 1972) would bring certain defeat in the fall election and might wreck the party for years. Safeguards against such an outcome include a runoff election or a national convention that has a significant proportion of uncommitted delegates. (The Democratic Party already has "unpledged delegates," who number nearly 20 percent of the total and include the party's top officials.)[25]

A regional primary system represents a second option. The parties would divide the states into regions (for example, the East, South, Midwest, and West), and all states within each would hold their primaries on the same Tuesday. The first regional primary would occur in early March, followed a month apart by the others. The order would change with each election, allowing each region to be first in the rotation once every sixteen years.

Rotating regional primaries are seen as a way to ensure that all states "are treated fairly."[26] However, they are treated fairly only in the sense that no state or set of states would always start the primary season. In any particular election year, some states would automatically be first while others would be seeded last. Disparities would also exist within each region; its delegate-rich states would get the most attention, just as California, New York, and Ohio dominated the candidates' Super Tuesday strategies in 2000.

Some argue that regional primaries would reduce candidates' travel time and conserve their budgets.[27] These gains are small, however. Candidates would still operate at breakneck speed, fitting as many stops as possible into their campaign schedules. They would also have to raise huge sums of money in advance of the campaign just to compete in the first round of a regional system. Almost no limit exists to what a candidate could spend on a primary that covers a dozen states.

A longstanding objection to regional primaries is that they could tip the race to a presidential hopeful from the first region. A nationally known candidate with broad support could normally be expected to prevail against a regional challenger, but regional bias could affect the outcome when no candidate of national stature was in the race.[28]

A regional system would also heavily burden the first region's voters. They would be forced to choose from among a large field of contenders without the benefit of preliminary contests. It would be as if the current system started with Super Tuesday instead of the Iowa caucuses. In 1999, the National Association of Secretaries of State (NASS)—the organization of state election officials—endorsed a modified regional primary system that addressed this problem. NASS recommended that the parties keep Iowa and New Hampshire in the opening positions. Although this arrangement was designed to encourage retail politics and enable less moneyed candidates to compete, it would also serve to activate voters in advance of the first regional primary.

Even so, their task would be imposing. Although the Iowa and New

Hampshire contests would create interest, voters would still be trying to sort out the candidates when the first regional primary takes place a few weeks later.[29] A well-funded candidate with name recognition and party support like Dole, Bush, or Gore could easily dominate the region's dozen or so contests. Even if the race did not end there, it's hard to imagine that hard-pressed opponents could survive the next round of a dozen primaries.

Voters in the remaining regions would then be effectively disenfranchised. They might well feel cheated. It is one thing when a system denies residents of single states a vote, as in the current system, and quite another when a system silences residents of every southern, western, midwestern, or northern state. Regional rivalries would be a natural outgrowth of the system as well as a source of resentment when a regional favorite was perceived to have lost out because of the order of the voting.

Regional primaries would not shorten the campaign. The formal process would start, as it does now, early in the calendar year, which means that the active campaign would kick off somewhere around Halloween. Moreover, whenever the races ended early, the conventions would still be months away.

In 2000, the GOP came within a step of adopting a new nominating system. The party's Brock Commission had proposed that future nominees be selected through a population-based system (also known as the Delaware plan,* or the inverted-pyramid system). The commission claimed the plan "would give more voters a say in determining which candidate the party puts forward for the general election" and "would achieve [the] goal of reducing front-loading."[30] However, George W. Bush, fearing a disruptive fight over the proposal, withdrew it before the GOP convention could vote on it.[31]

---

*The plan was the brainchild of Delaware Republican Party chairman Basil Battaglia. That the plan would originate with a Delaware official is not surprising. In recent elections, the state has tried unsuccessfully to raise the profile of its primary by placing it in close proximity to New Hampshire's. In 2000, Delaware went outside the Democratic Party's window and held its primary on February 5, four days after New Hampshire's. Under pressure from New Hampshire Democrats and others, the candidates more or less ignored the contest, which led the national press also to downplay it.

The Brock Commission's plan would have divided the states into four "pods." The dozen or so smallest states would be in the first pod, the next smallest states in the second, and so on, ending with the largest-population states in the fourth. States in the first pod would hold their primary or caucus on the first Tuesday in March or later. States in the second, third, and fourth pods would schedule their contests anytime on or after the first Tuesday in April, May, and June, respectively. Unlike the rotating regional primary system, the order of the vote would be the same in each election. The smallest-population states would always go first; the largest would always go last.[32]

The Brock Commission claimed that the system would level the playing field. Candidates would compete first in the smallest states, which would encourage retail politics and reduce the role of money. But this scenario is not realistic. Any campaign fought at once across a dozen states, whatever their size, is going to be waged with media and money. A lesser-known candidate could target a particular state in the hope that a victory there would impress journalists and party leaders. But it would be a small success compared with that of a candidate with the visibility, party backing, and money to organize effective field operations and run strongly in a half dozen or more states.

A stand-alone contest, such as the New Hampshire primary, is the only proven way to reduce the power of money. By campaigning for weeks on end in one state, and pouring every available resource into it (McCain spent $1.5 million in New Hampshire in 2000),[33] a lesser-known candidate can sometimes win and thereby gain the momentum necessary to compete successfully elsewhere. But the first round of the population-based system would be like a small-state Super Tuesday. States in the first pod would congregate on or near the first available date, forcing the candidates to spread their time and resources across numerous states, which would give a decisive edge to a candidate who entered the race with high public recognition and deep pockets.

A strong start would bring in additional money and party support, increasing the odds that the same candidate would dominate the contests of the second-pod states. Any opponent unable to break through by then would be viewed by party leaders as a spoiler and pressured to quit the race, as McCain was after Super Tuesday in 2000. Rarely would the campaign last beyond the third pod. No three-time loser could mount a credible campaign in the dozen largest states.

The Brock Commission reasoned that because half the delegates would be chosen in the fourth round, no candidate could "realistically secure the party's nomination until the final grouping of primaries."[34] But delegate counts are only part of the reality of a nominating race. No candidate who is broke and behind in the polls will continue to campaign because of a hypothetical chance of victory. And there's the real rub in the population-based system. Residents of large states such as California, New York, Texas, and Florida would repeatedly be denied a voice in the nominations.

By the second or third time they were shut out they would be infuriated. "What is this? The night of the living dead?" scoffed an Ohio official upon discovering his state's consignment to the fourth pod.[35] Indeed, Bush decided to withdraw the Brock Commission proposal partly in response to pressure from large-state Republicans who vowed to defeat it on the convention floor if necessary.

The population-based system could produce a huge drop in primary voting. Relatively high turnout could be expected in states of the first pod and, depending on the closeness of the race, the second or third. But turnout would collapse once the race was decided. With all the large-population states at the back end of the process, the national voting rate could reach record lows.

The population-based system would neither shorten nor tighten the campaign. The active phase would begin before the holidays and, typically, the races would end long before the conventions.

For all its flaws, the current campaign structure contains the seeds of a nominating system that would serve the public's needs better than the alternatives. The modified system would shorten the campaign dramatically, give voters time to come to grips with their choice, allow residents of every state a chance to cast a meaningful vote, and provide for a quick transition from the primary stage to the convention stage. The modification does not satisfy all needs, but it would successfully address the requirements set forth earlier in this chapter. Finally, because it is rooted in the current system, it is less likely than other reforms to create unanticipated problems.

The modification is fairly straightforward. The nominating process would start with a string of, say, five state contests spaced a week or two apart, followed by a month-long interval that would lead to a single day—Ultimate Tuesday—on which all forty-five remaining states would ballot.

For illustration purposes only,* let's assume that the campaign has five single-state contests with the first taking place in mid-April. The second would come two weeks later, in late April or early May. After another two weeks the third would be held. The fourth and fifth would then be scheduled for the next two Tuesdays. A month later, on the final Tuesday in June, all forty-five remaining states would hold their contests. Ultimate Tuesday, in which more than 90 percent of the elected convention delegates would be chosen, would determine the nominees. The party conventions would begin four to five weeks later. If the system had been in use in 2000, the election calendar would have had the following dates:

April 18	Single-state contest #1
May 2	Single-state contest #2
May 16	Single-state contest #3
May 23	Single-state contest #4
May 30	Single-state contest #5
June 27	Ultimate Tuesday (45 states)
July 31	First national convention starts
August 14	Second national convention starts

---

*My purpose in providing a fleshed-out example of the system is to show how it would work rather than to claim that it is optimal in its particulars. Adjustments could, and undoubtedly would be made, if the parties chose to develop a system based on the model. It could be argued, say, that there should be four or six single-state contests rather than five, or that there should be a six-week interval before Ultimate Tuesday rather than four weeks. The spacing of the single-state contests would also be subject to review. As illustrated, the system includes a longer interval (two weeks) between the first single-state contests than between the last ones (a week). In the early going, voters need more time to digest what has happened. By the fourth contest, the interval is arguably less important; the last two would serve as barometers of the candidates' support in other areas of the country.

Should a shorter campaign be desired, the first contest could be held in mid-May with Ultimate Tuesday occurring in late July and the conventions taking place in late August and early September. Either way, what is now a formal campaign of nine months would shrink to five or six months—more than enough time for a vigorous national campaign.

The parties would select the single-contest states just as they now grant Iowa and New Hampshire the opening positions. The parties might want to keep these two states at the front,* but they could rotate all or some of the positions in order to eventually give different states a chance to hold a stand-alone contest. The parties would undoubtedly seek a regional balance in their five selections.[36]

By the last of the single-state contests, the race could be expected to have narrowed to two major candidates, simplifying the voters' decision. Of the dozen contests since 1976, only the 1988 and 1992 Democratic races would have had three candidates still in contention on Ultimate Tuesday.

This arrangement would meet the requirements for a voter-centered system. First, the campaign would be shortened substantially. Second, interest created by the primaries would flow into the conventions because of their proximity to the concluding contests. Third, residents of all states would cast votes that counted. Fourth, the campaign would start with a flourish but then develop slowly enough to give voters a chance to make a prudent choice.

The change would dramatically boost interest because the campaign would reach into all the states. There are no "have-nots" in this system. The voting rate would also increase substantially. National turnout should be at least as high as that of recent contested primaries.

---

*New Hampshire has the stronger claim to an opening position. The Iowa caucuses do not have the same long tradition as the New Hampshire primary, which has been first in the nation since 1920. Moreover, participation in the Iowa caucuses has been at 10 percent or fewer of the state's adult population. On the other hand, the turnout rate in New Hampshire is twice that of nearly any other state and its residents take their role seriously in other ways. They may not pour into town halls to hear the candidates, but they do pay attention. One study found that they were 100 percent more likely to have particular knowledge of primary election candidates and issues than other Americans. However, New Hampshire voters seem increasingly determined to defy the oddsmakers, and their independence is facilitated by the state's allowance of crossover voting. The best example of their contrary views, although not the only one, is Pat Buchanan's victory there in the 1996 GOP race.

The system would level the playing field. In any primary-based system, a candidate with money to burn will always have an edge. But a financially weaker aspirant has a chance when the race starts in a single state and moves slowly toward a cluster of states. Single-state contests also serve to deplete the funds of heavily financed candidates. Recent front-runners, when hard pressed in states like Iowa and New Hampshire, have spent heavily. Five such contests in advance of Ultimate Tuesday would substantially deplete even a large war chest. Unless a candidate retained a huge financial edge after the fifth contest, money would not be a decisive factor on Ultimate Tuesday.

A small amount of money thins rapidly in a forty-five-state campaign, which would force the candidates to scramble for "free" airtime. News programs and interview shows would be a major focus of Ultimate Tuesday's campaign. So, too, would televised debates. In recent elections, the audience for primary debates has been roughly five times larger in states with a pending contest than in other states.[37] Because Ultimate Tuesday would encompass forty-five states, large audiences could be expected.

The proposed system has a final advantage.* Because it is based on known tendencies in the current system, it reduces the likelihood of unexpected problems. Unlike the alternatives, the change would not plunge the nominating process into uncharted territory. The biggest unknown is Ultimate Tuesday. It will have the appearance of a national primary, although a different reality: voters will have had ten weeks after the first contest to figure out the candidates. As a result, voters would be better prepared to make a wise choice on Ultimate Tuesday than the current system prepares them for Super

---

*This proposal does not solve the bias inherent in a process that begins with a single state or region. No state is a microcosm of the nation; for example, fewer than 2 percent of New Hampshire and Iowa residents are African American. A cluster of states from all regions of the country is obviously more demographically representative than any single state. However, the issue of representation also includes the question of whether voters know what they are choosing. Does the campaign start small so that later voters can benefit from the opening contests and make a more informed decision? Or does it start large with the greater risk that the electorate, though more representative demographically, will be uninformed about the choice it's making? What tips the balance for many who have thought about this dilemma is that a system that begins with single-state contests is more likely to produce a competitive campaign, with all the advantages this entails.

Tuesday or than a national primary system would prepare them for the nationwide vote.

Would the proposed system meet the parties' needs? Is there any reason to think that a system designed for the voters could also satisfy the parties? In this case, it could.

The proposed system basically fine-tunes the current one. It would add a few more single-state contests to the opening phase, stretch out the interval between the first contest and the cluster of decisive primaries, and require all states except those at the front to vote on the same day. It anticipates that, if the current system is not changed, states will continue to move their contests to Super Tuesday, virtually ensuring that the races will end there. That being the case, it makes sense for the parties to schedule all remaining states on the climactic day and to improve the run-up period by stretching it out and adding a few more single-state contests.

The proposed system would resolve or reduce several of the parties' specific concerns about the current process: the routine disenfranchisement of states and voters, the clustering of contests very close to the opening date, and the dampening of competition. The system would also enable the parties to accommodate states that feel Iowa and New Hampshire have undeservedly dominated the opening positions.[38] Over time, other states would have the opportunity to hold an early contest. The parties might want to reserve these positions for small and medium-sized states. Delegate-rich states like California, New York, and Texas would not need to be up front to exercise power. They would dominate attention on Ultimate Tuesday.

The change would solve a problem that keeps some states from holding their primaries on Super Tuesday, despite wanting a larger voice in the selection process. They have decided that March is too early for their statewide, congressional, and local primaries. Rather than incurring the huge expense of a second statewide ballot at a later time, these states have scheduled their nominating contests at the back of the calendar so that all their primaries can be held at once. They would not be forced to make this sacrifice in the proposed system because Ultimate Tuesday would be held in June.

Because the campaign would open with a series of single-state contests, it would inspire more competition than the current system. This aspect will trouble those party leaders who believe that the best nominating campaign is one where the front-runner breezes, largely unscathed, to victory. They assume that a quick and quiet race improves the party's chances in November.[39] There is scant evidence, however, that a hard-fought nominating race hurts a party's chances in the fall campaign.[40] Indeed, nominees and parties benefit from such a contest. Nominees will have had their messages tested and refined by challenges from their competitors and the press. They will have engaged in debates requiring them to think on their feet and defend their proposals.[41]

For the party, the benefits are at least as great. A competitive race mobilizes its base, including citizens who might not otherwise participate. Research indicates that individuals working for winning *and* losing candidates in a nominating race are more active on the party's behalf in the general election.[42] For example, in 1988, many of Pat Robertson's volunteers became involved in George Bush's general election campaign and subsequently stayed active in Republican politics.[43] "It is not necessarily in the party's interest to end the process quickly," the political scientists Ronald Rapoport and Walter Stone observe. "Doing so provides superficial relief from the conflict that necessarily occurs within the party over the nomination, but it does not permit the party to take advantage of that conflict."[44]

The proposed system might well mobilize the parties more fully than at any time since the 1970s. Today's front-loaded system compresses the number of states in play and the time they are in play. The proposed alternative would extend the time and include all the states, giving party activists everywhere a reason to get involved. Although the parties might be concerned that their role would be undercut by Ultimate Tuesday, when the candidates' focus would shift to media markets, the final stage could bring out the power of party activists. A candidate can be in only one place at a time, and party leaders can help fill the void, as they did in the Super Tuesday contests of 1996 and 2000.

Moreover, the excitement created by Ultimate Tuesday would spill over to the national convention. The process of rallying the full party in support of the winning candidate would carry straight into the convention, and even less interested citizens will want a closer look at the newly chosen nominee. The convention might even play a brokering role. Although an outright winner is likely to emerge, Ultimate Tuesday would sometimes feature three candidates, which could prevent any of them from obtaining a delegate majority. The convention would then choose the nominee. Any such confab would have its risks,* but it would give the party something it has not had in a long time: an expectant television audience.

Although the proposed system would benefit the parties, reform is difficult to accomplish. Even when, as in this case, the reform is an incremental one rather than a complete revamping of a process, change is hard to bring about. Reform always contends with inertia and entrenched interests, and strong leadership is not assured.

In 2001, DNC national chairman Terry McAuliffe engineered a new calendar for the 2004 election that will exacerbate the voters' problems. With virtually no public debate, he persuaded the DNC to approve a calendar that will move Iowa and New Hampshire a week closer to the beginning of the year and allow any other state to hold its primary as early as February 3. The pause after New Hampshire will be only one week, rather than the five weeks in 2000, and if a large number of states move into the early February date, Super Tuesday will occur a month earlier than in 2000. McAuliffe's goal is a quick conclusion to the nominating race so that Democrats can prepare for what he says "will be a tough fight against an incumbent with unlimited finances."[45]

---

*The risk in a brokered convention after primaries is that the front-running candidate's supporters might feel cheated if the nomination goes to another contender. That sentiment would be particularly acute in a national primary because it would be the sole source of a candidate's legitimacy. In the proposed system, however, the emphasis is on states rather than on the popular vote total. In a national primary, the winner would be the candidate who gets the most votes nationally. In the proposed system, the vote is tabulated in the same way it currently is. Each state is a separate contest, and delegates are apportioned to the candidates in accordance with their showing there. Any candidate who was still in the running after Ultimate Tuesday would have won in a number of states and thus have a claim to legitimacy. In all likelihood, a brokered convention under the proposed system would produce a fusion ticket with one of the contenders taking the vice-presidential nomination in return for supporting an opponent's bid for the presidential nomination.

McAuliffe's plan could hurt the Democrats' chances in 2004. If the party nominates a newcomer to national politics, he or she will be denied the testing period and widespread public attention that attends an extended nominating race. In any case, voters will be hurt by McAuliffe's plan. An already imposing system will become one they find nearly impossible to manage effectively. In 2000, they basically had about six weeks in which to make up their minds about the nominees. In 2004, they may have only half that much time.

Something better is needed. The problems of the front-loaded system have increased with each election, as has Americans' dissatisfaction with it. The parties should finish the reform effort they began in 2000. They may discover that the system proposed here, or a variation of it, will meet their needs. Or they may come up with something better. Whichever, a presidential election is the parties' best chance to engage and mobilize the public. It's an opportunity that today's parties should not waste.

KEY MOMENTS such as the primaries, conventions, and October debates are opportunities to bring Americans more fully into the campaign. Citizens do not have a fixed amount of attention to give. The more engaging these moments are, the more attention they will pay.

Reform advocates often overlook key moments when thinking about how to improve campaigns. They tend to see an election as an educational opportunity that depends on the quality of information made available to the voters.[46] It was in this vein that the Alliance for Better Campaigns and the National Commission on Federal Election Reform, for example, recommended that qualified candidates receive five minutes of free broadcast time each night during the last thirty days of the campaign to discuss their issues.

Although such proposals are constructive, they do not address the motivation problem.[47] They would increase the supply of useful information without increasing the demand for it. The challenge of informing the electorate depends less on supplying more information than of staging the campaign in a way that will get people interested enough to pay heed.[48] Voters are not like students in a classroom. They are more like the crowd at a ball game. The more exciting the game, the more attention spectators pay. And the more attention they pay, the more they understand what's happening on the field. This type of response is what the Jacksonians had in mind when they invented political campaigning. "The campaign as sport and spectacle" was how Alexis de Tocqueville described Jacksonian-era elections.[49]

Few recent events illustrate this idea better than the three-ring circus that Bush, Clinton, and Perot staged during the 1992 debates. It was political theater of a high order, and the audience grew in size with each meeting. One hundred million viewers, an all-time high, saw the final debate.[50] Moreover, as people watched and listened, they learned. Studies revealed a sharp rise in viewers' knowledge of the candidates and issues.[51]

A campaign's key moments are particularly important to the involvement of those with less interest in politics. Our Vanishing Voter surveys showed that the gap in involvement between the more and less interested shrank during key moments. The less motivated were always less likely to talk, think, and follow news of the election, but the gap narrowed during the contested primaries, the conventions, and the October debates.

Today's campaign wastes many of its key moments, including the late-scheduled primaries. They come and go almost unnoticed. In states that held primaries after Super Tuesday in 2000, only one in three residents was aware the state's vote would be held soon.[52] If the problem of meaningless primaries is to be fixed, the leadership will have to be provided by the political parties.

For other key moments, however, the leadership will have to come from the three major broadcast networks—ABC, CBS, and NBC. They are licensed to operate on public airwaves and ought to fulfill their obligation to serve the public's information needs. The medium of broadcast television is critical to the success of the conventions and debates. As the Alliance for Better Campaigns' Paul Taylor notes: "Presidential politics is more than a niche event. It ought to be played out in the biggest public square we have."[53]

The primary debates would be a place for the networks to start. These debates kick off the campaign and help to shape its issues. The 2000 Republican debates, for example, thrust campaign finance reform into the headlines.[54] Debates also give lesser-known candidates a chance to rise above the pack. McCain's surge in 2000 began with the debates, just as they jump-started Carter's campaign in 1976, John Anderson's in 1980, Gary Hart's in 1984, and Clinton's in 1992.[55]

Yet, as far as the networks are concerned, the debates might as well be happening in some other democracy. In 2000, the networks broadcast only two primary debates, neither in prime time. One was held late in the evening on ABC's *Nightline* and the other on Sunday morning on NBC's *Meet the Press*. Even so, four times as many viewers saw each of these debates as watched the average prime-time debate on cable television.

The networks claim that viewers are not interested in primary debates. "Fully nine or 10 or 11 months before the election, it's hard to get people's attention," said an NBC executive in 2000.[56] That's true enough before the New Hampshire primary, but it's not true once the first votes are cast. Moreover, cable cannot substitute for network participation. Broadcasting reaches the 25 million households untouched by cable, and the networks dominate the viewing hours even of most cable subscribers. If the three major networks in 2000 had each broadcast a Republican and a Democratic debate in prime time in the weeks before Super Tuesday, the six debates would have drawn an estimated 60 million viewers,[57] which would have been more than twice the number who saw the nearly two dozen debates shown on cable television.[58]

Other changes, too, would increase the debate audience. For one, primary debate sponsors need to recognize that television viewers expect a good show. Audience turnover for the primary debates is very high, and one can nearly hear viewers reach for the remote control when the debates are held on makeshift, poorly lit stages.[59] "These debates are sort of like phantom pain," complained *Hotline* editor Chris Crawford in 2000. "It's sort of it's-gone-away, but we still feel it."[60]

Debate timing also affects audience interest. Primary debates have been scheduled earlier and earlier, a trend that guarantees ever-smaller audiences. In 2000, the first debates were held three months before the New Hampshire primary, and three-fourths of all debates were held in advance of that contest. After the primary, audience ratings rose, but only a handful of debates were held in this later period.[61] Some pre-primary debates are helpful, but they should be concentrated in the interval *after* the first primary.

Since the 1950s the televised summer conventions have marked the official start to the general election. They were once the highlight of the campaign and its most intensive learning experience.[62] They are still a time for voters to discover more about the candidates. A recent analysis ranked convention speeches as the form of election communication that gives citizens their best opportunity to learn what the candidates represent.[63]

The summer conventions, however, are losing their audience. Throughout the 1970s the typical television household watched 12 hours of the conventions. In 2000, the average was less than 3 hours. To be sure, the convention audience is still large. Nearly 15 million households tuned in to each night of the 2000 conventions, and most Americans saw at least part of the proceedings. But that's a far cry from the past.

The conventions' reduced role in the nominating process has diminished their appeal. Although the McGovern-Fraser reform did not intend to undercut the conventions, viewers now have less reason to watch. They still like features of the conventions, but they say that the lack of suspense is a reason they don't pay more attention.[64]

The parties have chosen to eliminate nearly all controversy from the conventions. Their nightmare is a repeat of the 1968 Democratic convention, when street protests competed with the podium for viewers' attention and contributed to the Democrats' defeat in November. But the parties now avoid even smaller disruptions, like Pat Buchanan's angry call for a "culture war" at the 1992 GOP convention. Ironically, the absence of conflict appears only to reduce public appetite for convention television. The "bounce" that nominees get in the polls has been as large for mildly unruly conventions as for tame ones.[65]

Although parties should open up their conventions, these events may no longer be a suitable arena for honest debate. The nominating races now end so early that disputes might seem as staged as the rest of the proceedings. But a continuation of current practices will lead only to long-term decline. The conventions, which once served to draw young people into party politics, now produce few converts. In 2000, only 10 percent of adults under thirty deliberately tuned in the conventions. Four of five viewers in this age group came across the conventions while changing channels, and most of them watched for only a few minutes.

The conventions once had a captive audience. The networks provided gavel-to-gavel coverage, and most viewers did not have access to other programming. As cable entered American homes, however, viewers drifted toward entertainment programs, and convention audiences began to decline, as did the audiences for other public-affairs broadcasts. In fact, the 46 percent decline in convention ratings between 1976 and 2000 is not substantially greater than the 40 percent decline in the network evening news ratings during the same period.

Cutbacks in network coverage also reduced the convention audience. The networks lopped off convention hours at a faster rate than the decline in audience, thereby guaranteeing a further drop in viewing hours. Between 1976 and 2000, as convention ratings decreased by 50 percent, broadcast coverage was cut by more than 80 percent, from 60 hours to 10 hours per network.[66] If the networks had slashed their half-hour nightly newscasts at the same rate because of their declining ratings, each would now be five minutes in length.

Although the networks claim that the nominee's acceptance speech is now the only newsworthy aspect, they should not see the convention as just another news event.* It is a 170-year-old institution with a rich

---

*The conflict between the parties and the networks over convention coverage has led some observers to suggest that some sort of compromise is necessary. One proposal is that the parties shorten their conventions to two days, which the networks would cover in prime time. If the parties should want to do that for their own reasons, that would be fine, but the structure of the conventions should not be dictated by broadcasters' concerns. It might also be difficult to attract financial support from a host city for such a short event.

tradition and a continuing purpose.[67] The conventions may no longer have the power to nominate, but they give the nominees, one of whom will become president, their only real opportunity to address the American people at length and on their own terms.[68] It is not unreasonable to conclude that the nominees deserve this opportunity, and plenty of evidence indicates that citizens gain from it.[69]

The networks say their participation is less vital now because cable provides gavel-to-gavel coverage. But broadcast television is the only source for many Americans and is the key to capturing inadvertent viewers. Although deliberate viewers in 2000 were nearly as likely to watch the conventions on cable as on the networks, inadvertent viewers were three times more likely to be captured through a national channel (Figure 6.1). Such viewers constitute 50 percent of the total convention audience. Many of them watched for only a few minutes, but half stayed tuned for thirty minutes or more.

How much broadcast coverage is needed? A commitment by ABC, CBS, and NBC to carry an hour of prime-time coverage each of the

FIGURE 6.1

WHERE VIEWERS WATCHED THE CONVENTIONS

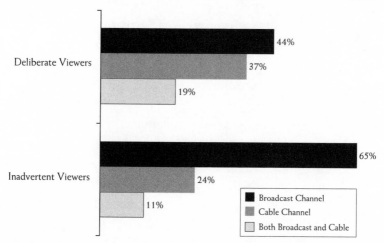

Viewers who deliberately tuned in the conventions were nearly as likely to rely on cable as on network television. Viewers who came across the conventions in the course of watching television were more likely to be captured by a broadcast network channel than by a cable channel.

first two nights and three prime-time hours each of the last two would solidify the conventions as a key moment in the campaign. The networks would be setting aside sixteen prime-time hours (eight for each party) every four years. Sixteen hours is four more hours than each network carried in 1996 and six more than was provided in 2000, but only a third of the hours allotted as recently as 1980.

These broadcasts should focus on the parties. In the 1970s, gavel-to-gavel coverage gave way to a form of convention television in which network anchors and correspondents fill large chunks of the airtime.[70] Journalists play an important role in the coverage, but they are not the main attraction. Viewers say journalists' commentary is the convention feature that they care least about. In our Vanishing Voter survey just before the 2000 Republican convention, only 14 percent said this aspect was of keen interest. A larger number said they were quite interested in seeing the nominee's acceptance speech (44 percent), the roll-call vote (36 percent), the nominee's biographical film (24 percent), and interviews with party leaders (21 percent).[71]

The televised October debates testify to the importance of spectacle. They have done more to enliven presidential campaigns than anything else since primaries were introduced in the early 1900s.

As the news analyst Daniel Schorr notes, the debates are not a perfect forum and sometimes magnify the inconsequential: Nixon's five-o'clock shadow, Ford's confused answer to a question about Eastern Europe, Dukakis's coldly analytical response when asked what he would do if his wife was raped and murdered, Gore's huffing and puffing while his opponent spoke. "When you see how many debates were won on quips, boners, and attitudes," says Schorr, "you may ask whether there isn't some better way to test our leaders."[72]

Nevertheless, the October debates are a compelling spectacle. No other scheduled political event draws an audience as large or diverse. And debates give viewers the unique opportunity to see the candidates perform without the aid of the prepared scripts that now define so much of what they say.[73] Citizens learn more about the candidates during the ninety minutes of an October debate than they do in most weeks of the campaign.[74]

Debates have been held in every election since 1976, although their continuation has been shaky at times. In 1980, President Carter agreed to just a single debate. In 1992, President Bush decided to participate only after it became clear that the debates were his last hope of overtaking Clinton. His son followed a similar course in 2000, agreeing to participate after he dropped behind in the polls. Nevertheless, press criticism now makes it difficult for candidates to duck the debates.[75] The elder Bush's dawdling in 1992 prompted a heckler dressed in a chicken costume to show up at his rallies. "Chicken George" was a regular figure on television newscasts until Bush agreed to participate.

Since 1987 the debates have been organized through a bipartisan body, the Commission on Presidential Debates (CPD). It has helped institutionalize the events through its success in getting the candidates to participate each time. It has also made the debates more responsive to the public. Until the CPD's sponsorship, the questions asked of the candidates were frequently entrusted to a panel of journalists. CPD's research found that citizens disliked this format,[76] as did commentators who believed the panelists were too intent on asking headline-grabbing "gotcha" questions.[77] The CPD changed the format, introducing the single-moderator and town-meeting debates that have been used since 1992.[78]

An issue that surfaces each election is control of the debates. Should the rules be set by an independent organization, such as the CPD? Or should the candidates themselves set the rules? Although analysts believe independent control is preferable, the front-running candidate can usually dictate some of the rules. To redress this inequity, analysts have recommended that candidates who accept public funding for their campaigns be required to participate in debates conducted under rules established by an independent body.[79] "No debate, no dollars," was how Senator Robert Dole expressed his support for the policy.[80] So far, Congress has rejected this approach.[81] Accordingly, the best strategy for protecting the debates' integrity is CPD's current one: an announcement several months before the debates of the times and places they will be held. This public announcement solidifies the schedule and makes it harder for a reluctant candidate to engage in delaying tactics that could scuttle some or all of the debates.

The participation of third-party candidates is the thorniest issue surrounding the debates. CPD was created with the support of the two major parties and has devised rules that disadvantage third parties. The most controversial of its rulings was Perot's exclusion from the 1996 debates. Most Americans wanted him to be included, and it's easy to see why. Perot was on the ballot in every state, had public funding, had nearly 10 percent support in the polls, and, four years earlier, had received more votes than any third-party candidate since Theodore Roosevelt in 1912. Moreover, Perot was the straw that stirred the drink in the 1992 debates, which contributed to the large size of the viewing audience. From the standpoint of viewer interest, his exclusion in 1996 was unquestionably a mistake.[82]

This CPD decision struck many as rank partisanship. Nevertheless, the third-party issue is inherently difficult. Several dozen third-party candidates run each time, and they cannot all be included in the debates.* Even the stronger third-party candidates, such as Ralph Nader in 2000, do not automatically deserve an invitation. The October debates are not a time to parade before the voters a candidate they have little interest in seeing.[83]

What, then, should be the qualifying standard for third-party candidates? The CPD uses several criteria, including poll standings, ballot listings, newsworthiness, and organizational resources, which are then weighed by a panel of journalists, political professionals, and political scientists in the context of two questions: Does the candidate have a viable campaign? Does the candidate have a "realistic" (that is, "more than theoretical") chance of winning?[84]

The second of these standards is too stringent. With the exception of Theodore Roosevelt in 1912 and for a while Perot in 1992, significant

---

*Third-party candidates ought to have vehicles (for example, cable TV appearances, including debates) earlier in the campaign that would test the strength of their message and position them for possible inclusion in the broadcast debates.

third-party candidates have not had a "realistic" chance of victory. Their importance has been their ability to force the major parties to respond to issues they would prefer to ignore. George Wallace did that in 1968.

The CPD's ties to the major parties have prompted some observers to want a change. The Task Force on Campaign Reform, which was funded by the Pew Charitable Trusts and included several leading political scientists, recommended that CPD "be significantly revamped or even replaced by a new, more independent . . . body capable not only of maintaining the cooperation of both major parties, but also of representing the interests of the broader public."[85]

However, elimination of the CPD would be a step backward in view of its success in keeping the debates going.[86] But CPD should expand its criteria for judging the significance of third-party candidates. Any such candidate who can "win" should be included in the debates. But so should any candidate who has captured the public's attention with a message it clearly wants to hear and consider.

Other major televised events could also be scheduled during the fall campaign. In 1991, for example, the Joan Shorenstein Center on the Press, Politics and Public Policy at Harvard's John F. Kennedy School of Government proposed that nine Sunday evenings between Labor Day and Election Day be set aside for candidate broadcasts, which would include speeches and interview programs as well as the debates.[87]

A broadcast series of this scope would place an undue burden on the candidates and networks. A less ambitious series, however, would be workable and could stimulate interest and learning. For example, the networks could each devote a prime-time hour to back-to-back candidate interviews hosted by the network anchor. The three broadcasts could have a common title (for instance, "Conversations with the Candidates") and be cross-promoted by the three networks. If the program dates were announced shortly after the CPD set the debate locations and times, the networks could work the programs into their fall line-ups and the candidates could fit them into their campaign schedules.

Would large numbers of Americans watch these programs? The sizeable audiences for candidate appearances on, for example, CNN's *Larry King Live* and ABC's *Oprah Winfrey Show* have quieted critics who once claimed the public is not interested in interview-type programs. A prime-time broadcast on ABC, CBS, or NBC featuring the network's anchor and the major-party presidential nominees would almost certainly attract an audience well in excess of 10 million viewers. That's not a debate-scale number but it's not small potatoes, either.

Viewers would seek these programs out, which is a reason they are preferable to some alternatives. For example, the five-minute candidate segments during the final month of the campaign that the Alliance for Better Campaigns and other entities have urged on broadcasters increase the supply of useful information, but, as noted earlier, they do not address the demand problem.[88] Why would large numbers of viewers make an effort to watch a canned five-minute segment?* Research indicates that these segments don't attract a dedicated audience and make only a small impression on those who see them.[89] On the other hand, the three hour-long interviews would attract viewers and stimulate campaign discussion. Gore's and Bush's appearances in 2000 on *The Oprah Winfrey Show* got people talking about the election. Hour-long programs featuring the candidates and the network anchors would do the same thing.

Would the candidates take part in a broadcast series of this type? They would refuse to participate if they believed the programs were designed to produce headlines at their expense. For this reason, each program should feature the network's anchor rather than a panel of its reporters. Candidates are more likely to trust the anchors to ask tough questions without lapsing into "gotcha" journalism.

Would the networks be willing to broadcast such a series? That's the

---

*The five-minute segments and the hour-long programs proposed here are not exclusive options. The networks could do both or they could choose to do the programs while the affiliates air the segments. The latter approach would be consistent with the recommendation of those who have argued that the networks ought to do more election programming but should have flexibility in choosing what to do.

vexing question. Network executives might see the interview programs as just another crazy demand for "free time."

Broadcasters profit immensely from election campaigns. In 2000, more than a billion dollars was spent on televised political advertising. Ad spending has increased with each election while live coverage has decreased.

Broadcasters argue that cable is now delivering much of the election programming they once provided. But this fact does not discharge their public service obligation nor substitute for their participation. Broadcasting provides the key to capturing the inadvertent audience and is the only television available to many Americans. As one analyst said: "It's a shame people have to pay to get access to [campaign events]."[90]

The networks would like to have it both ways. They want to tout their superior ratings to advertisers and then say that cable is just as good when it comes to election programs. Ironically, as digital cable spreads and the typical viewer has access to several hundred channels, the networks' participation will become even more important. As the number of channels grows, viewers stop surfing and limit their search to selected ones.[91] The broadcast networks will be virtually alone among television providers in their capacity to deliver a large audience. If elections are to serve as a rallying point for an increasingly fragmented audience, the networks will have to carry the load.

Although many of the free-time demands placed on the networks are unreasonable, they need to recognize more fully that the democracy in which they have a lucrative stake requires their participation. Each network now provides less than twenty hours of live election coverage. A network cannot realistically be expected, as it once did, to provide upwards of sixty hours of live election coverage, but it should furnish a reasonable amount, as defined not by its accountants but by the needs of the voters.

What's a reasonable amount? If the various recommendations suggested here were followed, for example, each network would provide 25 prime-time hours of live election coverage: 2 hours for primary election debates, 16 hours for the conventions, 6 hours for the general election debates, and 1 hour for a general election interview program. This programming would consume 0.6 percent of the network's prime-time hours in a four-year period.[92]

That's not too much to ask. The networks enjoy the incomparable privilege of operating on the public airwaves. According to a recent economic analysis, their broadcast licenses, which cost them virtually nothing, are worth more than $350 billion.[93] When they get a license, they sign an agreement to act in the public interest. What could be more consistent with that obligation than a commitment to extensive election coverage?[94]

That commitment should extend also to daily news coverage and encompass not only the networks but all news outlets. Election coverage has fallen sharply as newspapers and newscasts have squeezed public affairs to make room for softer stories. Presidential coverage dropped in 2000 from its level in 1996, just as, in that year, it dropped from its level of four years earlier. Reporting on statewide, congressional, and local races has declined even more dramatically. Many local news stations and some local papers no longer attempt to cover these elections, leaving televised advertising as the only substantial form of information available to voters.[95]

Election news drives day-to-day involvement in the campaign. As was shown in Chapter 3, the amount of time that people spend thinking, talking, and following news about a campaign is a direct consequence of the amount of attention it receives from the press. In turn, their level of attention affects how much they know about the candidates and the certainty with which they hold it. Although the press alone does not bear the burden of an informed and engaged electorate, such an electorate cannot develop in the absence of sustained and substantial news coverage.

In its reporting, the press should also recognize how some of its tendencies distort the campaign. None is more damaging of the public's desire to participate than the insinuation that candidates do not stand for anything. The fact is, candidates tend to keep their promises. To say otherwise is to drain the election of its meaning, for if nothing is on the level, then voting is a charade. Of course, the press should not always take candidates at their word. Candidates should be held accountable for the lies, dirty tricks, special favors, and other acts that carry them beyond recognized standards of public conduct. The press is better equipped than any other institution to blow the whistle on wrong-doing. But there is no challenge, and no merit, in blind criticism. The challenge comes in getting it right. Campaign promises may be wise or foolish, may represent signs of a healthy or a defective electoral system, but they are not automatically attempts to pull the wool over the eyes of unsuspecting voters.

Journalists should also recognize the proper limits of their own role. When journalists talk six minutes for every minute the candidates speak, as they have in recent campaigns, something is wrong. An election is not like *The Truman Show*. Candidates need to be in on the preparation of the script. Although there is a need for insightful analysis, it should not overwhelm the candidates' messages to the point where the campaign looks more chaotic, more manipulative, and more combative than it actually is.

ELECTION DAY is a final "key moment." Although the political and legal struggles waged in Florida in 2000 exposed a host of Election Day flaws, most of them had little bearing on whether people voted. Nevertheless, because Americans now know that faulty ballots and machines disqualify a significant percentage of all ballots cast,[96] the problem could discourage them from voting if it is not fixed. Congress and the states must correct the problem, which, as the National Commission on Federal Election Reform (NCFER) concluded, is one "that government actually can solve."[97] Common sense, money, and a concerted effort can fix it.

NCFER, which was chaired by former presidents Carter and Ford, also faulted the television networks' election night coverage in 2000. The networks' inaccurate projections of the Florida vote contributed to the ensuing confusion and uncertainty. NCFER recommended that the networks be prohibited from predicting election outcomes until the polls on the West Coast have closed.

This recommendation raises troubling First Amendment issues and is based on the unproven claim that projections depress West Coast turnout.[98] Moreover, from the standpoint of election interest, NCFER's proposal is wrongheaded. Election night is an occasion when Americans gather around their television sets to follow the state-by-state returns. Without the projections, they would have less reason to watch. The real problem with the projections is the recklessness that stems from the networks' competition to be the first to make a call. After the 2000 election the networks promised to improve their forecasting models and to act more responsibly. They should be given a chance to do so.

Election Day 2000 awakened Americans to the fact that they do not choose the president. This power rests with the Electoral College, which appears to be a fixture despite the distortions it introduces. Why should residents of toss-up states get the benefit of a more intense campaign, have their issue concerns weighted more heavily by the candidates, and have more reason to vote than residents of other states do? When, as in 2000, turnout goes up in some states and down in others depending on the closeness of a state's vote, something is wrong with the design of the electoral system. The Electoral College was a reasonable safeguard at the beginning of the Republic when state-centered government and fear of a popularly elected chief executive were pressing issues. It makes little sense today.

Although the Electoral College appears to be a fixture, other obstacles to full and equitable participation can be removed or reduced. Registration barriers are among them. More than two-thirds of nonvoters in 2000 were ineligible to participate because they hadn't registered.[99] Of these, one in three was a former registered voter who had moved and hadn't re-registered.[100] Roughly 80 percent had moved within the same state; Harvard University's Gary Orren has proposed that registration in such cases be transferred automatically from the old location to the new one.

Election Day registration would also reduce the hurdles facing these and other citizens.[101] The six states with Election Day registration have a voting rate that is 15 percentage points higher than the national average. Because these states also rank high on other participation indicators, the 15-point difference is not attributable entirely to same-day registration. Even by relative standards, however, the effectiveness of the policy is undeniable. In 2000, the same-day registration states averaged a 5.1 percent increase from their turnout levels in 1996, compared with 3.4 percent in battleground states and 2.2 percent nationwide. Analysts have concluded that universal same-day registration would result in more new voters than all other registration reforms combined.[102] Yet, officials in most states have steadfastly opposed the reform. Despite the ease with which it has been implemented in the states that have it, lawmakers elsewhere continue to argue that it would be an administrative burden.

Lawmakers have been more willing to lower the voting barriers for those who are already registered. Early voting, which allows people to vote in person before Election Day, is now available in thirteen states. Twenty-one states permit absentee balloting by any voter, not just those who can show they are unable to participate in person on Election Day. The state of Ohio even allows political parties to send mail-ballot applications to registered voters. The state of Oregon now conducts its elections entirely by mail.

Same-day registration is the most effective of these policies.* The 5.1 percent increase in turnout between 1996 and 2000 in same-day states exceeded the gain in the no-excuse absentee-ballot states (1.5 percent), the early voting states (2.2 percent), and even Oregon with its all-mail voting system (3.1 percent).[103] Same-day voting also has the advantage of requiring citizens to cast their ballots in person. The Constitution Project of Georgetown University's Public Policy Institute concluded that mail balloting pales alongside in-person voting: "The gathering of citizens to vote is a fundamental act of community and citizenship. It provides the greatest security for enabling voters to cast their ballots free of coercion. It facilitates prompt counting and verification of results."[104]

Same-day registration does not, as some opponents allege, threaten the integrity of the vote. Few individuals have used a false identity or

---

*Internet voting is an option that may come into widespread use someday. At the moment, security, fraud, and access issues make it an unattractive choice.

residence in order to register and vote on Election Day. Individuals also have not abused mail voting. Phil Keisling, Oregon's secretary of state, reported in 2001 that only one case of vote fraud had been prosecuted in the fifteen years that the state has used mail voting in elections of one kind or another.[105] The fact is, few people are willing to risk the penalty for illegal voting in order to add a single vote to the election total. The major perpetrators of ballot fraud have been unscrupulous officials who discover an opportunity to falsify, disqualify, or divert large numbers of ballots. The Task Force on Campaign Reform concluded that there is no evidence to indicate "that fraudulent voting has increased as a result of simplified registration."[106]

If fraud is a concern, provisional voting is an appropriate safeguard. In cases where a citizen's eligibility to register and vote is in question, a provisional ballot is cast. If the voter's claim to eligibility is later verified, the ballot is counted; if not, it is discarded. Provisional voting also protects citizens from careless or unethical officials. As many as 2 percent of voters who go to the polls find that their names have been improperly deleted from or left off the registration lists. No citizen should lose the vote for reasons of official error or misconduct, which led the National Commission on Federal Election Reform to recommend that every state adopt provisional voting.[107]

Nor should voters be disenfranchised because the polls close at an unreasonably early hour. The polls in every state should stay open at least until 8 p.m., although a 9 p.m. closing would be even better.* A late closing would give virtually everyone who wanted to vote an opportunity to do so. As with so many areas of election law, the public has a better sense of what's fair in terms of a closing hour than do the lawmakers. Although nearly half the states close their polls at 7 p.m., only 21 percent of the public believe that voting should end this early. Fifty-six percent say the polls should close at 9 p.m. or later. Among adults under thirty, 70 percent prefer a late closing.[108]

---

*In its recommendations, the NCFER implied that 8 p.m. is the preferred closing time. At that hour on the West Coast, the networks would be allowed to project state winners. However, 9 p.m. closing times with network projections allowed from the time of the first poll closings would have a more positive impact on turnout than NCFER's approach.

The National Commission on Federal Election Reform recommended, as have other groups, that Election Day be made a national holiday. NCFER proposed that in even-numbered years Veterans Day be observed on Election Day, arguing that the change would "increase availability of poll workers and suitable polling places and might make voting easier for some workers."[109] A national holiday would also help to impress upon children and teenagers the civic importance of voting, particularly if teachers, as they do now for many holidays, engaged students in holiday-related projects.

Nonvoters say they would be more inclined to participate if Election Day were a national holiday.[110] Such a designation would, at the least, stimulate other forms of participation, including rallies and canvassing. An unprecedented get-out-the-vote effort might result if Election Day became a national holiday. If it does, the other reforms proposed here would take on added importance. It would be a shame to hold a national holiday to celebrate the vote and then deny Election Day registration to otherwise eligible citizens. Late poll closings would also accommodate the many citizens returning home late from a long holiday weekend away.

Young adults would be a beneficiary. When asked about reforms that would increase their chance of voting, young adults are twice as likely as older ones to cite same-day registration, late poll closings, and an Election Day holiday.[111] Of these, same-day registration would be the most significant. For all sorts of reasons, young adults are less likely than others to be on the registration rolls when Election Day arrives. Many of them do a lot of things on the spur of the moment, and same-day registration would accommodate this response. The odds that they would get caught up in the moment would increase if Election Day were marked by a holiday. Once they cast that first vote, the odds increase greatly that they will participate in subsequent elections.[112]

Just as the major responsibility for strengthening the nominating system and campaign television rests with the political parties and broadcast networks, respectively, the responsibility for strengthening Election Day falls on public officials. For roughly a century, officials have used registration and voting rules to discourage participation. Thankfully, the most egregious abuses, such as literacy tests and poll taxes, have been eliminated.

It's now time to clear away the rest. The timing could not be better. As was explained in Chapter 5, the partisan advantages that once motivated discriminatory rules have largely disappeared. In any case, lawmakers of both parties should do what is right: open wide the polling booths.

POLICY RECOMMENDATIONS

FOR THE POLITICAL PARTIES
Change the nominating process in a way that will:
- shorten the overall length of the campaign;
- increase the competitive period so voters learn more about the candidates;
- give voters of every state a meaningful vote; and
- shorten the period between the end of the nominating races and the party conventions.

FOR EACH BROADCAST NETWORK
Increase coverage to include:
- a prime-time Republican and a prime-time Democratic primary debate;
- a total of eight prime-time hours for each of the party conventions; and
- a one-hour prime-time interview program with the candidates during the general election.

FOR PUBLIC OFFICIALS
Provide for full and equitable voter participation by:
- eliminating the Electoral College;
- adopting Election Day registration;
- instituting later poll-closing hours; and
- making Election Day a national holiday.

They should also do the right thing when it comes to the conduct of their campaigns: clean them up. Of all the reasons Americans give for their lack of election interest, the most troubling is their belief that candidates are not very worthy of respect: that they are beholden to their financiers, that they will say almost anything to get themselves elected, that they are more concerned with winning than with the public good. Perhaps, as some scholars argue, these irritants do not keep regular voters from going to the polls. But even if they serve only to diminish the satisfaction these citizens derive from electoral participation, the price is too high. Moreover, these irritants appear to dissuade some nonvoters, young adults particularly, from joining the electorate.[113]

Americans are tired of the contradiction between their civic sensibilities and the insensibilities of modern campaigning.[114] Spin, poll-driven issues, and attack politics have worn them down. Candidates should stop acting like neighbors who can't get over the fight they had twenty years ago about the location of a backyard fence.

Political leaders do not bear full responsibility for the public's disenchantment with election politics, but they are part of the problem and must be part of the solution. Unlike the citizen politicians of early times, who had a life outside of politics, most of today's politicians are professionals whose identity and livelihood are almost inseparable from the office they hold.

Their well-being has come at the public's expense, a fact most clearly seen in congressional elections. There are today more House districts where incumbents run unopposed than there are districts where both parties stand a realistic chance of victory. Although some congressional districts are naturally lopsided, many others are made so by the abuse of incumbency. When congressional staffs were greatly enlarged in the 1960s, it was argued that the change was needed to cope with the complexity of modern legislation and to offset the executive's information advantage. But these staffs now spend the bulk of their time ensuring the reelection of their member; they are reelection machines funded with taxpayer dollars. Incumbents also get five of every six dollars that PACs contribute to campaigns. Incumbents are positioned to help groups achieve their legislative goals and are likely to win: PACs know where to place their bets. The lifeblood of election politics, competition, has been drained from House races. With nearly three-fourths of these contests now being decided by margins of 60 percent or more, there is precious little reason for citizens in most of the 435 House districts to get involved. As a team of *Boston Globe* reporters said of the 2002 midterm elections: "The political balance in Washington may be determined by a fraction of voters in a couple of dozen . . . races scattered across the country.[115]

Unless elected officials start responding to a higher calling, disenchantment will continue to eat away at the foundation of election interest. The chief casualties will be the youngest among us. The United States has already produced a generation of citizens who believe election politics is barely worthy of their time and respect. Politicians should recognize the wisdom in James Madison's claim that leadership stems from the proper joining of personal ambition and public purpose.

IN 1878, the British statesman William Gladstone declared the U.S. Constitution to be "the most wonderful work ever struck off at a given time for the brain and purpose of man." Would anyone of his stature say the same about the design of today's presidential election system?

What words would describe a jerry-built system that includes an outdated Electoral College, a chaotic nominating process, tepid party conventions, and an Election Day administered by states and localities that differ in their registration procedures, polling hours, balloting measures, and commitment to full participation? What could be said of an election process that is easily the world's most time consuming, cumbersome, and expensive? What words would apply to a system that saddles citizens with unnecessary burdens, teases them into activity before brushing them aside, and arbitrarily excludes many of them—sometimes, whole states—from having a meaningful voice in its outcomes?

Americans deserve a presidential campaign process suited to their interests. It should be inviting—free of institutional barriers that dampen participation and enthusiasm. It should be gratifying—rewarding to all that give it their time and attention. It should be responsive—reflecting in its outcomes the will of the people. And it should be enjoyable—a spectacular celebration of that most basic of democratic rituals, an election campaign. As the scholar John Zaller has urged: "Let's make campaigns fun again."[116]

The parties, the networks, the candidates, and election officials have it within their power to give the American people this type of campaign. They should rise to the challenge.

Skeptics will say that rules don't really matter all that much. In their view, the force of circumstance and the interests of participants drive politics.[117] Although, as this book itself has argued, there is a certain truth in that claim, it is disabling if it is taken as the complete truth. Rules can make a difference, as constitutions regularly demonstrate. Moreover, rules are among the few aspects of elections that are subject to careful analysis.[118] Even the best rules don't always work as planned, but they are superior to the alternative. Electoral participation in the United States may have an uncertain future for other reasons, but only indifference would allow a poorly designed electoral system to remain a part of the problem.

The skeptics are right on one point. Structural change by itself is not enough. Other things must be done to invigorate the nation's political life. When turnout dropped sharply in the 1920s, Arthur M. Schlesinger and Erik McKinley Eriksson wrote "no stone should be left unturned" in the effort to lure voters back to the polls.[119] Today, the schools can do more to give students a decent civic education and to help them register so that the first election upon graduation is a step toward lifelong participation. Other entities—including the churches, the news media, the universities, the nonprofits, unions, and corporations—must also use their power to assist people in the exercise of the vote. Although the terrorist attacks on the World Trade Center and the Pentagon alerted Americans to the importance of civic involvement, this sentiment is likely to find a permanent outlet only if citizens are given constant urgings and opportunities.

The task is more imposing than many might imagine. A half century ago, when the United States was shocked by another surprise attack, the patriotic outpouring had many outlets, from enlistment to Victory Gardens. There was no want of volunteers, but there was also no want of opportunities. And out of this experience grew what many now call "the greatest generation." Its sacrifices in World War II are well known. What is less widely recognized is how that generation in subsequent years built voluntary organizations and, even today, votes at an extraordinarily high rate.

What was lacking in the aftermath of the more recent terrorist attacks were outlets for Americans' willingness to pitch in. Their civic attitudes soared, but their civic behavior did not, except for the flying of the flag. The organizations they might have joined fifty years ago are now run by professional managers, who solicit dues but do not invite active participants. The war in Afghanistan was fought by professional soldiers, the bioterrorism threat was relegated to professional scientists, homeland security was entrusted to professional law enforcement and intelligence officers. Even the appeal to sacrifice was missing. Americans were urged to keep spending, lest the economy sink.[120]

The modern campaign, too, is a thoroughly professional operation. Voters have no expectation that they will be asked to do anything more than send a check and vote on Election Day. This fact has not been lost on citizens, nor do they expect a change anytime soon. Four months after the September terrorist attacks, the Harwood Institute sought to discover whether Americans believed that the attacks would lead candidates and the media to behave better during the 2002 midterm elections. Most people were skeptical. Sixty-five percent believed that candidate name-calling would be just as bad as in past years and 80 percent thought that media sensationalism would be just as prevalent.[121]

The next few elections might see an upturn in participation, partly because civic attitudes have improved and partly because demographics—fewer young adults—favor it. But unless more is done, the momentum will not be sustained. No stone should be left unturned in the effort to bring Americans back to the polls. For if they cannot be encouraged to participate more fully, the nation will face the far greater challenge of how to maintain self-government when citizens don't vote.

Appendix

THE VANISHING VOTER PROJECT

The Vanishing Voter Project, a study by the Joan Shorenstein Center on the Press, Politics and Public Policy at Harvard University's Kennedy School of Government, was designed to understand the factors that affect public involvement in a presidential campaign. Supported by a generous grant from The Pew Charitable Trusts, the project focused on the 2000 presidential campaign.

Other studies had sought to enhance the presidential election process by improving the quality of campaign information. The Vanishing Voter Project concentrated instead on campaign involvement, on the assumption that it is the most pressing problem of today's electorate and also a key to alleviating other problems. For example, as involvement levels increase, people's attention to the campaign also increases, as does their inclination to talk about it with others. Heightened public involvement can also help to improve the quality of media and candidate communication. An involved electorate is a more demanding electorate, as has been seen time and again during presidential debates. Candidates and the media are normally on their best behavior when they know that citizens are watching.

Beyond the project's contribution to an understanding of voter involvement, its purpose was to contribute policy ideas on the structure of the presidential selection process. Given the many changes that have taken place in communication and politics in recent decades, it is remarkable that this structure has seldom been thoroughly examined for the purpose of determining its suitability to today's voters.

A key feature of the project was weekly national surveys that we used to track campaign involvement. From November 1999 through January 2001 we asked questions on a weekly omnibus survey conducted by International Communications Research (ICR). Each survey was in the field for five consecutive days and asked questions of approximately 1,000 people. Respondents were eighteen years of age or older and lived in the continental United States. The field period for most of our surveys was Wednesday through Sunday, although we occasionally ran questions on another ICR omnibus survey that was fielded Friday through Tuesday. In total, we ran questions on 99 surveys, collected data on 97,797 respondents, and asked several hundred unique survey questions.

Each weekly poll included a core set of questions asked throughout the campaign. Question wording and additional details for this core set are included below. Additional information on the survey questions is available from the author upon request.

We also monitored campaign news coverage from November 10, 1999, through November 7, 2000, to determine the relative amount of attention the election received during the various weeks of the campaign. The following newspapers were used for this purpose: the *New York Times, Boston Globe, Atlanta Constitution, Minneapolis Star Tribune,* and *Des Moines Register.* The topic and placement of each story was coded. We also examined the coverage given to nineteen campaign events (for example, the revelation that Bush had been arrested for driving while intoxicated in the 1970s). In assessing this coverage, we expanded our news organization list to include the *Houston Chronicle, Christian Science Monitor, Los Angeles Times, USA Today, Washington Post,* and the ABC, CBS, and NBC nightly newscasts.

CAMPAIGN INVOLVEMENT

Each week, we asked four questions designed to measure respondents' involvement in the presidential campaign. Responses to these questions were the basis for our weekly Voter Involvement Index—the average of the affirmative responses to the four questions. For the question about attention to the campaign, the affirmative responses are "a great deal" of attention and "quite a bit" of attention.

The four questions were asked of half samples. Each week, one-half of the sample, or approximately 500 respondents, were asked two of the questions, while the other half of the sample were asked the other two questions. We rotated the question pairings systematically throughout the campaign.

Q1. During the past week, how much attention did you pay to the presidential election campaign—a great deal, quite a bit, just some, only a little, or none?

Q2. Now we'd like you to think about the past day only. During the past day, have you been doing any thinking about the presidential campaign, or is this something you haven't been thinking about?

Q3. Can you recall a particular news story about the presidential campaign that you read, saw, or heard during the past day?

Q4. During the past day have you discussed the presidential campaign with anyone?

AFFECTIVE REACTION TO CAMPAIGN

Each week, we also asked four questions that were designed to measure people's affective reaction to the campaign. As with the involvement questions, we asked one-half of the sample two of the affective questions, while the other half were asked the remaining two questions. In addition, the order in which the response options were read was rotated randomly across the respondents, so that one-half of the respondents heard one option first while the other half heard the other option first.

Q1. We're interested in your reaction to what's happened in the presidential campaign during the past week. Would you say that the campaign has been boring or has it been interesting during the past week?

Q2. We're interested in your reaction to what's happened in the presidential campaign during the past week. Would you say that the campaign has been informative or has it been uninformative during the past week?

Q3. We're interested in your reaction to what's happened in the presidential campaign during the past week. Would you say that the tone of the campaign has been primarily negative or has it been primarily positive during the past week?

Q4. We're interested in your reaction to what's happened in the presidential campaign during the past week. Would you say that you have felt encouraged or discouraged by what has happened in the campaign during the past week?

AWARENESS OF CANDIDATE ISSUE POSITIONS

Our surveys included questions designed to gauge people's awareness of the presidential candidates' policy positions. During the nominating campaign, we asked a question on several surveys about each of the four major presidential candidates' issue positions. Each question was administered to one-quarter of the sample. The following questions were asked during the nominating period:

Q1. Next I have a question about gun control. Some people say that people should be required to register all the guns that they own. Others oppose this idea. Do you know whether Texas Governor George W. Bush favors or opposes the registration of all guns, or is this something you've not heard about yet?

Q2. Next I have a question about campaign financing. Some people say that large contributions of money to political campaigns should be banned. Others oppose this idea. Do you know whether Arizona Senator John McCain favors or opposes a ban on large political contributions, or is this something you've not heard about yet?

Q3. Next I have a question about health-care policy. Some people say that the federal government should provide health insurance for all low-income Americans. Others oppose this idea. Do you know whether former Senator Bill Bradley favors or opposes government-paid health insurance for all low-income Americans, or is this something you've not heard about yet?

Q4. Next I have a question about school vouchers. Some people say that parents should be allowed to use tax dollars to send their children to a private or parochial school. Others oppose this idea. Do you know whether Vice President Al Gore favors or opposes allowing parents to use tax dollars for this purpose, or is this something you've not heard about yet?

After the two major parties' nomination races were decided, we began asking an expanded battery of issue-knowledge questions. Every week from mid-April through the November election we asked six questions about Bush's positions and six questions about Gore's positions. One-quarter of the sample were asked about both candidates' issue positions. We rotated the candidate order so that one-half of the respondents were asked about Bush's positions first, while the other half were asked about Gore's positions first. Within each block of candidate questions, the order in which the different issue questions were asked was rotated randomly during the interviews. The following questions were asked in the post-primary phase:

Q1. Now we'd like to ask you some questions about the major presidential candidates, George W. Bush and Al Gore. First some questions about George W. Bush. If you are unsure of an answer, feel free to say you're not sure and we'll go on to the next question. Do you happen to know whether Bush favors or opposes requiring people to register all guns they own?

Q2. Do you happen to know whether Bush favors or opposes a substantial cut in defense spending?

Q3. Do you happen to know whether Bush favors or opposes a large cut in personal income taxes?

Q4. Do you happen to know whether Bush favors or opposes a ban on very large contributions to political candidates?

Q5. Do you happen to know whether Bush favors or opposes placing new restrictions on abortions?

Q6. Do you happen to know whether Bush favors or opposes giving low-income people a tax credit that they can use to buy private health insurance?

Q7. Now we have some questions about Al Gore. Again, if you are unsure of an answer, feel free to say you're not sure and we'll go on to the next question. Do you happen to know whether Gore favors or opposes allowing parents to use tax dollars to send their children to a private or parochial school?

Q8. Do you happen to know whether Gore favors or opposes expanding Medicare for retirees to cover the costs of prescription drugs?

Q9. Do you happen to know whether Gore favors or opposes a ban on offshore oil drilling in federal waters as a way of protecting the environment?

Q10. Do you happen to know whether Gore favors or opposes allowing workers to invest a portion of their payroll taxes in private retirement accounts rather than having all of it go toward social security?

Q11. Do you happen to know whether Gore favors or opposes affirmative-action policies that would allow the use of race as a consideration in college admissions and government contracts?

Q12. Do you happen to know whether Gore favors or opposes placing substantial restrictions on trade with China because of its human rights record?

STATE DIFFERENCES IN CAMPAIGN INVOLVEMENT

Because of the large number of surveys conducted during the project, we were able to utilize state comparisons in order to assess how the structure of the campaign affected involvement.

For the nominating period, we divided states into two groups based on the timing of their nominating contests. States that held their primaries or caucuses on or before March 7, 2000 (Super Tuesday), were considered "early-contest states." "Late-contest states" were those that held their nominating contests after March 14. In order to get a true comparison of states that participated fully in the nominating campaign and those that did not, we excluded from the analysis states with contests between March 8 and March 14, because the candidates had done some campaigning in those states in anticipation of their contests and because of the intense national news coverage in the week following Super Tuesday.

For the general election campaign, in order to assess the impact of the Electoral College on involvement, we distinguished those states that the candidates treated as "battleground" states from those considered "safe" states. Using *The Cook Political Report,* we identified thirteen battleground states: Florida, Iowa, Maine, Michigan, Minnesota, Missouri, New Hampshire, New Mexico, Oregon, Pennsylvania, Tennessee, West Virginia, and Wisconsin.

Table A.1 displays the Voter Involvement Index broken down by state. The states are ordered by their overall involvement ranking across all of our weekly surveys from November 1999 through December 2001. The table also includes average involvement and state rankings for separate phases of the campaign. (Because of time-zone differences, Alaska and Hawaii were excluded from the Vanishing Voter weekly telephone surveys and are therefore not included in Table A.1.)

Appendix

TABLE A.1

STATE-BY-STATE CAMPAIGN INVOLVEMENT, 2000 ELECTION

State	Involvement Index During Entire Campaign	Rank During Entire Campaign	Involvement During Contested Primaries	Rank During Contested Primaries	Involvement During Summer Months	Rank During Summer Months	Involvement During General Election	Rank During General Election
Alabama	34.83	36	35.68	41	39.74	6	39.01	41
Arizona	41.71	3	52.35	2	37.77	13	52.80	5
Arkansas	36.14	26	36.20	37	30.65	41	47.23	21
California	39.68	6	46.48	7	38.25	11	47.43	19
Colorado	34.89	35	38.57	30	28.29	46	42.88	36
Connecticut	38.00	17	44.72	11	37.05	17	49.05	12
Delaware	31.34	46	33.61	45	32.64	33	37.78	44
District of Columbia	53.76	1	57.58	1	57.83	1	63.89	1
Florida	39.99	5	42.67	17	38.50	10	50.64	9
Georgia	34.90	34	38.03	31	31.17	36	44.03	33
Idaho	33.56	41	39.64	26	33.05	30	40.90	38
Illinois	38.55	13	45.45	9	39.55	8	47.42	20
Indiana	36.31	24	39.96	24	37.88	12	44.22	32
Iowa	36.00	29	45.07	10	29.71	42	40.10	40
Kansas	36.18	25	39.04	27	33.12	29	43.19	35
Kentucky	32.88	43	34.65	42	26.49	48	48.35	13
Louisiana	36.04	28	37.93	33	31.15	37	47.12	22

State	Involvement Index During Entire Campaign	Rank During Entire Campaign	Involvement During Contested Primaries	Rank During Contested Primaries	Involvement During Summer Months	Rank During Summer Months	Involvement During General Election	Rank During General Election
Maine	33.28	42	41.67	20	29.17	43	35.53	47
Maryland	40.75	4	43.31	14	42.54	2	48.19	14
Massachusetts	39.54	7	48.80	4	33.23	28	48.08	16
Michigan	37.45	20	48.69	5	30.67	40	51.02	8
Minnesota	34.34	39	35.79	39	31.10	38	45.21	30
Mississippi	34.73	37	34.36	43	33.51	27	41.28	37
Missouri	35.59	30	37.16	36	34.78	23	45.66	28
Montana	38.62	12	42.27	18	34.92	22	44.49	31
Nebraska	32.59	44	37.25	35	28.61	45	35.66	46
Nevada	36.76	22	33.04	48	42.52	3	38.55	43
New Hampshire	42.56	2	52.31	3	31.43	35	59.58	2
New Jersey	38.02	16	42.16	19	39.76	5	40.76	39
New Mexico	34.63	38	35.72	40	28.74	44	45.82	26
New York	38.02	15	43.90	13	34.67	25	47.68	18
North Carolina	35.42	32	40.70	22	30.84	39	46.81	24
North Dakota	29.61	49	29.04	49	27.56	47	43.43	34
Ohio	35.54	31	35.95	38	37.14	15	46.96	23

TABLE A.1 CONTINUED

TABLE A.1 (CONTINUED)

STATE-BY-STATE CAMPAIGN INVOLVEMENT, 2000 ELECTION

State	Involvement Index During Entire Campaign	Rank During Entire Campaign	Involvement During Contested Primaries	Rank During Contested Primaries	Involvement During Summer Months	Rank During Summer Months	Involvement During General Election	Rank During General Election
Oklahoma	37.60	19	38.80	29	32.52	34	49.40	10
Oregon	36.68	23	38.89	28	35.24	21	48.18	15
Pennsylvania	36.13	27	37.95	32	37.23	14	45.52	29
Rhode Island	35.32	33	33.18	47	37.14	16	45.70	27
South Carolina	37.35	21	47.27	6	36.19	18	37.52	45
South Dakota	30.79	47	44.17	12	32.94	32	35.42	48
Tennessee	37.94	18	41.24	21	36.16	19	51.22	7
Texas	39.34	9	43.11	16	38.92	9	46.59	25
Utah	33.92	40	33.59	46	33.53	26	38.96	42
Vermont	38.35	14	39.65	25	39.58	7	53.01	3
Virginia	38.90	11	43.18	15	35.60	20	49.39	11
Washington	39.31	10	46.12	8	34.72	24	52.96	4
West Virginia	32.48	45	33.62	44	33.02	31	35.36	49
Wisconsin	39.37	8	40.38	23	39.77	4	52.33	6
Wyoming	30.15	48	37.78	34	25.64	49	48.06	17
Average	36.65		40.59		34.74		45.72	
Standard Deviation	3.83		5.71		5.34		5.96	

Notes

1. Vanishing Voter survey, Nov. 10–14, 2000.
2. Vanishing Voter survey, Nov. 3–7, 2000.
3. Vanishing Voter survey, Nov. 10–14, 2000.
4. Vanishing Voter survey, Nov. 3–7, 2000.
5. Sam Roberts is a composite; the quote was created by melding sentiments that Florida citizens expressed to reporters after Election Day 2000.
6. CNN survey, November 2000.
7. CNN's "Democracy in America," Nov. 5, 2000.
8. U.S. Census Bureau data, 1960 and 1996 elections.
9. Federal Election Commission data, 2002.
10. Richard A. Brody, "The Puzzle of Political Participation in America," in Anthony King, ed., *The New American Political System* (Washington, D.C.: American Enterprise Institute, 1978), pp. 287–324.
11. See Angus Campbell et al., *The American Voter* (New York: Wiley, 1960), pp. 412–13, 479–81.
12. V. O. Key, Jr., *Public Opinion and American Democracy* (New York: Knopf, 1967), p. 329.
13. William C. Havard, ed., *The Changing Politics of the South* (Baton Rouge: Louisiana State University Press, 1972), p. 20.
14. Charles N. Fortenberry and F. Glenn Abney, "Mississippi, Unreconstructed and Unredeemed," in ibid., p. 507.
15. Ibid.
16. Thad Beyle and Ferrell Guillory, "Presidential Turnout in Southern States, 1960–2000," *South Now*, no. 1 (June 2001): 3.

17. Address to Congress, March 15, 1965.

18. Havard, *Changing Politics,* p. 20.

19. Ibid., pp. 512–14.

20. National Election Studies 1960 survey.

21. Walter Dean Burnham, *The Current Crisis in American Politics* (New York: Oxford University Press, 1982), p. 128.

22. See, for example, Frances Fox Piven and Richard A. Cloward, *Why Americans Still Don't Vote: And Why Politicians Want It That Way* (Boston: Beacon, 2000), p. 191.

23. See, for example, David Glass, Peverill Squire, and Raymond Wolfinger, "Voter Turnout: An International Comparison," *Public Opinion* 6 (December 1983/January 1984): 52.

24. Raymond E. Wolfinger and Steven J. Rosenstone, *Who Votes?* (New Haven, Conn.: Yale University Press, 1980).

25. North Dakota does not have a registration requirement; its residents need only provide proof of residency in order to vote on Election Day.

26. The Federal Election Commission reported that 154 million were registered to vote in 2000. Estimates based on registration increases in 1988 and 1992 (the two most recent presidential election years prior to the Motor Voter Act) suggest that registration in 2000 would have been somewhat more than 140 million without the legislation.

27. Michael P. McDonald and Samuel Popkin, "The Myth of the Vanishing Voter," p. 2. Paper presented at the annual meeting of the American Political Science Association, Washington, D.C., Aug. 30–Sept. 3, 2000.

28. See, for example, Peter Bruce, "How the Experts Got Voter Turnout Wrong Last Year," *Public Perspective,* October/November 1997, pp. 39–43.

29. U.S. Census Bureau data.

30. McDonald and Popkin, "Myth of the Vanishing Voter."

31. Ibid., p. 38.

32. Ibid., p. 3.

33. Brody, "Puzzle of Political Participation in America," p. 291.

34. Walter Dean Burnham, "The System of 1986: An Analysis," in Paul Kleppner et al., eds., *The Evolution of American Electoral Systems* (Westport, Conn.: Greenwood, 1981), p. 100. McDonald and Popkin's estimate for 1960 is slightly lower: 69 percent.

35. Walter Dean Burnham's analysis, cited in Robert D. Putnam, *Bowling Alone: The Collapse and Revival of American Community* (New York: Simon & Schuster, 2000), p. 33.

36. Austin Ranney, *Participation in American Presidential Nominations: 1976* (Washington, D.C.: American Enterprise Institute, 1977), p. 20; Ranney, ed., *The American Elections of 1980* (Washington, D.C.: American Enterprise Institute, 1981), pp. 353, 364; Jack Moran and Mark Fenster, "Voter Turnout in Presidential Primaries," *American Politics Quarterly* 10 (October 1982): 453–76.

37. League of Women Voters of Connecticut Web site, Aug. 20, 2001.

38. Jack C. Doppelt and Ellen Shearer, *Nonvoters: America's No-Shows* (Thousand Oaks, Calif.: Sage, 1999), pp. 5–6.

39. "Voters Stay Home in Most Areas," *Syracuse Post-Standard*, Nov. 8, 2001, p. 3.

40. *Chicago Tribune*, Nov. 6, 1996.

41. Quoted in Doppelt and Shearer, *Nonvoters*, p. 10.

42. Cited in Piven and Cloward, *Why Americans Still Don't Vote*, p. 5.

43. Daniel Boorstin, *The Genius of American Politics* (Chicago: University of Chicago Press, 1953).

44. See Lawrence Goodwyn, *The Populist Movement* (New York: Oxford University Press, 1978).

45. Cited in James L. Sundquist, *Dynamics of the Party System: Alignment and Realignment of Political Parties in the United States* (Washington, D.C.: Brookings Institution, 1983), p. 157.

46. Sidney Verba, Kay Lehman Schlozman, and Henry Brady, *Voice and Equality: Civic Voluntarism in American Politics* (Cambridge, Mass.: Harvard University Press, 1995), p. 468.

47. See, for example, Stephen E. Bennett and David Resnick, "The Implications of Nonvoting for Democracy in the United States," *American Journal of Political Science* 34 (1990): 771–802; John R. Petrocik, "Voter Turnout and Electoral Preference: The Anomalous Reagan Elections," in Kay L. Schlozman, ed., *Elections in America* (Boston: Allen & Unwin, 1987), pp. 239–59.

48. Ruy A. Teixeira, *The Disappearing American Voter* (Washington, D.C.: Brookings Institution, 1992), pp. 96–97.

49. Walter Dean Burnham, "The Class Gap," *The New Republic*, May 9, 1988, pp. 30, 32.

50. See Benjamin Highton and Raymond E. Wolfinger, "The Political Implications of Higher Turnout," *British Journal of Political Science* 31 (2001): 179–223.

51. The final Vanishing Voter poll before the 2000 election found that Americans of low income (bottom 20 percent) preferred Gore to Bush by

3 percent and were 47 percent less likely than those of high income (top 20 percent) to say they intended to vote. These findings are consistent with what other polls found.

52. CNN post-election polls, 1994.

53. Sidney Verba and Norman H. Nie, *Participation in America: Political Democracy and Social Equality* (New York: Harper & Row, 1972), p. 271; James D. Wright, *The Dissent of the Governed: Alienation and Democracy in America* (New York: Academic Press, 1976), p. 276.

54. Steven J. Rosenstone and John Mark Hansen, *Mobilization, Participation, and Democracy in America* (New York: Macmillan, 1993), p. 247.

55. Seymour Martin Lipset, *Political Man* (Baltimore: Johns Hopkins University Press, 1981), p. 164. Originally published in 1960.

56. Gary R. Orren, "The Linkage of Policy to Participation," in Alexander Heard, ed., *Presidential Selection* (Durham, N.C.: Duke University Press, 1987), p. 78.

57. John Stuart Mill, *Utilitarianism, Liberty, and Representative Government* (New York: Dutton, 1910), p. 217.

58. Putnam, *Bowling Alone*, p. 35.

59. See, for example, Max Kaase and Alan Marsh, "Distribution of Political Action," in Samuel H. Barnes et al., *Political Action: Mass Participation in Five Western Democracies* (Beverly Hills, Calif.: Sage, 1979), pp. 168–69, 198.

60. Putnam, *Bowling Alone*, p. 41.

61. Federal Election Commission data.

62. National Election Studies data.

63. Alan Schroeder, *Presidential Debates: Forty Years of High-Risk TV* (New York: Columbia University Press, 2000), p. 201.

64. Ibid.

65. Nielsen Media Research data for all debate audience references.

66. *CBS News:* presidential debate broadcast, Oct. 3, 2000.

67. Kathy Kiely, "Wealth of Debates Keeps the Hopefuls Talking," *USA Today,* Jan. 26, 2000, p. 8A.

68. Zachary Karabell, "The Rise and Fall of the Televised Political Convention," p. 4. Discussion Paper D-33, Joan Shorenstein Center on the Press, Politics and Public Policy, John F. Kennedy School of Government, Harvard University, October 1998.

69. Ibid. Concluding quote: *New York Times,* Aug. 19, 1952; cited in Gladys Engel Lang and Kurt Lang, *Politics and Television: Re-Viewed* (London: Sage, 1984), p. 60.

70. "Networks, Parties Trade Charges Over Plunge in Convention Coverage," *The Political Standard,* August 2000, p. 1.

71. Vanishing Voter survey. The figure is the percentage who reported on the day after Thanksgiving that they had discussed the campaign within the past twenty-four hours.

72. Vanishing Voter surveys in February and April included issue awareness questions.

73. Vanishing Voter survey, Aug. 4–9, 2000. Question was asked of respondents interviewed from August 7 to 9.

74. Vanishing Voter survey, Nov. 3–7, 2000.

75. Michael X. Delli Carpini and Scott Keeter, *What Americans Know About Politics and Why It Matters* (New Haven, Conn.: Yale University Press, 1996), p. 133.

76. Bernard R. Berelson, Paul F. Lazarsfeld, and William McPhee, *Voting: A Study of Opinion Formation in a Presidential Campaign* (Chicago: University of Chicago Press, 1954), p. 374.

77. Wilson Carey McWilliams, "The Meaning of the Election," in Gerald M. Pomper et al., *The Election of 2000* (New York: Chatham House, 2001), p. 177.

78. Gallup poll, Nov. 19, 2000.

79. Quoted in McWilliams, "Meaning of the Election," p. 177. McWilliams is a keen election analyst. The 1876 campaign example is derived from his commentary on the 2000 campaign.

80. David M. Shribman, "Is Politics Dead or Only Just Sleeping?" *Boston Globe,* Dec. 12, 1999, p. D3.

81. See Jerrold G. Rusk, "The American Electoral Universe: Speculation and Evidence," *American Political Science Review* 68 (1974): 1028–49.

82. Walter Dean Burnham, *Critical Elections and the Mainsprings of American Politics* (New York: Norton, 1970), p. 84.

83. Stanley Kelley, Jr., Richard E. Ayres, and William G. Bown, "Registration and Voting: Putting First Things First," *American Political Science Review* 61 (June 1967): 359–79.

84. Quoted in Ralph Volney Harlow, *The Growth of the United States* (New York: Holt, 1943), p. 312.

85. Arthur M. Schlesinger and Erik McKinley Eriksson, "The Vanishing Voter," *The New Republic,* Oct. 15, 1924, p. 165.

86. U.S. Bureau of the Census, *Historical Statistics of the United States, Colonial Times to 1970,* Part 2 (Washington, D.C.: U.S. Government Printing Office, 1975), p. 1071.

87. Schlesinger and Eriksson, "Vanishing Voter," pp. 164–65.

88. Margaret Talbot, "Who Wants to Be a Legionnaire?" *New York Times Book Review,* June 25, 2000, p. 12.

89. Project Vote Smart national survey, July/August 2000.

90. E. E. Schattschneider, *The Semi-Sovereign People: A Realist's View of Democracy in America* (New York: Holt, Rinehart and Winston, 1960), p. 132.

CHAPTER TWO
PARTIES AND CANDIDATES: POLITICS OF THE MOMENT

1. Vanishing Voter survey, Nov. 3–7, 2000.

2. Ibid.

3. Vanishing Voter survey, Jan. 17–21, 2001.

4. Vanishing Voter survey, Nov. 10–14, 2000.

5. James L. Sundquist, *Dynamics of the Party System: Alignment and Realignment of Political Parties in the United States* (Washington, D.C.: Brookings Institution, 1983), p. 290.

6. See Arthur M. Schlesinger, Jr., *Crisis of the Old Order, 1919–1933* (Boston: Houghton Mifflin, 1957).

7. Press conference statement, May 22, 1932. Cited in Sundquist, *Dynamics of the Party System,* p. 207.

8. *Time,* July 18, 1932, p. 8, and July 25, 1932, p. 8. Cited in Sundquist, *Dynamics of the Party System,* p. 207.

9. Quoted in Sundquist, *Dynamics of the Party System,* p. 209.

10. Angus Campbell et al., *The American Voter* (New York: Wiley, 1960).

11. An exception is Martin P. Wattenberg. See his *The Decline of American Political Parties, 1952–1996* (Cambridge, Mass.: Harvard University Press, 1998).

12. See Paul S. Herrnson, *Party Campaigning in the 80's* (Cambridge, Mass.: Harvard University Press, 1988).

13. Quoted in "Perspectives," *Newsweek,* Jan. 13, 1992, p. 17.

14. Paul Taylor, *See How They Run: Electing the President in the Age of Mediaocracy* (New York: Knopf, 1990), p. 6.

15. This interpretation is taken from Walter Lippmann, *Public Opinion* (New York: Free Press, 1965), pp. 178–79. Originally published in 1922.

16. See Joseph Charles, *The Origins of the American Party System* (New York: Harper & Row, 1961).

17. See Richard P. McCormick, *The Second American Party System* (Chapel Hill: University of North Carolina Press, 1966).

18. James MacGregor Burns, *The Vineyard of Liberty* (New York: Knopf, 1982), p. 368.

19. Alexis de Tocqueville, *Democracy in America* (Garden City, N.Y.: Doubleday/Anchor, 1960), p. 60. Originally published in installments between 1835 and 1840.

20. Everett Carll Ladd, *Transformations of the American Party System: Political Coalitions from the New Deal to the 1970s*, 2nd ed. (New York: Norton, 1978), p. 32.

21. Sundquist, *Dynamics of the Party System*, p. 106.

22. Cited in V. O. Key, Jr., *Politics, Parties, and Pressure Groups*, 4th ed. (New York: Crowell, 1958), p. 235.

23. See William Allen White, "The Boss System," in Richard Hofstadter, ed., *The Progressive Movement: 1900–1915* (Englewood Cliffs, N.J.: Prentice-Hall, 1963), pp. 104–107.

24. Ladd, *Transformations of the American Party System*, p. 32.

25. Sundquist, *Dynamics of the Party System*, p. 134; Paul Allen Beck and Frank J. Sorauf, *Party Politics in America* (New York: HarperCollins, 1992), p. 214.

26. Walter Dean Burnham, "Theory and Voting Research," *American Political Science Review* 68 (1974): 1002–23.

27. William Allen White, *Autobiography of William Allen White* (New York: Macmillan, 1946), p. 427. Quoted in Ladd, *Transformations of the American Party System*, p. 34.

28. Ladd, *Transformations of the American Party System*, p. 34.

29. Ibid.

30. See Edmund Morris, *Theodore Rex* (New York: Random House, 2001).

31. Seymour Martin Lipset, *Political Man* (Baltimore: Johns Hopkins University Press, 1981), p. 194.

32. Andrew W. Dobelstein, *Politics, Economics, and Public Welfare* (Englewood Cliffs, N.J.: Prentice-Hall, 1980), p. 5.

33. William C. Havard, Jr., "From Past to Future: An Overview of Southern Politics," in Havard, Jr., ed., *The Changing Politics of the South* (Baton Rouge: Louisiana State University Press, 1972), pp. 705–706.

34. Ladd, *Transformations of the American Party System*, p. 134. This paragraph in its particulars draws from Ladd's observations, pp. 130–34.

35. John M. Allswang, *A House for All Peoples: Ethnic Politics in Chicago, 1890–1936* (Lexington: University of Kentucky Press, 1971), p. 53.

36. V. O. Key, Jr., *The Responsible Electorate: Rationality in Presidential Voting, 1936–1960* (Cambridge, Mass.: Belknap Press of Harvard University Press, 1966), p. xi.

37. Kristi Andersen, *The Creation of a Democratic Majority, 1928–1936* (Chicago: University of Chicago Press, 1979).

38. Ladd, *Transformations of the American Party System,* pp. 121–24; Seymour Martin Lipset, "Religion and Politics in the American Past and Present," in Lipset, ed., *Revolution and Counterrevolution: Change and Persistence in Social Structures* (New York: Basic Books, 1968), pp. 305–73.
39. Edward G. Carmines and James A. Stimson, *Issue Evolution: Race and the Transformation of American Politics* (Princeton, N.J.: Princeton University Press, 1989), p. 6.
40. Walter Dean Burnham, *Critical Elections and the Mainsprings of American Politics* (New York: Norton, 1970), p. 27.
41. Walter Dean Burnham was among the few scholars to consider the possibility that public policy and society had progressed to a point where the realignment cycle might have stopped oscillating. See ibid., p. 173.
42. Cited in Ladd, *Transformations of the American Party System,* p. 196.
43. U.S. Bureau of the Census, *Statistical Abstract of the United States, 1988* (Washington, D.C.: U.S. Government Printing Office, 1987), p. 454.
44. It is still the case that poverty in America is higher than in Western Europe. See Timothy Smeeding, "Doing Poorly: The Real Income of American Children in Comparative Perspective," Luxembourg Income Study Working Paper No. 127, Maxwell School of Citizenship and Public Affairs, Syracuse University, 1995.
45. See, for example, Daniel Patrick Moynihan, *Maximum Feasible Misunderstanding* (New York: Free Press, 1969).
46. See, for example, the extensive discussion of this subject in Carmines and Stimson, *Issue Evolution.*
47. Ladd, *Transformations of the American Party System,* p. 111.
48. Ibid.
49. Richard M. Scammon and Ben J. Wattenberg, *The Real Majority* (New York: Coward-McCann, 1970), p. 43; see also Kevin Phillips, *The Emerging Republican Majority* (New Rochelle, N.Y.: Arlington House, 1969).
50. Burnham, *Critical Elections,* pp. 384–90.
51. Speech of Martin Luther King, Jr., in Washington, D.C., Aug. 2, 1963.
52. National Election Studies data, 1972.
53. Carmines and Stimson, *Issue Evolution,* pp. 63, 105, 150.
54. Samuel Lubell, *The Hidden Crisis in American Politics* (New York: Norton, 1971), p. 278.
55. Norman H. Nie, Sidney Verba, and John R. Petrocik, *The Changing American Voter* (Cambridge, Mass.: Harvard University Press, 1976), p. 52.

56. See David Broder, *The Party's Over: The Failure of Politics in America* (New York: Harper & Row, 1972).

57. See, for example, Jack L. Walker, *Mobilizing Interest Groups in America* (Ann Arbor: University of Michigan Press, 1991).

58. Steven Schier, "Activation in American Politics," Web posting, 2001, p. 8.

59. Federal Election Commission data.

60. National Election Studies data.

61. Ibid.

62. Jeff Fishel, *Presidents and Promises: From Campaign Pledge to Presidential Performance* (Washington, D.C.: Congressional Quarterly Press, 1985), p. 28.

63. National Election Studies data indicate that only Goldwater, Humphrey, McGovern, and Carter (1980), all of whom lost, were less popular than Reagan was in 1980.

64. Thomas E. Patterson, *The American Democracy,* 2nd ed. (New York: McGraw-Hill, 1993), pp. 275–76.

65. See David C. King, "The Polarization of American Parties and Mistrust of Government," in Joseph S. Nye, Jr., Philip D. Zelikow, and David C. King, *Why People Don't Trust Government* (Cambridge, Mass.: Harvard University Press, 1997), pp. 157–62.

66. See, for example, Alan Crawford, *Thunder on the Right* (New York: Pantheon, 1980).

67. Robert Wuthnow, "The Political Rebirth of American Evangelicals," in Robert C. Liebman and Robert Wuthnow, eds., *The New Christian Right: Mobilization and Legitimation* (Hawthorne, N.Y.: Aldine, 1983), pp. 167–85.

68. Quoted in Steven E. Schier, *By Invitation Only: The Rise of Exclusive Politics in the United States* (Pittsburgh: University of Pittsburgh Press, 2000), p. 5.

69. *Congressional Quarterly Weekly Report,* various dates.

70. Lawrence R. Jacobs and Robert Y. Shapiro, "Debunking the Pandering Politician Myth," *Public Perspective* 5 (April/May 1997): 4.

71. E. J. Dionne, Jr., *Why Americans Hate Politics* (New York: Touchstone, 1991), p. 354; see also King, "Polarization of American Parties," p. 168.

72. Quoted in Charlotte Grimes, "Danforth, Others Seek Better Race Relations," *St. Louis Post-Dispatch,* May 18, 1992, p. B1.

73. Dick Morris, *Behind the Oval Office* (New York: Random House, 1997).

74. David Broder, text of the Lucius W. Nieman Lecture, Marquette University, Milwaukee, March 28, 2001, p. 3.

75. Ibid., pp. 2–3.
76. Vanishing Voter survey, Nov. 3–7, 2000.
77. Nie, Verba, and Petrocik, *Changing American Voter,* p. 30.
78. National Election Studies survey, 2000.
79. See, for example, ibid.; Broder, *The Party's Over;* and Burnham, *Critical Elections.*
80. Ladd, *Transformations of the American Party System,* p. 374.
81. James Bryce, *The American Commonwealth,* vol. 2 (Indianapolis, Ind.: Liberty Fund, 1995), pp. 699–707.
82. Roderick Hart, *Campaign Talk: Why Elections Are Good for Us* (Princeton, N.J.: Princeton University Press, 2000), pp. 19, 58, 70, 113, 115, 155.
83. David D. Kirkpatrick, "Media Talk: Why the Mind Shrivels for the Body Politic," *New York Times,* Oct. 16, 2000, p. C16.
84. Abraham McLaughlin, "After Election, Are Promises Kept?" *Christian Science Monitor,* Sept. 14, 2000, Web download.
85. Robert D. Putnam, *Bowling Alone: The Collapse and Revival of American Community* (New York: Simon & Schuster, 2000), p. 40.
86. Wattenberg, *Decline of American Political Parties.*
87. National Election Studies data, 1952–2000.
88. Theodore J. Lowi and Benjamin Ginsberg, *American Government: Freedom and Power* (New York: Norton, 1990), p. 517.
89. Ladd, *Transformations of the American Party System,* p. 382.
90. Although it might seem relatively easy to measure levels of voter turnout among particular groups, it has not been because of the tendency of respondents to claim to vote when they don't. For opposing views on the question of whether the class gap has grown, see, for example, Walter Dean Burnham, "The Turnout Problem," in A. James Reichley, *Elections American Style* (Washington, D.C.: Brookings Institution, 1987); David Darmofal, "Socioeconomic Bias in Turnout Decline: Do the Voters Remain the Same?" Paper presented at the annual meeting of the American Political Science Association, Atlanta, September 1999; Jan E. Leighley and Jonathan Nagler, "Socioeconomic Class Bias in Turnout, 1964–1988: The Voters Remain the Same," *American Political Science Review* 86, no. 3 (1992): 725–36.
91. The question was asked in several surveys. Across all of them, 46 percent in the bottom third, 36 percent in the middle third, and 32 percent in the upper third said the election's outcome would have little or no effect on their lives.
92. Carmines and Stimson, *Issue Evolution,* p. 11.

93. Vanishing Voter surveys, multiple dates. Among the non–college educated who were strong partisans, turnout was 11 percentage points lower for those who could not find words to describe the parties, and among weak partisans and independents, it was 20 points lower. Among those who had been to college, the differences were much smaller, 4 points and 13 points, respectively.

94. As candidate-centered campaigns developed, participation in presidential primaries increased but has since declined substantially.

95. Frank Sorauf, *Political Parties in American Democracy* (Boston: Little, Brown, 1964), pp. 38–39.

96. Richard Jensen, "American Election Campaigns." Paper delivered at the Midwest Political Science Association meeting, Chicago, May 1968.

97. For a discussion of early television newscasts, see Martin Mayer, *About Television* (New York: Harper & Row, 1972), pp. 203–205.

98. Michael Robinson, "Television and American Politics 1956–1976," *The Public Interest* 3 (1977): 18.

99. See, for example, Robert MacNeil, *The People Machine* (New York: Harper & Row, 1968).

100. Robinson, "Television and American Politics," p. 17.

101. Richard Rubin, *Press, Party, and President* (New York: Norton, 1980), p. 187.

102. See, for example, Howard L. Reiter, *Selecting the President: The Nominating Process in Transition* (Philadelphia: University of Pennsylvania Press, 1985).

103. See F. Christopher Arterton, "Campaign Organizations Confront the Media-Political Environment," in James David Barber, ed., *Race for the Presidency: The Media and the Nominating Process* (Englewood Cliffs, N.J.: Prentice-Hall, 1978), pp. 3–24.

104. Fox Butterfield, "Dukakis Says Race Was Harmed by TV," *New York Times,* April 22, 1990, sec. 1, p. 23. Quoted in Philip Wander and David McNeil, "The Coming Crisis in American Politics," *Political Communication Review* 16 (1991): 38.

105. Taylor, *See How They Run,* p. 25.

106. Center for Media and Public Affairs data, 2000.

107 Todd Gitlin, "The Candidate Factory: Providing a Better Product for a Bored America," *Boston Review,* Web release, p. 2.

108. Bryce, *American Commonwealth,* vol. 2, p. 879. Idea for use of the quote is from Richard R. Lau et al., "The Effects of Negative Political Advertisements: A Meta-Analytic Assessment," *American Political Science Review* 93, no. 4 (December 1999): 851.

109. Arthur M. Schlesinger and Erik McKinley Eriksson, "The Vanishing Voter," *The New Republic,* Oct. 15, 1924, p. 165.

110. Taylor, *See How They Run,* p. 6.

111. Hart, *Campaign Talk,* p. 136.

112. Darrell West, *Air Wars: Television Advertising in Election Campaigns, 1952–1992* (Washington, D.C.: Congressional Quarterly Press, 1993), p. 48.

113. See Hart, *Campaign Talk,* p. 135. One of the studies he cites is Lynda Lee Kaid, "Videostyle in the 1996 Presidential Advertising." Paper presented at the annual meeting of the National Communication Association, San Diego, November 1996.

114. Anthony Corrado, "Financing the 2000 Elections," in Gerald M. Pomper et al., *The Election of 2000* (New York: Chatham House, 2001), pp. 208–209.

115. Thomas E. Patterson, *Out of Order: How the Decline of Political Parties and the Growing Power of the News Media Undermine the American Way of Electing Presidents* (New York: Knopf, 1993), p. 20.

116. Quoted in David Shaw, "On the Campaign Trail, Bad News Wins Out," *Los Angeles Times,* April 18, 1996, p. A22.

117. Thomas B. Edsall, "Elections Can Hinge on Persuading Likely Opponents Not to Vote," *Washington Post,* April 29, 1984, p. A2. Cited in Alexander Heard, *Made in America: Improving the Nomination and Election of Presidents* (New York: HarperCollins, 1991), p. 121.

118. See, for example, Richard Lau and Gerald M. Pomper, "Effects of Negative Campaigning on Turnout in U.S. Senate Elections, 1988–1998," *Journal of Politics* 63, no. 5 (August 2001): 804–19.

119. Stephen Ansolabehere and Shanto Iyengar, *Going Negative: How Political Advertisements Shrink and Polarize the Electorate* (New York: Free Press, 1995).

120. Vanishing Voter survey; average is based on the three surveys in which the question was asked.

121. James W. Ceaser, *Presidential Selection: Theory and Development* (Princeton, N.J.: Princeton University Press, 1979), p. 11.

122. Richard Stengel and Eric Pooley, "Masters of the Message: Inside the High-Tech Machine That Set Clinton and Dole Polls Apart," *Time,* Nov. 18, 1996, p. 93.

123. McLaughlin, "After Election, Are Promises Kept?"

124. Patterson, *Out of Order,* p. 13.

125. John Aldrich, *Why Parties?: The Origin and Transformation of Party Politics in America* (Chicago: University of Chicago Press, 1995), p. 4.

126. Paul Weaver, "Is Television News Biased?" *The Public Interest* 27 (1972): 69.

127. Ibid.

128. Michael Robinson, "Improving Election Information in the Media," p. 2. Paper presented at Voting for Democracy Forum, Washington, D.C., September 1983.

129. *NBC Nightly News with Tom Brokaw,* Oct. 3, 2000.

130. Vanishing Voter survey, various dates.

131. Doris A. Graber, *Processing the News: How People Tame the Information Tide* (New York: Longman, 1984), p. 141.

132. Gerald Pomper with Susan Lederman, *Elections in America: Control and Influence in Democratic Politics,* 2nd ed. (New York: Longman, 1980), ch. 8; Michael G. Krukones, *Promises and Performance: Presidential Campaigns as Policy Predictors* (Lanham, Md.: University Press of America, 1984); Ian Budge and Richard I. Hofferbert, "Mandates and Policy Outputs: U.S. Party Platforms and Federal Expenditures," *American Political Science Review* 84 (1990): 111–32; and Fishel, *Presidents and Promises,* pp. 38, 42–43. The studies do not distinguish the candidates' promises in terms of their scope or impact.

133. McLaughlin, "After Election, Are Promises Kept?"

134. Ibid.

135. Maura Clancy and Michael Robinson, "General Election Coverage, Part I," in Michael J. Robinson and Austin Ranney, eds., *The Mass Media in Campaign '84* (Washington, D.C.: American Enterprise Institute, 1985), p. 29.

136. Ibid.

137. Patterson, *Out of Order,* p. 146.

138. Thomas E. Patterson, *The Mass Media Election: How Americans Choose Their President* (New York: Praeger, 1980), pp. 36–37.

139. Larry J. Sabato, *Feeding Frenzy: How Attack Journalism Has Transformed American Politics* (New York: Free Press, 1991), p. 1.

140. Example from Charles Krauthammer, "The Pornography of Self-Revelation," *Time,* Aug. 10, 1992, p. 72.

141. Kiku Adatto, "Sound Bite Democracy: Network Evening News Presidential Campaign Coverage, 1968 and 1988," p. 5. Research Paper R-2, Joan Shorenstein Center on the Press, Politics and Public Policy, John F. Kennedy School of Government, Harvard University, June 1990.

142. Taylor, *See How They Run,* pp. 22–23.

143. Gallup polls, 1936–2000.

CHAPTER THREE
THE NEWS MEDIA: THE POLITICS OF ANTI-POLITICS

1. Vanishing Voter survey, Jan. 17–21, 2001.
2. Ibid.
3. Ibid.
4. Robert Lichter, "A Plague on Both Parties: Substance and Fairness in TV Election News," *Harvard International Journal of Press/Politics* 6, no. 6 (Summer 2001): 16.
5. "Election Coverage: The Last Lap," Project for Excellence in Journalism Web report, March 6, 2002.
6. *CBS Evening News,* Sept. 15, 2000.
7. Edith Efron, *The News Twisters* (Los Angeles: Nash, 1971).
8. David Niven, "Partisanship and Negativity in Media Coverage of Presidents George Bush and Bill Clinton," *Harvard International Journal of Press/Politics* 6, no. 6 (Summer 2001): 32.
9. "Campaign 2000—The Primaries," *Media Monitor* (Center for Media and Public Affairs, Washington, D.C.) 14, no. 2 (March/April 2000): 4; "Hess Report on Campaign Coverage in Nightly News," Brookings Institution, Nov. 7, 2000, Web release.
10. *NBC Nightly News with Tom Brokaw,* Oct. 5, 2000.
11. Project for Excellence in Journalism data, Web download, March 7, 2002. Figures based on twenty-seven news sources (more than 2,000 stories) over a two-month period of the 2000 campaign.
12. Tim Groeling and Samuel Kernell, "Is Network News Coverage of the President Biased?" *Journal of Politics* 60, no. 4 (1998): 1063–87.
13. S. Robert Lichter and Ted J. Smith, "Bad News Bears," *Media Critic,* Winter 1994, pp. 81–87.
14. See, for example, Kathleen Hall Jamieson, *Dirty Politics* (New York: Oxford University Press, 1992).
15. Quoted in Thomas E. Patterson, "More Style than Substance: Television News in U.S. National Elections," *Political Communication and Persuasion* 8 (1991): 157.
16. James Carey, "Lawyers, Voyeurs, and Vigilantes," *Media Studies Journal,* Spring/Summer 1999, p. 20.
17. The audience reach of the nineteenth-century press also moderated their impact. Most Americans then did not read a daily paper because they could not afford one, were illiterate, or lived in remote areas. In 1820, when the United States had a population of 9.6 million, there were only 24 dailies with a combined circulation of roughly 50,000 copies. Even

as late as 1870, when the population was 38.6 million, dailies had a circulation of only 2.6 million. Edwin Emery, *The Press and America: An Interpretive History of Journalism*, 2nd ed. (Englewood Cliffs, N.J.: Prentice-Hall, 1962), pp. 174, 345.

18. Walter Lippmann, *Public Opinion* (New York: Free Press, 1965), p. 214. Originally published in 1922.

19. Thomas E. Patterson, *Out of Order: How the Decline of Political Parties and the Growing Power of the News Media Undermine the American Way of Electing Presidents* (New York: Knopf, 1993), p. 20 for 1960–92; Center for Media and Public Affairs data for 1996 and 2000.

20. Leonard Downie, Jr., and Robert G. Kaiser, *The News About the News: American Journalism in Peril* (New York: Knopf, 2002).

21. Bill Kovach and Tom Rosenstiel, *The Elements of Journalism: What Newspeople Should Know and the Public Should Expect* (New York: Crown, 2001).

22. Ben Bradlee, *A Good Life: Newspapering and Other Adventures* (New York: Simon & Schuster, 1995), p. 352.

23. Hendrik Hertzberg, "Talk of the Town," *The New Yorker*, July 30, 2001, p. 25.

24. Paul Weaver, "Is Television News Biased?" *The Public Interest* 27 (1972): 69.

25. Quoted in Michael Robinson and Margaret Sheehan, *Over the Wire and on TV* (New York: Sage Foundation, 1983), p. 226.

26. Weaver, "Television News," p. 69.

27. Patterson, *Out of Order*, p. 82.

28. Carl Leubsdorf, "The Reporter and the Presidential Campaign," *ANNALS* (1976): 6.

29. Weaver, "Television News," p. 69.

30. Daniel R. Hallin, "Sound Bite News," *Journal of Communication* 42 (1992): 11.

31. Timothy Crouse, *The Boys on the Bus* (New York: Ballantine, 1974), p. 323.

32. *CBS Evening News*, Oct. 9, 1972. Reported in Thomas E. Patterson and Robert D. McClure, *The Unseeing Eye: The Myth of Television Power in National Elections* (New York: Putnam, 1976), p. 32.

33. Hallin, "Sound Bite News," p. 10.

34. Robinson and Sheehan, *Over the Wire*.

35. Catherine A. Steele and Kevin G. Barnhurst, "The Journalism of Opinion," *Critical Studies in Mass Communication* 13 (1996): 198.

36. *CBS Evening News*, Jan. 7, 1980.

37. Kiku Adatto, "Sound Bite Democracy: Network Evening News Presidential Campaign Coverage, 1968 and 1988," p. 4. Research Paper R-2, Joan

Shorenstein Center on the Press, Politics and Public Policy, John F. Kennedy School of Government, Harvard University, June 1990.

38. Hallin, "Sound Bite News," pp. 5–24.

39. Adatto, "Sound Bite Democracy," p. 4.

40. Lichter, "Plague on Both Parties," p. 17.

41. These figures are based on the content analysis of the Center for Media and Public Affairs. The center reports that Bush and Gore had 102 minutes of combined speaking time on the ABC, CBS, and NBC nightly newscasts. Since a viewer could watch only one newscast on a given night, the average exposure would be about 17 minutes for each candidate.

42. "Campaign 2000 Final," *Media Monitor* 14, no. 6 (November/December 2000): 2.

43. Patterson, *Out of Order*, p. 75.

44. Quoted in Marvin Kalb, "The Rise of the New News," p. 13. Discussion Paper D-34, Joan Shorenstein Center on the Press, Politics and Public Policy, John F. Kennedy School of Government, Harvard University, October 1998.

45. Crouse, *Boys on the Bus*, p. 323.

46. Michael Schudson, *What Time Means in a News Story* (New York: Gannett Center for Media Studies, Columbia University, 1986), Occasional Paper no. 4, p. 1.

47. Weaver, "Television News," p. 69.

48. Patterson and McClure, *The Unseeing Eye*, p. 46.

49. Michael J. Robinson, "Public Affairs Television and the Growth of Political Malaise: The Case of 'The Selling of the Pentagon,'" *American Political Science Review* 70, no. 3 (1976): 409–32. Robinson was the first scholar to develop and investigate the notion that television journalism would have an adverse effect on public attitudes, but was not the first to suggest it. Kurt and Gladys Lang had articulated the idea a decade earlier. See Kurt Lang and Gladys Engel Lang, "The Mass Media and Voting," in Bernard Berelson and Morris Janowitz, *Reader in Public Opinion and Communication* (New York: Free Press, 1966).

50. Arthur H. Miller, Edie N. Goldenberg, and Lutz Erbring, "Type-Set Politics: Impact of Newspapers on Public Confidence," *American Political Science Review* 73 (1979): 67–84.

51. Michael Schudson, *The Power of News* (Cambridge, Mass.: Harvard University Press, 1995), ch. 7.

52. See, for example, Max Kampelman, "The Power of the Press," *Policy Review*, Fall 1978, pp. 7–41; Irving Kristol, "Crisis Over Journalism," in George Will, ed., *Press, Politics, and Popular Government* (Washington,

D.C.: American Enterprise Institute, 1972), p. 50; Robinson and Sheehan, *Over the Wire,* p. 2.

53. Jorgen Westerstahl and Folke Johansson, "News Ideologies as Molders of Domestic News," *European Journal of Communication* 1 (1986): 141, 146–47.
54. Quoted in David Shaw, "Beyond Skepticism: Have the Media Crossed the Line into Cynicism?" *Los Angeles Times,* April 17, 1996, p. A1.
55. Ibid.
56. Quoted in Kalb, "Rise of the New News," pp. 13–14.
57. Anecdote told to the author by former U.S. senator Alan Simpson.
58. Westerstahl and Johansson, "News Ideologies," pp. 146–47.
59. Shaw, "Beyond Skepticism," p. A1.
60. Thomas Mann and Norman Ornstein, eds., *Congress, the Press and the Public* (Washington, D.C.: American Enterprise Institute and Brookings Institution, 1994), pp. 59–129.
61. Larry J. Sabato, *Feeding Frenzy: How Attack Journalism Has Transformed American Politics* (New York: Free Press, 1991), p. 1.
62. Catherine A. Steele and Kevin G. Barnhurst, "The Growing Dominance of Opinionated Journalism in U.S. Presidential Campaign Television Coverage, 1968 and 1988," p. 9. Unpublished paper, Syracuse University.
63. Kristi Andersen and Stuart J. Thorson, "Public Discourse or Strategic Game? Changes in Our Conception of Elections," *Studies in American Political Development* 3 (1989): 271–73.
64. Steve Bell, "Kill the Messenger: The Public Condemns the News Media," *USA Today Magazine,* January 2000, pp. 61–62.
65. Example from Steele and Barnhurst, "Growing Dominance of Opinionated Journalism," pp. 3–4, 10–11.
66. Patterson, *Out of Order,* pp. 136–37.
67. Shaw, "Beyond Skepticism," p. A1.
68. Niven, "Partisanship and Negativity," p. 32.
69. Quoted in Shaw, "Beyond Skepticism," p. A1.
70. Sissela Bok, "School for Scandal," Discussion Paper D-4, Joan Shorenstein Center on the Press, Politics and Public Policy, John F. Kennedy School of Government, Harvard University, April 1990.
71. Quoted in Shaw, "Beyond Skepticism."
72. Sabato, *Feeding Frenzy,* p. 1.
73. "Keeping an Eye on Congress," *Media Monitor* 3 (November 1989): 3.
74. Representative Jack Brooks, quoted by Carol Matlack, "Crossing the Line," *National Journal* 21 (March 25, 1989): 724–29.
75. "The Honeymoon That Wasn't," *Media Monitor* 7, no. 7 (September/October 1993): 2–5.

76. Ibid., pp. 2–3.
77. *Congressional Quarterly Weekly Report,* Dec. 31, 1994, p. 3620.
78. "Congress's Sour Finish," *New York Times,* Oct. 8, 1994, p. 22.
79. "No Newt Is Good Newt," *Media Monitor* 9 (March/April 1995): 2.
80. Ibid., pp. 1–6.
81. See Robert Blendon, "Bridging the Gap Between the Public's and Econo- mists' Views of the Economy," *Journal of Economic Perspectives* 11, no. 1 (Summer 1997): 105–18.
82. William John Fox, "Junk News," p. 12. Discussion Paper D-26, Joan Shorenstein Center on the Press, Politics and Public Policy, John F. Kennedy School of Government, Harvard University, August 1997.
83. "The Bad News Campaign," *Media Monitor* 10, no. 2 (March/April 1996): 3–6.
84. David Broder, "War on Cynicism," *Washington Post,* July 6, 1994, p. A19.
85. Maureen Dowd, "Raffish and Rowdy," *New York Times,* March 31, 1996, p. E15.
86. Seventy-three percent blamed Congress and 2 percent blamed the press. The remaining 25 percent said the blame was equally shared.
87. Nielsen Media Research data.
88. According to the National Opinion Research Center surveys, daily news- paper readership dropped from about three-fourths of the public to half between 1970 and 1995.
89. Frank Luther Mott, *American Journalism: A History, 1690–1960* (New York: Macmillan, 1962), pp. 114–15.
90. Emery, *The Press and America,* p. 350.
91. Ibid., pp. 422–23.
92. Quoted in James McCartney, "News Lite," *American Journalism Review,* June 1997, pp. 19, 21. See also Walter Cronkite, *A Reporter's Life* (New York: Knopf, 1996).
93. Remark made at a Kennedy School Forum event, Harvard University, May 9, 1997.
94. Quoted in McCartney, "News Lite," p. 23.
95. Ibid., pp. 19–21.
96. Thomas E. Patterson, *Doing Well and Doing Good: How Soft News and Critical Journalism Are Shrinking the News Audience and Weakening Democracy—And What News Outlets Can Do About It* (Cambridge, Mass.: Joan Shorenstein Center on the Press, Politics and Public Policy, 2000), p. 4.
97. Robert Lichter and Jeremy Torobin, ". . . But Broadcasters Don't Seem to

Think So," *The Political Standard* (newsletter of the Alliance for Better Campaigns) 3, no. 1 (February 2000): 2.

98. Patterson, *Doing Well and Doing Good,* pp. 3–4.
99. Committee of Concerned Journalists, "News Magazine Cover Appeal," Web release, May 5, 1998.
100. Committee of Concerned Journalists, "Changing Definitions of News," Web release, May 4, 1998. The study, conducted by the Project for Excellence in Journalism and the Medill News Service, was based on the three major broadcast networks, the front-page coverage of the *New York Times* and *Los Angeles Times,* and the cover stories of *Time* and *Newsweek.*
101. Lawrence N. Hanson, "Reflections: The Press Looks at Itself, Politicians, and the Public," *Joyce Foundation Report* (Washington, D.C., 1992), p. 8.
102. Ibid.
103. Michael J. Robinson, "The Media in 1980: Was the Message the Message?" in Austin Ranney, ed., *The American Elections of 1980* (Washington, D.C.: American Enterprise Institute, 1981), p. 191.
104. R. W. Apple, Jr., "Just Too Slick, Willie," *New York Times,* March 11, 1994, Web download.
105. "Is Attack Pack Back?" *Media Monitor* 8, no. 2 (March/April 1994): 1.
106. Marvin Kalb, *One Scandalous Story: Clinton, Lewinsky, and Thirteen Days that Tarnished American Journalism* (New York: Free Press, 2001).
107. Bill Kovach and Tom Rosenstiel, *Warp Speed: America in the Age of Mixed Media* (New York: Century Foundation, 1999), p. 99.
108. Ibid., pp. 22–23.
109. Bradlee, *Good Life,* p. 339.
110. Cited in Thomas E. Patterson, *Out of Order* (New York: Vintage, 1994), p. 248. This material does not appear in the 1993 Knopf hardcover edition.
111. Fredric T. Smoller, *The Six O'Clock Presidency: A Theory of Presidential Press Relations in the Age of Television* (New York: Praeger, 1990); *Media Monitor,* various issues.
112. Bartholomew H. Sparrow, *Uncertain Guardians: The News Media as a Political Institution* (Baltimore: Johns Hopkins University Press, 1999), p. 43.
113. See Mann and Ornstein, *Congress, the Press and the Public.* See also Sparrow, *Uncertain Guardians,* p. 43.
114. Patterson, *Doing Well and Doing Good,* p. 4.
115. Mark Rozell, "Press Coverage of Congress," in Mann and Ornstein, *Congress, the Press, and the Public,* p. 109.
116. "More News Is Bad News for Bush," *Media Monitor* 3 (March 1991): 3.

117. National Election Studies, 1960–2000.
118. Humphrey Taylor, "Confidence in Leadership of Nation's Institutions Slips a Little But Remains Relatively High," Harris Initiative, Inc., Web release, Feb. 7, 2001.
119. Shaw, "Beyond Skepticism," p. A1.
120. Patterson, *Out of Order,* p. 23.
121. "They're No Friends of Bill," *Media Monitor* 8 (July/August 1994): 1–6.
122. Rozell, "Press Coverage of Congress," p. 109.
123. Shanto Iyengar, "Making Voters Autonomous." Paper presented at the National Conference for Digital Government Research, Los Angeles, May 21–23, 2001; see also Shanto Iyengar and Stephen Ansolabehere, *Going Negative: How Attack Ads Shrink and Polarize the Electorate* (New York: Free Press, 1995).
124. Joseph N. Cappella and Kathleen Hall Jamieson, *Spiral of Cynicism* (New York: Oxford University Press, 1997), p. 150.
125. Ibid., p. 159.
126. Ibid.
127. See, for example, Matthew Robert Kerbel, *Edited for Television: CNN, ABC, and the American Presidential Campaign* (Boulder, Colo.: Westview, 1998), p. 205.
128. Wendy M. Rahn and John Transue, "Social Trust and Value Change: The Decline in Social Capital in American Youth, 1976–1995," *Political Psychology* 19 (1998): 545–65.
129. See, for example, W. Lance Bennett, "The Uncivic Culture: Communication, Identity, and the Rise of Lifestyle Politics," *PS: Political Science and Politics* 31, no. 4 (December 1998): 741–61.
130. Cited in Robert Putnam, "Bowling Alone: America's Declining Social Capital," *Journal of Democracy* 6, no. 1 (January 1995): 73.
131. Cappella and Jamieson, *Spiral of Cynicism,* p. 39.
132. Richard Morin and Claudia Deane, "As Turnout Falls, Apathy Emerges as Driving Force," *Washington Post,* Nov. 4, 2000, Web version, p. 2.
133. Ibid.
134. Ibid., p. 3.
135. Ruy A. Teixeira, *The Disappearing American Voter* (Washington, D.C.: Brookings Institution, 1992), p. 33.
136. Ibid.
137. Steven J. Rosenstone and John Mark Hansen, *Mobilization, Participation, and Democracy in America* (New York: Macmillan, 1993), p. 150.
138. This way of phrasing the effect of childhood socialization is taken from

Robert Putnam, *Bowling Alone: The Collapse and Revival of American Community* (New York: Simon & Schuster, 2000).

139. Warren E. Miller and J. Merrill Shanks, *The New American Voter* (Cambridge, Mass.: Harvard University Press, 1996), p. 58.

140. Vanishing Voter survey.

141. Teixeira, *Disappearing American Voter*, p. 78.

142. Morin and Deane, "As Turnout Falls, Apathy Emerges as a Driving Force," p. 3.

143. Miller and Shanks, *New American Voter*, p. 41.

144. Putnam, *Bowling Alone*, p. 33.

145. Thomas B. Jankowski and Charles D. Elder, "Transforming the Puzzle Again: Age, Cohort, and Declining Turnout." Paper delivered at the annual meeting of the American Political Science Association, San Francisco, Aug. 30–Sept. 2, 2001.

146. Paul Weaver, *News and the Culture of Lying* (New York: Free Press, 1994).

147. "1993—The Year in Review," *Media Monitor* 8, no. 11 (January/February 1994).

148. "1994—The Year in Review," *Media Monitor* 9, no. 1 (January/February 1995).

149. Gallup poll, Aug. 1994.

150. Theodore H. White, *The Making of the President, 1972* (New York: Bantam, 1973), p. 327.

151. Neil Postman, *Amusing Ourselves to Death: Public Discourse in the Age of Show Business* (New York: Viking, 1985).

152. Comparison based on Center for Media and Public Affairs data, 1992 and 2000; see also "Hess Report on Campaign Coverage in Nightly News," Brookings Institution, Nov. 7, 2000, Web release.

153. Comparisons based on Center for Media and Public Affairs data, 1996 and 2000.

154. Lichter and Torobin, ". . . But Broadcasters Don't Seem to Think So," p. 2.

155. See, for example, Thomas E. Patterson, *The Mass Media Election: How Americans Choose Their President* (New York: Praeger, 1980), pp. 159–65. Our Vanishing Voter weekly surveys revealed a link ($r = .58$) between aggregate involvement and information levels.

156. Conversation with former CNN news president Rick Kaplan, July 19, 2001.

157. Cited in Frank Rich, "The End of the Beginning," *New York Times*, Sept. 29, 2001, p. A23. The reference to press coverage of Tenet's testimony appeared first in a *Washington Post* column by Geneva Overholser.

158. Carl Sessions Stepp, "Long and Short of It," *American Journalism Review* Web release, Dec. 8, 1999.

159. Committee of Concerned Journalists, "Changing Definition of News," Web release, May 4, 1998.

160. Remark by Richard Holbrooke at a Joan Shorenstein Center Brown Bag, John F. Kennedy School of Government, Harvard University, Oct. 4, 2001.

161. Rich, "End of the Beginning."

162. Quoted in Richard Harwood, "Searching for Facts in a Sea of Speculation," *Nieman Reports*, Summer 1999, p. 62.

163. Vanishing Voter survey, Oct. 10, 2001.

164. Quoted in Neil Hickey, "Money List: How Pressure for Profit Is Perverting Journalism," *Columbia Journalism Review*, July/August 1998, p. 10.

165. See, for example, Tom Rosenstiel, Carl Gottlieb, and Lee Ann Brady, "Time of Peril for TV News," Project for Excellence in Journalism, 2000.

166. Patterson, *Doing Well and Doing Good*.

167. Richard Kaplan, "After '9-11': Which War Will the Networks Fight?" p. 25. Research paper, Joan Shorenstein Center on the Press, Politics and Public Policy, John F. Kennedy School of Government, Harvard University, November 2001.

168. Patterson, *Doing Well and Doing Good*, p. 8.

169. Deborah Potter and Walter Gantz, "Bringing Viewers Back to Local TV," NewsLab survey, 2000.

170. Observation of the *Washington Post*'s Leonard Downie, Jr., luncheon talk, Harvard University, Feb. 26, 2002.

171. Patterson, *Doing Well and Doing Good*, p. 10.

172. Downie and Kaiser, *News About the News*.

173. Suggested by North Carolina State Professor Robert Entam in correspondence with author, February 2002.

174. Meg Greenfield, "The Art of Choosing Sides," *Newsweek*, Oct. 25, 1980.

175. George Will, "Debates Keep Them Off the Streets," syndicated column of Oct. 15, 1980.

176. *NBC Nightly News with Tom Brokaw*, Oct. 29, 1996.

177. Carey, "Lawyers, Voyeurs, and Vigilantes," pp. 16–17.

CHAPTER FOUR
THE LONG CAMPAIGN: THE POLITICS OF TEDIUM

1. Vanishing Voter survey, Jan. 17–21, 2001.

2. Vanishing Voter survey, Jan. 12–16, 2000.

3. Ibid.

4. Robert Friedman, "Perot: Co-Opting Legitimate Issues," *St. Petersburg Times,* Nov. 21, 1993, p. 4.

5. See Thomas E. Patterson, *The Mass Media Election: How Americans Choose Their President* (New York: Praeger, 1980).

6. Vanishing Voter survey, Feb. 6, 2000.

7. The Vanishing Voter Project's media tracking found that election coverage in major news outlets increased by 60 percent in response to the first primary debate.

8. *CNN Inside Politics,* Dec. 2, 1999.

9. All debate audience data from Nielsen Media Research.

10. CBS made a belated offer just before Super Tuesday to host a debate between the four top candidates—Bush, McCain, Bradley, and Gore. Whether network executives believed that the candidates would participate in a debate that included candidates of the opposite party is an open question. Only Bradley accepted the offer, and the debate was not held. It is worth noting, however, that CBS was the first network to embrace the recommendation of a 1998 White House panel and the Alliance for Better Campaigns that five minutes of airtime be made available to presidential candidates each night during the last thirty days of the 2000 campaign.

11. Quoted in Martin Tolchin, "How Senators View the Senate," *New York Times,* Nov. 25, 1984, p. 40.

12. Alan Mayer, "Bush Breaks Out of the Pack," *Newsweek,* Feb. 4, 1980, p. 30.

13. William R. Keech and Donald R. Matthews, *The Party's Choice* (Washington, D.C.: Brookings Institution, 1976), pp. 103–105.

14. Quoted in Paul T. David, Ralph M. Goldman, and Richard C. Bain, *The Politics of National Party Conventions* (Washington, D.C.: Brookings Institution, 1960), p. 296.

15. For a review of the McGovern-Fraser Commission's objectives, see Austin Ranney, *Participation in American Presidential Nominations: 1976* (Washington, D.C.: American Enterprise Institute, 1977), p. 6.

16. William Crotty and John S. Jackson III, *Presidential Primaries and Nominations* (Washington, D.C.: American Enterprise Institute, 1977), pp. 44–49.

17. Vanishing Voter news release, Dec. 16, 1999.

18. Patterson, *Mass Media Election,* ch. 6.

19. Vanishing Voter surveys, Dec. 1–5, 8–12, 21–26, 1999.

20. Vanishing Voter survey, 2000.

21. Vanishing Voter news release, Feb. 10, 2000.

22. Austin Ranney, *Channels of Power* (New York: Basic Books, 1983), p. 93.

23. Patterson, *Mass Media Election,* pp. 108–109.
24. Vanishing Voter national survey, Feb. 4–9 and March 29–April 2, 2000.
25. See Gerald M. Pomper et al., *The Election of 2000* (New York: Chatham House, 2001).
26. Samuel L. Popkin, *The Reasoning Voter: Communication and Persuasion in Political Campaigns* (Chicago: University of Chicago Press, 1991).
27. Scott Keeter and Cliff Zukin, *Uninformed Choice: The Failure of the New Presidential Nominating System* (New York: Praeger, 1983).
28. Patterson, *Mass Media Election,* chs. 10–13.
29. William G. Mayer, *In Pursuit of the White House 2000* (New York: Chatham House, 2000).
30. Jules Witcover, *Marathon: The Pursuit of the Presidency* (New York: Viking, 1977), p. 202.
31. Keeter and Zukin, *Uninformed Choice,* pp. 110, 136.
32. Scott Lindlaw, "Wilson Signs Bill Moving Up California Presidential Primary," Associated Press wire story, Sept. 29, 1999.
33. Vanishing Voter news release, July 13, 2000.
34. Quoted in "Heavy Campaigning Leads to Better Informed Citizens," *The Political Standard* (a publication of the Alliance for Better Campaigns), April 2000, p. 6.
35. Figures from Vanishing Voter weekly release of April 21, 2000.
36. Patterson, *Mass Media Election,* p. 68.
37. William Schneider, "And Now the GOP Is Rewriting Its Rules," *National Journal,* April 12, 1997, p. 734.
38. Figure is based on candidate financial disclosure statements filed with the Federal Election Commission.
39. Barbara Norrander, "Candidate Attrition During the Presidential Nominating System," p. 2. Paper presented at the Joan Shorenstein Center on the Press, Politics and Public Policy Roundtable, John F. Kennedy School of Government, Harvard University, Oct. 16, 2000.
40. Ibid.
41. Vanishing Voter national survey, June 7–11, 2000.
42. Civic Service national poll (personal interviews with roughly 1,500 respondents), Feb. 1–15, 1980.
43. Vanishing Voter national survey, March 24–April 2 and March 31–April 5, 2000.
44. Quoted in Eileen Shields-West, *The World Almanac of Presidential Campaigns* (New York: World Almanac, 1992), p. 163. Shields-West is also the source of other information in this example.

45. See Howard Reiter, *Selecting the President: The Nominating Process in Transition* (Philadelphia: University of Pennsylvania Press, 1985).

46. Quoted in Burt Solomon and Alexis Simendinger, "It's All About the Bounce," *National Journal Convention Review,* July 1, 2000, p. 6.

47. *New Standard,* Aug. 16, 1996, Internet copy.

48. Ibid.

49. Vanishing Voter survey, July 26–30 and Aug. 18–22, 2000.

50. Ratings and viewing hours from Nielsen Media Research.

51. Thomas E. Patterson, "Lessons from the Last Convention," p. 3. Paper presented at Shorenstein Center panel at the the Democratic National Convention, Los Angeles, August 2000.

52. This rough estimate is based on Vanishing Voter surveys. That the size of the inadvertent audience is a function of the hours of broadcast coverage is apparent from the increase in this audience as network convention coverage increases. It might be thought that, as a convention unfolds, inadvertent viewers would decline as a proportion of the total audience because people are more aware that the convention is under way. In fact, however, the inadvertent audience peaked on the fourth, and final, convention night. It was the night when ABC, CBS, and NBC provided the most hours of coverage.

53. Vanishing Voter surveys, Aug. 1–2, 2–6, 15–16, 16–17, 2000.

54. Quoted in Solomon and Simendinger, "It's All About the Bounce," p. 6.

55. Vanishing Voter weekly report, Aug. 30, 2000.

56. Zachary Karabell, "The Rise and Fall of the Televised Political Convention," p. 7. Discussion Paper D-33, Joan Shorenstein Center on the Press, Politics and Public Policy, John F. Kennedy School of Government, Harvard University, October 1998.

57. Vanishing Voter news release, Aug. 11, 2000.

58. See, for example, "Battle of the Sound Bites: Coverage of the 1992 Presidential Election Campaign, *Media Monitor* 6 (August/September 1992).

59. Vanishing Voter weekly report, Aug. 25, 2000.

60. Everett Carll Ladd, *Transformations of the American Party System: Political Coalitions from the New Deal to the 1970s,* 2nd ed. (New York: Norton, 1978), p. 194.

61. Vanishing Voter national surveys, 2000.

62. Vanishing Voter national surveys, Aug. 18–22, Sept. 13–17, 2000.

63. Vanishing Voter national surveys, September 2000.

64. Nielsen Media Research data, for all debate audience references.

65. Paul Taylor, "A Nation of Pundit-Cynics," *Political Standard* 3 (October 2000): 2.

66. See Sidney Kraus, *Televised Presidential Debates and Public Policy*, 2nd ed. (Mahwah, N.J.: Erlbaum, 2000); see also Marion Just, Ann Crigler, and Lori Wallach, "Thirty Seconds or Thirty Minutes," *Journal of Communication* 51 (1990): 120–32.

67. Vanishing Voter national survey, Oct. 18–22, 2000.

68. NBC/*Wall Street Journal* poll, reported on *NBC Nightly News*, Oct. 22, 1992.

69. Vanishing Voter national survey, Oct. 4–8, 11–15, 18–22, 2000.

70. Thomas E. Patterson, *Out of Order: How the Decline of the Political Parties and the Growing Power of the News Media Undermine the American Way of Electing Presidents* (New York: Knopf, 1993), p. 238.

71. Vanishing Voter news release, Oct. 12, 2000.

72. Vanishing Voter national surveys, early to mid October 2000.

73. Average of Vanishing Voter national surveys, Nov. 5 and 7, 2000.

74. Ibid.

75. Ibid.

76. Patterson, *Mass Media Election*, p. 168.

77. Bernard R. Berelson, Paul F. Lazarsfeld, and William McPhee, *Voting: A Study of Opinion Formation in a Presidential Campaign* (Chicago: University of Chicago Press, 1954), p. 227.

78. Vanishing Voter national survey, Nov. 3–7, 2000.

CHAPTER FIVE   ELECTION DAY: THE POLITICS OF INEQUITY

1. Vanishing Voter survey, Nov. 3–7, 2000.

2. Ibid.

3. Vanishing Voter survey, Jan. 17–21, 2001.

4. See, for example, David Gonzalez, "The Race Factor: Blacks, Citing Flaws, Seek Inquiry into Florida Vote," *New York Times*, Nov. 10, 2000, p. A13.

5. Dean Baquet, "Feuds and Favoritism Keep Old Voting Machines in New York," *New York Times*, June 5, 1990, p. B12.

6. Ronnie Dugger, "Annals of Democracy: Counting Votes," *The New Yorker*, Nov. 7, 1988, p. 43.

7. Ibid., p. 104. Quoted in Alexander Heard, *Made in America: Improving the Nomination and Election of Presidents* (New York: HarperCollins, 1991), p. 130.

8. "CBS News Coverage of Election Night 2000: Investigation, Analysis, Recommendations," *CBS News,* January 2001, pp. 16–22.

9. See, for example, Douglas A. Fuchs, "Election-Day Radio-Television and Western Voting," *Public Opinion Quarterly* 30, no. 2 (1966): 226–36; Harold Mendelsohn, "Western Voting and Broadcasts of Results on Presidential Election Day," *Public Opinion Quarterly* 30, no. 2 (1966): 212–25; Seymour Sudman, "Do Exit Polls Influence Voting Behavior?" *Public Opinion Quarterly* 50, no. 3 (1986): 331–39; Michael W. Traugott, "The Impact of Media Polls on the Public," in Thomas E. Mann and Gary R. Orren, eds., *Media Polls in American Politics* (Washington, D.C.: Brookings Institution, 1992), pp. 125–49; and Sam Tuchman and Thomas E. Cronin, "The Influence of Election Night Television Broadcasts in a Close Election," *Public Opinion Quarterly* 35, no. 3 (1971): 315–46.

10. See, for example, Michael X. Delli Carpini, "Scooping the Voters? The Consequences of the Networks' Early Call of the 1980 Presidential Race," *Journal of Politics* 46 (1984): 866–85; John E. Jackson, "Election Night Reporting and Voter Turnout," *American Journal of Political Science* 27, no. 4 (1983): 615–35; and Raymond Wolfinger and Peter Linquiti, "Tuning In and Turning Out," *Public Opinion* 4 (1981): 56–60.

11. Richard A. Brody, "The Puzzle of Participation in America," in Anthony King, ed., *The New American Political System* (Washington, D.C.: American Enterprise Institute, 1978), p. 292.

12. Robert W. Jackson, "Political Institutions and Voter Turnout in the Industrial Democracies," *American Political Science Review* 81 (June 1987): 419.

13. "CBS News Coverage of Election Night 2000," p. 77.

14. In our post-election Vanishing Voter surveys, a small percentage of respondents claimed they tried to vote only to find the polls had closed. Our surveys did not include a question that asked directly whether respondents had not voted because the polls had closed, and we have no reliable way to estimate how many would-be voters did not participate for this reason.

15. Vanishing Voter surveys ending Oct. 29, Oct. 31, Nov. 5, and Nov. 7, 2000.

16. Federal Election Commission, "The Impact of the National Voter Registration Act of 1993," Washington, D.C., 2001, p. 1.

17. Stephen Knack, "Does 'Motor Voter' Work? Evidence from State-Level Data," *Journal of Politics* 57 (1995): 796–811; Michael D. Martinez and David Hill, "Did Motor Voter Work?" *American Politics Quarterly* 27, no. 3 (1999): 296–315.

18. Raymond E. Wolfinger and Jonathan Hoffman, "Registering and Voting

with Moter Voter," *PS: Political Science and Politics* 34 (March 2001): 85–90.

19. Through 1984 the decrease from 1960 was 13 percentage points. Turnout fell in 1988 despite registration drives by both parties, making it likely that the 15 point threshold was exceeded. See Heard, *Made in America,* p. 118.

20. U.S. Census Bureau, *Current Population Reports,* March 2000 Mobility Survey, Table 1.

21. Steven J. Rosenstone and John Mark Hansen, *Mobilization, Participation, and Democracy in America* (New York: Macmillan, 1993), p. 207; Stanley Kelley, Jr., Richard E. Ayres, and William G. Bown, "Registration and Voting: Putting First Things First," *American Political Science Review* 61 (June 1967): 359–79; Steven J. Rosenstone and Raymond E. Wolfinger, "The Effect of Registration Laws on Voter Turnout," *American Political Science Review* 72 (March 1978): 22–45.

22. Rosenstone and Hansen, *Mobilization,* pp. 207–208.

23. Percentage calculated from Federal Election Commission data.

24. Rosenstone and Hansen, *Mobilization,* p. 209; Ruy A. Teixeira, *The Disappearing American Voter* (Washington, D.C.: Brookings Institution, 1992), p. 113.

25. Mark J. Fenster, "The Impact of Allowing Day of Registration Voting on Turnout in the United States from 1960 to 1992," *American Politics Quarterly* 22 (1994): 74–87.

26. Vanishing Voter survey, Nov. 3–7, 2000.

27. Benjamin Ginsberg, *The Consequences of Consent* (New York: Random House, 1982), p. 49.

28. Paul Kleppner, *Who Voted?: The Dynamics of Electoral Turnout, 1870–1980* (New York: Praeger, 1982), pp. 158–59.

29. Cited in Frances Fox Piven and Richard A. Cloward, *Why Americans Still Don't Vote: And Why Politicians Want It That Way* (Boston: Beacon, 2000), p. 252.

30. Report of the Task Force on Campaign Reform, "Campaign Reform," in Larry M. Bartels and Lynn Vavreck, eds., *Campaign Reform: Insights and Evidence* (Ann Arbor: University of Michigan Press, 2000), p. 237; Brent Thompson, "The Motor Voter Boondoggle," *Washington Times,* Nov. 18, 1996.

31. Other liberalized voting efforts of recent years do not appear to have a substantial partisan bias and the proposed initiatives do not have features that would suggest they would be different in this respect. See

Report of the Task Force on Campaign Reform, "Campaign Reform," p. 238; Robert M. Stein, "Early Voting," *Public Opinion Quarterly* 62 (1998): 57–69.

32. Craig Leonard Brians and Bernard Grofman, "When Registration Barriers Fall, Who Votes?: An Empirical Test of a Rational Choice Model," *Public Choice* 21 (1999): 161–76.

33. Committee for the Study of the American Electorate report, Aug. 30, 2001.

34. Rosenstone and Hansen, *Mobilization,* p. 183.

35. See Richard W. Boyd, "Decline of U.S. Voter Turnout: Structural Explanations," *American Politics Quarterly* 9 (April 1981): 141–46.

36. Rosenstone and Hansen, *Mobilization,* pp. 183–84.

37. Malcolm Jewell and David Olson, *American State Politics and Elections* (Homewood, Ill.: Irwin Press, 1978), p. 50.

38. Pippa Norris, *Count Every Voice: Democratic Participation Worldwide* (New York: Cambridge University Press, 2002), ch. 4; see also Anthony King, *Running Scared* (New York: Free Press, 1997), p. 157.

39. Kenneth C. Davis, *Don't Know Much About History* (New York: Avon, 1995), p. 424.

40. Vote margins from Federal Election Commission, *2000 Presidential Election and Popular Vote,* Web download, December 2000.

41. Quoted in Burt Solomon, "What Were They Thinking?" *National Journal,* Nov. 18, 2000, p. 3665.

42. Kathleen A. Francovic and Monika L. McDermott, "Public Opinion in the 2000 Election: The Ambivalent Electorate," in Gerald M. Pomper et al., *The Election of 2000* (New York: Chatham House, 2001), p. 91.

43. Wilson Carey McWilliams, "The Meaning of the Election," in Pomper et al., *The Election of 2000,* p. 178. See also "The Case for the Electoral College," *New York Times* editorial, Dec. 13, 2000, p. A34.

44. Statement of Betsy Cain, President of the League of Women Voters, House Committee on Judiciary, Sept. 4, 1997.

45. *New York Times* editorial, Dec. 12, 2000, Web download.

46. Peter Marks, "TV Spots Are Concentrated in Bush-Gore Battlegrounds," *New York Times,* Sept. 19, 2000, Web story.

47. Peter Marks, "The Forgotten State: Dearth of Ads Makes Race in Kansas a Snooze," *New York Times,* Oct. 27, 2000, p. A26.

48. The thirty stories estimate is a conservative calculation based on data of Project for Excellence in Journalism and the Center for Media and Public Affairs.

49. Quoted in Marks, "Forgotten State," p. A26. See also Thomas E. Patterson and Robert D. McClure, *The Unseeing Eye: The Myth of Television Power in National Elections* (New York: Putnam, 1976), pp. 109–22.

50. Quoted in Marks, "Forgotten State," p. A26.

51. Quoted in Lewis Chester, Godfrey Hodgson, and Bruce Page, *An American Melodrama: The Presidential Campaign of 1968* (New York: Viking, 1969), p. 620. Cited in Joseph A. Pika and Richard A. Watson, *The Presidential Contest*, 5th ed. (Washington, D.C.: Congressional Quarterly Press, 1996), p. 80.

52. Pika and Watson, *Presidential Contest*, p. 81.

53. F. Christopher Arterton, "Campaign '92: Strategies and Tactics of the Candidates," in Gerald M. Pomper, *The Election of 1992: Reports and Interpretations* (Chatham, N.J.: Chatham House, 1993), p. 87. Example taken from Pika and Watson, *Presidential Contest*, pp. 81–82.

54. Committee for the Study of the American Electorate report, Aug. 30, 2001.

55. Data gathered by the Vanishing Voter Project.

56. Vanishing Voter national survey, Oct. 4–8, 11–15, 18–22, 25–29 and Nov. 1–5, 2000.

57. Quoted in Marks, "Forgotten State," p. A26. See also Darrell M. West, *Air Wars: Television Advertising in Election Campaigns*, 3rd ed. (Washington, D.C.: Congressional Quarterly Press, 2002).

58. About a third of nonvoters have a college degree or have spent time in college. For the analysis here, we use college and noncollege experience to define high potential voters and low potential voters, respectively.

59. Vanishing Voter survey data, multiple surveys.

60. Heard, *Made in America*, p. 117.

CHAPTER SIX

A MODEL CAMPAIGN: THE POLITICS OF PARTICIPATION

1. Vanishing Voter survey, Nov. 10–14, 2000.

2. Vanishing Voter survey, Jan. 17–21, 2001.

3. Ibid.

4. See William Crotty, *Political Reform and the American Experiment* (New York: Crowell, 1977), p. x.

5. Everett Carll Ladd, "Party Reform and the Public Interest," *Political Science Quarterly* 102 (Fall 1987): 355–70.

6. At the time of the McGovern-Fraser reform, seventeen states held primaries but not all of them were in play each election. It was fairly common for a prominent politician in a state to run for president as its "favorite son" as a means of gaining control of his party's delegation and of having his name entered into nomination. These candidates were not regarded as serious presidential contenders but typically won the primary, in part because serious contenders were reluctant to run against them.

7. James R. Benninger, "Winning the Presidential Nomination: National Polls and State Primary Elections, 1936–1972," *Public Opinion Quarterly* 40 (Spring 1976): 25.

8. Quoted in "Can We Make It a Better Race Next Time?" *New York Newsday*, Nov. 3, 1992, p. 73.

9. "Beyond 2000 Hearing," hearing of the Democratic National Committee Rules and Bylaws Committee, Washington, D.C., Nov. 20, 1999, p. 100.

10. "Beyond 2000 Hearing," hearing of the Democratic National Committee Rules and Bylaws Committee, Louisville, Jan. 22, 2000, p. 47.

11. Quoted in "RNC Primary Commission Recommends Changes to Enhance Voter Participation in Presidential Nominating System," Republican National Committee news release, May 2, 2000.

12. Austin Ranney, *Channels of Power* (New York: Basic Books, 1983), p. 93.

13. These results were related to the author by one of the designers of the poll, which was conducted for a leading newspaper. The results were not published, ostensibly on the grounds they were too complicated to explain. A survey I conducted earlier in the 1976 campaign measured candidate support differently, but provides evidence of the same phenomena.

14. Vanishing Voter weekly report, July 2000.

15. "Beyond 2000 Hearing," Nov. 20, 1999, p. 13.

16. Kathleen Hall Jamieson, quoted in "Heavy Campaigning Leads to Better Informed Citizens," *The Political Standard* (Newsletter of the Alliance for Better Campaigns), April 2000, p. 6; see also Scott Keeter and Cliff Zukin, *Uninformed Choice: The Failure of the New Presidential Nominating System* (New York: Praeger, 1983), pp. 161–64; Larry M. Bartels, *Presidential Primaries and the Dynamics of Public Choice* (Princeton, N.J.: Princeton University Press, 1988), p. 289.

17. Testimony of Ronald B. Rapoport and Walter J. Stone, hearing of the Advisory Commission on the Presidential Nominating Process for the 1996 Election, Nov. 18, 1999; Center for the Study of the American Electorate for the 2000 election.

18. Gallup poll, Feb. 9–14, 1952.
19. Harris poll, May 9–10, 1972.
20. Thomas E. Patterson, "Public Involvement and the 2000 Nominating Campaign." Paper presented at Vanishing Voter Project Conference, Washington, D.C., April 27, 2000.
21. William G. Mayer, "Perspectives on the Current Presidential Election System," in Advisory Commission on the Presidential Nominating Process (a.k.a. Brock Commission), *Nominating Future Presidents* (Washington, D.C.: Republican National Committee, 2000), p. 114.
22. James L. Lengle and Byron Shafer, "Primary Rules, Political Power and Social Change," *American Political Science Review* 70, no. 1 (March 1976): 290.
23. Cited in James S. Fishkin, "Reforming the Invisible Primary: Thoughts on Presidential Selection and Media Coverage," p. 4. Paper delivered at the Mass Media and Electoral Process Conference, Princeton University, April 30–May 1, 1992.
24. Neither the GOP's Brock Commission nor the Democrats' Rules and Bylaws Committee gave serious consideration to a national primary.
25. Some proponents say a national primary should be preceded by a party convention. Its purpose would be to issue a statement of principles (not a full platform) and to endorse (not nominate) a presidential candidate. A similar arrangement is in effect for statewide offices in several states, including New York and Colorado. The endorsed candidate would have the party's support and imprimatur in the national primary. Any candidate who received a specified percentage (say, 25 percent) of the convention votes or who gathered enough petitions nationwide could challenge in the primary. A challenge would not always materialize, but the possibility would encourage convention delegates to pay attention to public opinion. A pre-primary convention would reestablish the party as the main force in nominating politics. Presidential hopefuls would have to court party chairs, governors, members of Congress, and other party leaders. For voters, a pre-primary convention would serve as the triggering event that pulled them into the campaign in advance of the national primary. Nevertheless, a pre-primary convention has little support within the parties. It strikes many leaders as elitist and cumbersome. Cost is also an issue. State parties struggle to raise the money to send their delegations to one national convention, much less two. As a Democratic Party official said during the 2000 hearings on the nominating process: "I find it hard to believe that we're going to move away from reliance on voters making the selections in primaries and having an

advance process by the party, which would be tantamount to a second convention."

26. California Secretary of State Bill Jones, quoted in *The Political Standard,* March 1999, Internet copy.

27. Alexander Heard, *Made in America: Improving the Nomination and Election of Presidents* (New York: HarperCollins, 1991), p. 46.

28. NBC's Tom Brokaw and others have proposed a thoughtful alternative to the traditional regional formulation. Noting that the major political divide in the United States tends to be along North-South lines, they suggest dividing the states into regions according to the country's four major time zones. Northern and southern states would be together in regions. Although this arrangement seems clearly better than the traditional formulation, it has not attracted much support.

29. A study by researchers at the Annenberg School for Communication found that the amount of campaigning in a state has a measurable effect on what people learn; in 2000, residents of Super Tuesday states were significantly less informed than residents of Iowa, New Hampshire, South Carolina, and Michigan, where the candidates campaigned more heavily. In a regional system, candidates would have to spread their efforts across a dozen states at once, making it unlikely that residents of a state would acquire significant amounts of information. See David Dutwin, "Knowledge in the 2000 Primary Elections," *ANNALS* 572 (November 2000): 17–25.

30. Brock Commission, *Nominating Future Presidents,* p. 38.

31. The Brock Commission divided 36–13 in its support for the population-based plan. Most of the opposition came from the large-state delegates, who intended to block the plan when it came up for a vote at the GOP convention (a reason Bush withdrew it).

32. Size would not be the only factor in play in a population-based system. There is no southern state among the dozen least populous states. If the parties at some point should decide to adopt the population-based system, it might make sense to include a regional factor in the selection of the states for each pod. The three least populous states from each of the four regions, for example, could be placed in the first pod.

33. Linda Fowler, Constantine Spiliotes, and Lynn Vavreck, "The Role of Issue Advocacy Groups in the New Hampshire Primary," Dartmouth College, Web download, November 2000. McCain's spending includes $941,207 in TV/radio ad buys in New Hampshire, Vermont, and Massachusetts.

34. Brock Commission, *Nominating Future Presidents,* p. 38.

35. Martin Plissner, "Twilight of the Pods: Is a National Primary Inevitable?" Unpublished paper, May 1999.

36. The parties could even decide to go their separate ways and select different states for the opening positions, which would mean that all states would hold at least one party's primary on Ultimate Tuesday. In general, however, the parties have tried to coordinate their choices. Because of the high cost of conducting a statewide election, legislatures are reluctant to schedule the Democratic and Republican primaries on different days, although they might make an exception for a primary that, as in this case, would put them in the national spotlight. The parties, too, usually prefer same-day primaries; if theirs is the second one, they are at a disadvantage in competing for the support of uncommitted voters.

37. Although audience ratings for primary debates are generally low, they are much higher in states that are about to hold a primary or caucus. In 2000, for example, ratings in New Hampshire and Iowa were about five times higher than in other states. In 1992, a nationally televised debate before Georgia's primary attracted 10 percent of Georgia households compared with about 2 percent of households nationwide.

38. See, for example, the testimony of Senator Carl Levin in "Beyond 2000 Hearing," Nov. 20, 1999, pp. 25–35.

39. See the testimony of Terry Michael at the hearing of the DNC Rules and Bylaws Committee, Nov. 20, 1999.

40. Mayer, "Perspectives," p. 114.

41. See Ronald B. Rapoport and Walter J. Stone's memo in *Nominating Future Presidents*, p. 139.

42. Walter J. Stone, Lonna Rae Atkeson, and Ronald B. Rapoport, "Turning On or Turning Off? Mobilization and Demobilization Effects of Participation in Presidential Nominating Campaigns," *American Journal of Political Science* 36 (August 1992): 665–91.

43. Walter J. Stone and Ronald B. Rapoport, "Candidate Perception Among Nomination Activists: A New Look at the Moderation Hypothesis," *Journal of Politics* 56 (November 1994): 1034–52; Gregory S. Pastor, Walter J. Stone, and Ronald B. Rapoport, "Candidate-Centered Sources of Party Change: The Case of Pat Robertson, 1988," *Journal of Politics* 61 (May 1999): 423–44.

44. Rapoport and Stone, in Brock Commission, *Nominating Future Presidents*, p. 146.

45. *Cincinnati Post* editorial, Nov. 28, 2001.

46. See, for example, Thomas E. Patterson and Robert D. McClure, *The*

Unseeing Eye: The Myth of Television Power in National Elections (New York: Putnam, 1976); Thomas E. Patterson, *The Mass Media Election: How Americans Choose Their President* (New York: Praeger, 1980).

47. Bruce Buchanan, "Regime Support and Campaign Reform," in Larry M. Bartels and Lynn Vavreck, eds., *Campaign Reform: Insights and Evidence* (Ann Arbor: University of Michigan Press, 2000), p. 187; for a general look at voter incentives, see, for example, Anthony Downs, *An Economic Theory of Democracy* (New York: Harper & Row, 1957).

48. See Lynn Vavreck, "How Does It All 'Turnout'?: Exposure to Attack Ads, Campaign Interest, and Participation in American Presidential Elections," in Bartels and Vavreck, eds., *Campaign Reform*, p. 178.

49. Quoted in Kristi Andersen and Stuart J. Thorson, "Public Discourse or Strategic Game?: Changes in Our Conception of Elections," *Studies in American Political Development* 3 (1980): 264.

50. Commission on Presidential Debates data.

51. See Sidney Kraus, *Televised Presidential Debates and Public Policy,* 2nd ed. (Mahwah, N.J.: Erlbaum, 2000).

52. Vanishing Voter national surveys. In the week just before their state's primary, respondents were asked when it would be held—in a week, a few weeks, more than a month, or whether they weren't sure.

53. Quoted in Kathy Kiely, "Wealth of Debates Keeps the Hopefuls Talking," *USA Today,* Jan. 26, 2000, p. 8A.

54. See, for example, Susan A. Hellweg, Michael Pfau, and Steven R. Brydon, *Televised Presidential Debates: Advocacy in Contemporary America* (New York: Praeger, 1992), p. 123; Myles Martel, *Political Campaign Debates: Images, Strategies, and Tactics* (New York: Longman, 1983), p. 52; Gary Orren, "The Nomination Process: Vicissitudes of Candidate Selection," in Michael Nelson, ed., *The Elections of 1984* (Washington, D.C.: Congressional Quarterly Press, 1985), p. 54; Michael Pfau, "The Influence of Intraparty Political Debates on Candidate Performance," *Communication Research* 14 (1987): 687–97.

55. Quoted in Kiely, "Wealth of Debates," p. 8A.

56. The average prime-time broadcast program draws about 10 million viewers. There is good reason to think that a debate held when the primaries are under way would draw an audience of that size. The audiences for the *Nightline* and *Meet the Press* debates were above average for their time slots. (Two of the cable debates produced the highest ratings ever for their cable networks, MSNBC and Fox.) If there had been six debates on broadcast television, and each had an average audience for a prime-time slot, 60 million viewers would have tuned in.

57. Nielsen Media Research figures indicate a combined total of about 27 million viewers for the 2000 primary debates on cable.

58. The October debates are organized by the Commission on Presidential Debates, which selects the sites, arranges the staging, screens the moderators, and determines who will be allowed to participate. No commission oversees the primary debates and, given the fluid nature of the nominating process, such a commission might simply impede debate scheduling. Nevertheless, the production quality of many primary debates makes them unappealing to viewers. Moreover, the hasty scheduling of many of these debates precludes a press buildup that would attract additional viewers. Unlike the October debates, which get a huge buildup, some of the primary debates get so little advance coverage that the large majority of Americans have no idea they are being held.

59. Cited in Fishkin, "Reforming the Invisible Primary," p. 49.

60. Quoted in "Election Coverage 2000," Project for Excellence in Journalism, June 5, 2001, Web release.

61. Heard, *Made in America*, p. 56.

62. Bartels and Vavreck, *Campaign Reform*, pp. 131–33.

63. The candidates' acceptance speeches are the top-ranked feature.

64. Thomas E. Patterson, "Lessons from the Last Convention." Paper presented at the Shorenstein Center panel at the Democratic National Convention, Los Angeles, Aug. 13, 2000.

65. Nielsen Media Research data.

66. "Beyond 2000 Hearing," Jan. 22, 2000, p. 47.

67. Heard, *Made in America*, p. 157.

68. This evidence is described and cited in Chapter 5.

69. See Zachary Karabell, "The Rise and Fall of the Televised Political Convention," Discussion Paper D-33, Joan Shorenstein Center on the Press, Politics and Public Policy, John F. Kennedy School of Government, Harvard University, October 1998.

70. Bartels and Vavreck, *Campaign Reform*, p. 136.

71. Thomas E. Patterson, "Is There a Future for the On-the-Air Televised Conventions?" Paper presented at the Shorenstein Center panel at the Republican National Convention, Philadelphia, July 30, 2000, p. 5.

72. Daniel Schorr, "Televised Debates Magnify the Trivial," *Political Standard*, Alliance for Better Campaigns newsletter, October 2000, p. 3.

73. Bartels and Vavreck, *Campaign Reform*, p. 219.

74. The Vanishing Voter surveys indicate that information levels were basically flat from week to week during most weeks of the 2000 campaign

and even declined in some weeks. However, these levels rose significantly during the debate weeks.

75. Report of the Twentieth Century Fund Task Force on Presidential Debates, *Let America Decide* (New York, 1995), p. 117.

76. Commission on Presidential Debates, *Review of 1992 Presidential Debates* (Washington, D.C., May 4, 1993), pp. 21–36; see also James B. Lemert et al., *News Verdicts, the Debates, and Presidential Campaigns* (New York: Praeger, 1991), pp. 257–58.

77. *Let America Decide*, p. 74.

78. Ibid, p. 95.

79. See Kraus, *Televised Presidential Debates and Public Policy*, p. 282; *Let America Decide*, p. 145.

80. Quoted in *Let America Decide*, p. 140.

81. For example, two such bills were introduced in Congress in 1993 but neither was brought to the floor for a vote. More than a score of such bills have been introduced during the past two decades.

82. Buchanan, "Regime Support," p. 189.

83. See testimony by Frank Fahrenkopf and Diana Carlin in hearings before the Subcommittee on Elections, U.S. House of Representatives, Committee on House Administration, June 17, 1993, 103rd Congress, 1st session.

84. *Let America Decide*, pp. 149–51; Bartels and Vavreck, *Campaign Reform*, p. 221.

85. Bartels and Vavreck, *Campaign Reform*, pp. 220–21.

86. See Bruce Buchanan, *Electing a President: The Markle Commission Research on Campaign '88* (Austin: University of Texas Press, 1991), p. 166.

87. John Ellis, "Nine Sundays: A Proposal for Better Presidential Campaign Coverage." Report of the Joan Shorenstein Center on the Press, Politics and Public Policy, John F. Kennedy School of Government, Harvard University, 1991.

88. Buchanan, "Regime Support," p. 187.

89. Annenberg Public Policy Center, *Free Air Time and Campaign Reform* (Philadelphia: University of Pennsylvania, 1997).

90. Quoted in Kiely, "Wealth of Debates," p. 8A.

91. Jim Rutenberg, "Cable Networks Look for Ways to Stand Out," *New York Times*, Aug. 20, 2001, p. 9.

92. See Bartels and Vavreck, *Campaign Reform*, p. 224.

93. Analysis by Thomas Wolzein of the investment house Sanford C. Bernstein, reported at a National Association of Broadcasters meeting. Cited in *The Political Standard* 4 (May 2001): 4.

94. "McCain, Coalition Leaders Criticize Broadcast Industry," *The Political Standard* 3 (September 2000): 2.

95. "Searching for Political News and Finding Political Ads," *The Political Standard* 4 (November/December 2001): 10.

96. According to the Caltech/MIT Voter Technology Project, which examined balloting in the 2000 presidential election, roughly 1.5 to 2 million votes were lost because of faulty equipment and confusing ballots, another 1.5 to 3 million were lost because of registration mix-ups, and up to 1 million were lost because of polling place operations.

97. *Executive Report of the National Commission on Federal Election Reform*, August 2001, p. 5.

98. See, for example, Douglas A. Fuchs, "Election-Day Radio-Television and Western Voting," *Public Opinion Quarterly* 30, no. 2 (1966): 226–36; Harold Mendelsohn, "Western Voting and Broadcasts of Results on Presidential Election Day," *Public Opinion Quarterly* 30, no. 2 (1966): 212–25; Seymour Sudman, "Do Exit Polls Influence Voting Behavior?" *Public Opinion Quarterly* 50, no. 3 (1986): 331–39; Michael W. Traugott, "The Impact of Media Polls on the Public," in Thomas E. Mann and Gary R. Orren, eds., *Media Polls in American Politics* (Washington, D.C.: Brookings Institution, 1992): pp. 125–49; Sam Tuchman and Thomas E. Cronin, "The Influence of Election Night Television Broadcasts in a Close Election," *Public Opinion Quarterly* 35, no. 3 (1971): 315–46; Michael X. Delli Carpini, "Scooping the Voters? The Consequences of the Networks' Early Call of the 1980 Presidential Race," *Journal of Politics* 46 (1984): 866–85; John E. Jackson, "Election Night Reporting and Voter Turnout," *American Journal of Political Science* 27, no. 4 (1983): 615–35; and Raymond Wolfinger and Peter Linquiti, "Tuning In and Turning Out," *Public Opinion* 4 (1981): 56–60.

99. Vanishing Voter national survey, Nov. 8–12, 2000.

100. Residential mobility is one of the major barriers to voting. See Steven J. Rosenstone and John Mark Hansen, *Mobilization, Participation, and Democracy in America* (New York: Macmillan, 1993), p. 157; Peverill Squire, Raymond E. Wolfinger, and David P. Glass, "Residential Mobility and Voter Turnout," *American Political Science Review* 81 (March 1987): 45–65.

101. Although automatic registration of the European type would be the easiest solution, personal registration is an American tradition that lawmakers are determined to keep. According to our Vanishing Voter survey, by three to two, respondents said they prefer a personal registration system.

102. See Ruy A. Teixeira, *The Disappearing American Voter* (Washington, D.C.: Brookings Institution, 1992), p. 113. His analysis suggests 60 percent of new voters would be attributable to Election Day registration. Although Teixeira's analysis was conducted before enactment of the Motor Voter Act, its logic suggests the percentage would be even higher today. See also Rosenstone and Hansen, *Mobilization,* pp. 207–209; Frances Fox Piven and Richard A. Cloward, *Why Americans Still Don't Vote: And Why Politicians Want It That Way* (Boston: Beacon, 2000), p. 207.

103. Committee for the Study of the American Electorate data.

104. Quoted in Norman J. Ornstein, "The Dangers of Voting Outside the Booth," *New York Times,* Aug. 3, 2001, p. A23.

105. Quoted in The Center for Voting and Democracy Web release, Nov. 14, 2001.

106. Report of the Task Force on Campaign Reform, "Campaign Reform," in Bartels and Vavreck, *Campaign Reform,* p. 237.

107. National Commission on Federal Election Reform, *To Assure Pride and Confidence in the Electoral Process* (Charlottesville: Miller Center for Public Affairs, University of Virginia, 2001), p. 6.

108. Vanishing Voter national survey.

109. National Commission on Federal Election Reform, *To Assure Pride and Confidence in the Electoral Process,* p. 7.

110. Vanishing Voter national survey, Jan. 17–21, 2001.

111. Vanishing Voter survey data.

112. See Warren E. Miller and J. Merrill Shanks, *The New American Voter* (Cambridge, Mass.: Harvard University Press, 1996).

113. Lynn Vavreck, "How Does It All 'Turnout'?" in Bartels and Vavreck, *Campaign Reform,* p. 81.

114. Buchanan, "Regime Support," p. 188.

115. Sue Kirchhoff et al., "Power in the Balance," *Boston Globe,* March 4, 2002, p. D1.

116. John Zaller, "Let's Make Politics Fun Again." Paper presented at a Princeton University conference on campaign reform, 1998.

117. Howard L. Reiter, *Selecting the President: The Nominating Process in Transition* (Philadelphia: University of Pennsylvania Press, 1985), p. 142.

118. Austin Ranney, "Changing the Rules of the Nominating Game," in James David Barber, ed., *Choosing the President* (Englewood Cliffs, N.J.: Prentice-Hall, 1974), p. 74.

119. Arthur M. Schlesinger and Erik McKinley Eriksson, "The Vanishing Voter," *The New Republic,* Oct. 15, 1924, p. 147. The rest of this paragraph

and the book's final sentence are indebted to the final paragraph of their article, even to the choice of the phrasing and some of the words in the final sentence.

120. Based on remarks of Robert Putnam and Theda Skocpol, Harvard University roundtable, Feb. 20, 2001.

121. Harwood Institute/Gallup survey, Jan. 4–20, 2002.

Bibliography

Adatto, Kiku. "Sound Bite Democracy: Network Evening News Presidential Campaign Coverage, 1968 and 1988." Research Paper R-25 Joan Shorenstein Center on the Press, Politics and Public Policy, John F. Kennedy School of Government, Harvard University, June 1990.

Aldrich, John H. *Before the Convention: Strategies and Choices in Presidential Nomination Campaigns.* Chicago: University of Chicago Press, 1980.

———. *Why Parties?: The Origin and Transformation of Party Politics in America.* Chicago: University of Chicago Press, 1995.

Ansolabehere, Stephen, Roy Behr, and Shanto Iyengar. *The Media Game: American Politics in the Television Age.* New York: Macmillan, 1992.

Arterton, F. Christopher. "Campaign Organizations Confront the Media-Political Environment." In James David Barber, ed., *Race for the Presidency.* Englewood Cliffs, N.J.: Prentice-Hall, 1978.

Barber, James David. *The Pulse of Politics.* New York: Norton, 1980.

———, ed. *Race for the Presidency: The Media and the Nominating Process.* Englewood Cliffs, N.J.: Prentice-Hall, 1978.

Barnhurst, Kevin G., and John Nerone. *The Form of News: A History.* New York: Guilford Press, 2001.

Bartels, Larry M. *Presidential Primaries and the Dynamics of Public Choice.* Princeton, N.J.: Princeton University Press, 1988.

———, and Lynn Vavreck, eds. *Campaign Reform: Insights and Evidence.* Ann Arbor: University of Michigan Press, 2000.

Bennett, Lance. *News: The Politics of Illusion.* New York: Longman, 1996.

Berelson, Bernard R., Paul F. Lazarsfeld, and William McPhee. *Voting: A Study of Opinion Formation in a Presidential Campaign.* Chicago: University of Chicago Press, 1954.

Bradlee, Ben. *A Good Life: Newspapering and Other Adventures.* New York: Simon & Schuster, 1995.

Broder, David. *The Party's Over: The Failure of Politics in America.* New York: Harper & Row, 1972.

Broh, C. Anthony. "Horse-race Journalism: Reporting the Polls in the 1976 Elections." *Public Opinion Quarterly* 44 (1980): 514–29.

Buchanan, Bruce. *Electing a President: The Markle Commission Research on Campaign '88.* Austin: University of Texas Press, 1991.

Burnham, Walter Dean. *Critical Elections and the Mainsprings of American Politics.* New York: Norton, 1970.

———. *The Current Crisis in American Politics.* New York: Oxford University Press, 1982.

Campbell, Angus, et al. *The American Voter.* New York: Wiley, 1960.

Cappella, Joseph N., and Kathleen Hall Jamieson. *Spiral of Cynicism.* New York: Oxford University Press, 1997.

Carmines, Edward G., and James A. Stimson. *Issue Evolution: Race and the Transformation of American Politics.* Princeton, N.J.: Princeton University Press, 1989.

Ceaser, James W. *Reforming the Reforms.* Cambridge, Mass.: Ballinger, 1982.

Commission on Party Structure and Delegate Selection. *Mandate for Reform.* Washington, D.C.: Democratic National Committee, 1970.

Crouse, Timothy. *The Boys on the Bus.* New York: Ballantine, 1974.

Delli Carpini, Michael X., and Scott Keeter. *What Americans Know About Politics and Why It Matters.* New Haven, Conn.: Yale University Press, 1996.

Dionne, E. J., Jr. *Why Americans Hate Politics.* New York: Simon & Schuster, 1991.

Doppelt, Jack C., and Ellen Shearer. *Nonvoters: America's No-Shows.* Thousand Oaks, Calif.: Sage, 1999.

Downie, Leonard, Jr., and Robert G. Kaiser. *The News About the News: American Journalism in Peril.* New York: Knopf, 2002.

Edelman, Murray. *Constructing the Political Spectacle.* Chicago: University of Chicago Press, 1988.

Edsall, Thomas Byrne, and Mary D. Edsall. *Chain Reaction: The Impact of Race, Rights, and Taxes on American Politics.* New York: Norton, 1991.

Efron, Edith. *The News Twisters.* Los Angeles: Nash, 1971.

Entman, Robert M. *Democracy Without Citizens: Media and the Decay of American Politics.* New York: Oxford University Press, 1989.

Epstein, Edward Jay. *News from Nowhere: Television and the News.* New York: Random House, 1973.

Fallows, James. *Breaking the News: How the Media Undermine American Democracy*. New York: Pantheon, 1996.

Gergen, David. *Eyewitness to Power: The Essence of Leadership, Nixon to Clinton*. New York: Simon & Schuster, 2000.

Graber, Doris A. *Processing the News: How People Tame the Information Tide*. New York: Longman, 1984.

Hallin, Daniel. "Sound Bite News: Television Coverage of Elections, 1968–1988." Occasional Paper, Media Studies Project, Woodrow Wilson International Center for Scholars, Washington, D.C., 1990.

Hart, Roderick. *Campaign Talk: Why Elections Are Good for Us*. Princeton, N.J.: Princeton University Press, 2000.

———. *Seducing America*. New York: Oxford University Press, 1994.

Heard, Alexander. *Made in America: Improving the Nomination and Election of Presidents*. New York: HarperCollins, 1991.

Hess, Stephen. *The Presidential Campaign*, rev. ed. Washington, D.C.: Brookings Institution, 1978.

Holbrook, Thomas. *Do Campaigns Matter?* Thousand Oaks, Calif.: Sage, 1996.

Iyengar, Shanto. *Is Anyone Responsible?: How Television Frames Political Issues*. Chicago: University of Chicago Press, 1991.

———, and Stephen Ansolabehere. *Going Negative: How Attack Ads Shrink and Polarize the Electorate*. New York: Free Press, 1995.

———, and Donald R. Kinder. *News That Matters: Television and American Opinion*. Chicago: University of Chicago Press, 1987.

Jamieson, Kathleen Hall. *Dirty Politics*. New York: Oxford University Press, 1992.

———. *Packaging the Presidency: A History and Criticism of Presidential Campaign Advertising*, 2nd ed. New York: Oxford University Press, 1992.

———, and David S. Birdsell. *Presidential Debates: The Challenge of Creating an Informed Electorate*. New York: Oxford University Press, 1988.

Just, Marion R., et al. *Crosstalk: Citizens, Candidates, and Media in a Presidential Campaign*. Chicago: University of Chicago Press, 1996.

Keech, William R., and Donald R. Matthews. *The Party's Choice:* Washington, D.C.: Brookings Institution, 1976.

Keeter, Scott, and Cliff Zukin. *Uninformed Choice: The Failure of the New Presidential Nominating System*. New York: Praeger, 1983.

Kerbel, Matthew Robert. *Edited for Television: CNN, ABC, and the American Presidential Campaign*. Boulder, Colo.: Westview Press, 1998.

Kernell, Samuel. *Going Public: New Strategies of Presidential Leadership*. Washington, D.C.: Congressional Quarterly Press, 1986.

Kessel, John H. *Presidential Campaign Politics: Coalition Strategies and Citizen Response*. Chicago: Dorsey, 1988.

Key, V. O., Jr. *The Responsible Electorate: Rationality in Presidential Voting, 1936–1960*. Cambridge, Mass.: Belknap Press of Harvard University Press, 1966.

Keyssar, Alexander. *The Right to Vote: The Contested History of Democracy in the United States*. New York: Basic Books, 2000.

Kirkpatrick, Jeane J., et al. *The Presidential Nominating Process: Can It Be Improved?* Washington, D.C.: American Enterprise Institute, 1980.

Kleppner, Paul. *Who Voted?: The Dynamics of Electoral Turnout, 1870–1980*. New York: Praeger, 1982.

Kovach, Bill, and Tom Rosenstiel. *The Elements of Journalism: What Newspeople Should Know and the Public Should Expect*. New York: Crown, 2001.

Kraus, Sidney. *Televised Presidential Debates and Public Policy*, 2nd ed. Mahwah, N.J.: Erlbaum, 2000.

Kurtz, Howard. *Spin Cycle: Inside the Clinton Propaganda Machine*. New York: Free Press, 1998.

Ladd, Everett Carll. *Transformations of the American Party System: Political Coalitions from the New Deal to the 1970s*, 2nd ed. New York: Norton, 1978.

———. *Where Have All the Voters Gone?* New York: Norton, 1978.

Lazarsfeld, Paul, Bernard Berelson, and Hazel Gaudet. *The People's Choice*. New York: Columbia University Press, 1968. Published originally in 1944.

Lichter, S. Robert, David Murray, and Joel Schwartz. *It Ain't Necessarily So: How Media Make and Unmake the Scientific Picture of Reality*. Lanham, Md.: Rowman & Littlefield, 2001.

Lippmann, Walter. *Public Opinion*. New York: Free Press, 1965. Originally published in 1922.

Mayer, William G. *In Pursuit of the White House 2000*. New York: Chatham House, 2000.

McChesney, Robert W. *Capitalism and the New Information Age*. New York: Monthly Review Press, 1997.

McCubbins, Mathew D., et al. *Under the Watchful Eye: Managing Presidential Campaigns in the Television Age*. Washington, D.C.: Congressional Quarterly Press, 1992.

McGinnis, Joe. *The Selling of the President 1968*. New York: Trident, 1969.

Miller, Warren E., and J. Merrill Shanks. *The New American Voter*. Cambridge, Mass.: Harvard University Press, 1996.

Minow, Newton N., and Clifford M. Sloan. *For Great Debates: A New Plan for Future Presidential Television Debates*. New York: Priority Press, 1987.

Neuman, W. Russell. *The Paradox of Mass Politics: Knowledge and Opinion in the American Electorate.* Cambridge, Mass.: Harvard University Press, 1986.

———, Marion R. Just, and Ann Crigler. *Common Knowledge: News and the Construction of Meaning.* Chicago: University of Chicago Press, 1992.

Nie, Norman H., Sidney Verba, and John R. Petrocik. *The Changing American Voter,* enl. ed. Cambridge, Mass.: Harvard University Press, 1979.

Norris, Pippa. *A Virtuous Circle: Political Communications in Postindustrial Societies.* New York: Cambridge University Press, 2000.

Page, Benjamin. *Choices and Echoes in Presidential Elections.* Chicago: University of Chicago Press, 1978.

Patterson, Thomas E. *Doing Well and Doing Good: How Soft News and Critical Journalism Are Shrinking the News Audience and Weakening Democracy— And What News Outlets Can Do About It.* Cambridge, Mass.: Joan Shorenstein Center on the Press, Politics and Public Policy, 2000.

———. *The Mass Media Election: How Americans Choose Their President.* New York: Praeger, 1980.

———. *Out of Order: How the Decline of the Political Parties and the Growing Power of the News Media Undermine the American Way of Electing Presidents.* New York: Knopf, 1993.

———, and Robert D. McClure. *The Unseeing Eye: The Myth of Television Power in National Elections.* New York: Putnam, 1976.

Petrocik, John R. *Party Coalitions: Realignment and the Decline of the New Deal Party System.* Chicago: University of Chicago Press, 1981.

Piven, Frances Fox, and Richard A. Cloward. *Why Americans Still Don't Vote: And Why Politicians Want It That Way.* Boston: Beacon, 2000.

Polsby, Nelson W. *Consequences of Party Reform.* New York: Oxford University Press, 1983.

Pomper, Gerald, with Susan Lederman. *Elections in America: Control and Influence in Democratic Politics,* 2nd ed. New York: Longman, 1980.

Popkin, Samuel L. *The Reasoning Voter: Communication and Persuasion in Presidential Campaigns.* Chicago: University of Chicago Press, 1991.

Postman, Neil. *Amusing Ourselves to Death: Public Discourse in the Age of Show Business.* New York: Viking, 1985.

Putnam, Robert D. *Bowling Alone: The Collapse and Revival of American Community.* New York: Simon & Schuster, 2000.

Ranney, Austin. *Participation in American Presidential Nominations: 1976.* Washington, D.C.: American Enterprise Institute, 1977.

Reiter, Howard L. *Selecting the President: The Nominating Process in Transition.* Philadelphia: University of Pennsylvania Press, 1985.

Robinson, Michael. "Public Affairs Television and the Growth of Political Malaise: The Case of 'The Selling of the Pentagon.'" *American Political Science Review* 70, no. 3 (1976): 409–32.

———, and Margaret Sheehan. *Over the Wire and on TV*. New York: Russell Sage Foundation, 1983.

Rosenstone, Steven J., and John Mark Hansen. *Mobilization, Participation, and Democracy in America*. New York: Macmillan, 1993.

Rubin, Richard. *Press, Party, and President*. New York: Norton, 1980.

Sabato, Larry J. *Feeding Frenzy: How Attack Journalism Has Transformed American Politics*. New York: Free Press, 1991.

Schattschneider, E. E. *The Semi-Sovereign People: A Realist's View of Democracy in America*. New York: Holt, Rinehart and Winston, 1960.

Schroeder, Alan. *Presidential Debates: Forty Years of High-Risk TV*. New York: Columbia University Press, 2000.

Schudson, Michael. *Discovering the News*. New York: Basic Books, 1978.

———. *The Power of News*. Cambridge, Mass.: Harvard University Press, 1995.

———. *What Time Means in a News Story*. Occasional Paper no. 4, Gannett Center for Media Studies, Columbia University, New York, 1986.

Semetko, Holli, et al. *The Formation of Campaign Agendas*. Hillsdale, N.J.: Erlbaum, 1991.

Seymour-Ure, Colin. *The Political Impact of Mass Media*. Beverly Hills, Calif.: Sage, 1974.

Sparrow, Bartholomew H. *Uncertain Guardians: The News Media as a Political Institution*. Baltimore, Md.: Johns Hopkins University Press, 1999.

Sundquist, James L. *Dynamics of the Party System: Alignment and Realignment of Political Parties in tne United States*. Washington, D.C.: Brookings Institution, 1983.

Swerdlow, Joel L. *Beyond Debate: A Paper on Televised Presidential Debates*. New York: Twentieth Century Fund, 1984.

Taylor, Paul. *See How They Run: Electing the President in an Age of Mediaocracy*. New York: Knopf, 1990.

Teixeira, Ruy A. *The Disappearing American Voter*. Washington, D.C.: Brookings Institution, 1992.

Tulis, Jeffrey. *The Rhetorical Presidency*. Princeton, N.J.: Princeton University Press, 1987.

Verba, Sidney, Kay Lehman Schlozman, and Henry Brady. *Voice and Equality: Civic Voluntarism in American Politics*. Cambridge, Mass.: Harvard University Press, 1995.

Walsh, Kenneth T. *Feeding the Beast: The White House versus the Press*. New York: Random House, 1996.

Wattenberg, Martin P. *The Decline of American Political Parties, 1952–1996*. Cambridge, Mass.: Harvard University Press, 1998.

———. *The Rise of Candidate-Centered Politics*. Cambridge, Mass.: Harvard University Press, 1991.

Weaver, Paul. "Is Television News Biased?" *The Public Interest* 27 (Winter 1972): 69.

———. *News and the Culture of Lying*. New York: Free Press, 1994.

West, Darrell M. *Air Wars: Television Advertising in Election Campaigns, 1952–1992*. Washington, D.C.: Congressional Quarterly Press, 1993.

White, Theodore. *America in Search of Itself: The Making of the President, 1956–1980*. New York: Harper & Row, 1982.

———. *The Making of the President, 1960*. New York: Atheneum, 1961.

Zaller, John. *The Nature and Origins of Mass Opinion*. New York: Cambridge University Press, 1992.

Index

245

A NOTE ABOUT THE AUTHOR

Thomas E. Patterson teaches at the Joan Shorenstein Center on the Press, Politics and Public Policy at Harvard University's John F. Kennedy School of Government. For many years he taught at Syracuse University. He is the author of several previous books on politics and the media, including *Out of Order*. He lives in Brookline, Massachusetts.

A NOTE ON THE TYPE

This book was set in Minion, a typeface produced by the Adobe
Corporation specifically for the Macintosh personal computer and
released in 1990. Designed by Robert Slimbach, Minion combines
the classic characteristics of old-style faces with the full comple-
ment of weights required for modern typesetting.

COMPOSED BY STRATFORD PUBLISHING SERVICES, BRATTLEBORO, VERMONT

PRINTED AND BOUND BY BERRYVILLE GRAPHICS, BERRYVILLE, VIRGINIA

DESIGNED BY ROBERT C. OLSSON